THOMAS AQUINAS ON THE JEWS

Studies in Judaism and Christianity

Exploration of Issues in the Contemporary Dialogue between Christians and Jews

Editor in Chief for
Stimulus Books
Lawrence Boadt, CSP

Editors
Lawrence Boadt, CSP
Rabbi Leon Klenicki
Kevin A. Lynch, CSP
Rev. Dennis McManus
Dr. Ann Riggs
Rabbi Leonard Schoolman
Dr. Elena Procario-Foley
Michael Kerrigan, CSP

A STIMULUS BOOK

THOMAS AQUINAS ON THE JEWS

Insights into His Commentary on Romans 9–11

Steven C. Boguslawski, OP

With a Foreword by
Rev. John E. Lynch, CSP

A STIMULUS BOOK

PAULIST PRESS • NEW YORK • MAHWAH, N.J.

BM
535
.B594
2008

The Scripture quotations contained herein are from the New Revised Standard Version: Catholic Edition Copyright © 1989 and 1993, by the Division of Christian Education of the National Council of the Churches of Christ in the United States of America. Used by permission. All rights reserved.

Cover design by Cynthia Dunne
Book design by The HK Scriptorium, Inc.

Copyright © 2008 by the Stimulus Foundation

All rights reserved. No part of this book may be reproduced or transmitted in any form or by any means, electronic or mechanical, including photocopying, recording, or by any information storage and retrieval system without permission in writing from the Publisher.

Library of Congress Cataloging-in-Publication Data

Boguslawski, Steven C.
   Thomas Aquinas on the Jews : insights into his commentary on Romans 9–11 / Steven C. Boguslawski.
      p. cm.
   Includes bibliographical references.
   ISBN-13: 978-0-8091-4233-0 (alk. paper)
   1. Judaism—Relations—Christianity. 2. Christianity and other religions—Judaism. 3. Christianity and antisemitism—History. 4. Thomas, Aquinas, Saint, 1225?–1274. 5. Thomas, Aquinas, Saint, 1225?–1274. In Epistolam ad Romanos expositio. 6. Bible. N.T. Romans—Commentaries. 7. Judaism (Christian theology)—History of doctrines—Middle Ages, 600–1500. I. Title.
   BM535.B594 2008
   261.2'6092—dc22
                                                                                                    2007030502

Published by Paulist Press
997 Macarthur Boulevard
Mahwah, New Jersey 07430

www.paulistpress.com

Printed and bound in the
United States of America

Contents

Foreword by John E. Lynch, CSP ix

Preface xv

1. Introduction to Thomas Aquinas' *Commentary on Romans* 1

2. Medieval Church Policy toward the Jews 19

3. The Jews in the *Summa Theologiae* 36

4. Predestination and Election in Aquinas
   and Thomas' Received Tradition 54

5. Election and Predestination in *CRO* 9 and 11 87

6. The Contribution of Aquinas' *Commentary on Romans*
   to the Contemporary Debate on Romans 9–11 123

Selected Bibliography 137

*For my parents,
Mary and Henry,
and for p.p.h.*

Acknowledgments

God has given me excellent mentors and good friends throughout my life.

I owe a particular debt to my Jesuit professors, Joseph A. Fitzmyer, SJ, Francis T. Gignac, SJ, and James Swetnam, SJ, who exemplified and demanded careful biblical scholarship and inspired me to pursue New Testament studies.

My Dominican brethren of the Province of Saint Joseph warrant special thanks for the financial support and the educational opportunities afforded me at Providence College in Providence, Rhode Island; the Dominican House of Studies in Washington, DC; the Pontifical Biblical Institute in Rome; and at Yale. The brethren at Saint Mary Priory in New Haven, Connecticut, in particular, repeatedly provided the daily means to pursue this project and to bring it to a successful completion. I am especially grateful to Br. Gerard Thayer, OP, for his unfailing hospitality. I would be remiss indeed if I did not mention the hidden contribution of Cajetan Sheehan, OP (*requiescat in pace*), whose fidelity to prayer kept reminding me of my purpose as a Dominican religious while engaged in research, teaching, or educational administration. He is truly missed by me.

There are mentors who became close friends and who shared their lecture halls and their dinner tables with me: Abraham Malherbe and Leander Keck, in particular. While at Yale, my dissertation co-directors, Wayne Meeks and Marilyn McCord Adams, provided the example and challenge to read the texts of Romans and Aquinas ever more carefully. What is lacking in this study is attributable entirely to me.

There are close friends who became mentors of another sort by their constancy; foremost among these is Juan Diego Brunetta, OP. I thank him for his friendship and his commitment to Dominican priestly life, as well as for his editorial acumen, which was always executed with clarity and wit. Allen and Anita Hunt shared their home and family with me for the three wonderful years they lived north of the Mason-Dixon line. The strength of their faith and their ever-ready sanctuary remain a precious gift to me. Sr. Mary Ann, OP, and the nuns of the Monastery of Our Lady of Grace in North Guilford, Connecticut, were more generous than I can recount or repay.

I want to express my gratitude to Nancy de Flon whose careful editing of the manuscript for Paulist Press prevented many an error or lack of clarity. That this present study is part of the Stimulus Series remains a distinct honor, given that I formerly served as director of The Pope John Paul II Cultural Center, whose mission is to foster the "conversation" between faith and culture, particularly through interreligious dialogue. The late, beloved Pope John Paul II remains a most reliable guide (both by his teaching and personal example) to urge us on.

Finally, I want to acknowledge the kind support of His Eminence Adam Cardinal Maida, as well as the Sacred Heart Major Seminary community, where I served as rector and began my revision of the manuscript. Now it is my hope that my Dominican brethren who are the "rising generation" being trained at the Dominican House of Studies (where I currently serve as president) will benefit from this reappraisal of our "older brother(s) in religion," St. Thomas Aquinas, as well as the Jewish people. My deepest desire, however, is that this present work will encourage those engaged in Jewish–Catholic dialogue in our own day, knowing that "God's gifts and call are irrevocable" (Rom 11:29). May the Lord, who has begun this good work in you, bring it to completion.

Washington, DC
8 September 2006
Birth of Mary

Foreword

The rise of the universities in the thirteenth and fourteenth centuries capped an intellectual revival that had been under way over the previous 150 years. Now that much of the wisdom of the Greco-Roman world and the writings of the fathers of the church had been collected and made available, scholars were faced with the more demanding challenge of analysis and synthesis. The universities soon dominated the life of medieval Europe, exerting more influence than they would at any period up until the nineteenth century. Scholarship knew no boundaries. Without passports but equipped with the universal Latin language, pupils and teachers were free to pursue knowledge wherever it attracted them.

The universities were organized along the lines of a medieval craft guild. A student had to pass through an apprenticeship in which he acquired a basic knowledge of the field; he then became a "journeyman," teaching under the supervision of a master; finally, he received a license that made him eligible for membership in the association of masters and accorded him a right to teach anywhere. To receive a license in theology at Paris, for example, one had to complete six years in the arts faculty, studying dialectic or logic and philosophy, and eight more in the theology faculty.

University teaching was carried on through the lecture and the disputation. In the lecture, a master read (*lectio*) and commented upon a prescribed text. In theology the texts were the Bible and the *Sentences of Peter Lombard,* a collection of excerpts from the fathers of the church on various theological matters composed about 1140. The disputation was in the form of a debate. A theological question was posed to which a negative or a positive response could be given, such as, "Can the existence of God be proved by reason?" These disputations were published individually, or grouped according to subject matter, or organized into extensive syntheses, such as the *Summa Theologiae* of St. Thomas.

St. Thomas Aquinas was a university master or professor par excellence. He was born of noble parentage in 1225 at Roccasecca, midway between Rome and Naples. While studying logic and natural philosophy at the imperial university in Naples, Thomas was attracted to join the Order of Preachers recently founded by St. Dominic. In 1245 the order sent him to study under St. Albert the Great in Paris. Three years later he followed St. Albert to Cologne, where he continued his program. Under Albert's tutelage, from 1250 to 1252 Thomas lectured cursorily (i.e., literally) on Isaiah, Jeremiah, and Lamentations. For the next four years, while pursuing graduate theological studies in Paris, he lectured and wrote a *Commentary on the Sentences of Peter Lombard*, which, in theological faculties, served roughly as a doctoral dissertation down to the time of Martin Luther.

Inducted as a full-fledged master or doctor in 1256, Thomas remained at Paris, lecturing on the Bible and engaging in theological disputations. In 1259 he returned to Italy, where he resumed his biblical commentaries and began work on his *Summa Theologiae*, an orderly survey of theology for beginners. In 1268 his Dominican superiors recalled him to Paris to counteract the philosophers who were using Aristotle to undermine the faith. In addition to commenting on all the major works of Aristotle, Thomas continued to work on his *Summa*, to lecture on scripture, and to engage in the usual academic disputations. Summoned back to Italy in 1272, he lectured again on the epistles of St. Paul and sought to complete the *Summa*. Before he was able to finish it, he apparently suffered a breakdown in December 1273 that ended his productive career. He died the following March, not quite fifty years old. During that brief period, he authored over ninety works that in an 1871–72 edition encompassed thirty-four volumes. A critical edition of all his writings, underway since 1882, has currently reached twenty-nine volumes.

Thomas Aquinas was canonized in 1323 and, by 1567, when he was declared a doctor of the church, most outstanding Catholic theologians could be numbered among his followers. He was the only person mentioned in the entire 1917 *Code of Canon Law,* which legislated in canons 589.1 and 1366.2 that all priests were to receive their philosophical and theological instruction according to the "method, doctrine, and principles" of St. Thomas. Although the study of St. Thomas was neglected in the decades following the Second Vatican Council, Pope John Paul II, in an extended section of his important 1998 encyclical *Fides et ratio,* highlighted the enduring originality of Thomas' thought, especially in vindicating the harmony of faith and reason (nos. 43–45). The pope here called attention to the dialogue that Thomas undertook with the Arab and Jewish thought of his time.

In any investigation of a bygone era, one must be careful not to impose current societal standards. Throughout history, it must be emphasized that religion was viewed not as a matter of personal preference, as in our Western democracies, but as the most important ingredient in forging a people's identity. Diversity would be divisive of the body politic, a threat not to be tolerated. The public practice of any but a legally recognized religion was generally forbidden, as is the case in too many countries today. For the first three hundred years of this era Christians were considered adherents of an illegal religion and, therefore, persecuted in Judaea as well as elsewhere in the Roman Empire. As Christianity gradually became the dominant religion in Europe, paganism and other primitive religions disappeared. Although forced conversions were theologically unacceptable and prohibited by the church, uniformity was too often purchased at the expense of intimidation. The political reality was expressed vividly during the period of the Protestant Reformation in the slogan *cuius regio, eius religio* ("The ruler of a country determines its religion").

The survival of Judaism, however, proved to be a remarkable exception and this for theological reasons. St. Paul, Christianity's most authoritative spokesman next to St. Peter, insisted that the Jews were to be respected as God's chosen people; God never takes back his gifts or revokes his choice (Rom 11:28–29). When Christianity gained ascendancy, official church policy not only prohibited forced conversions but also vindicated the traditional rights Jews had secured under Roman law. St. Gregory the Great (590–604) enunciated the principle, often repeated in papal documents, that "in those things granted them they should have no infringement of their rights." Without doubt this principle has been more noted in its breaking than in its keeping, but it does account for the continued existence of the Jewish people until modern times.

Even for renowned contemporary scholars who have spent a lifetime in its study, St. Paul's Epistle to the Romans has been characterized as "overwhelming." Certainly it ranks first in importance among all Paul's writings, if not all the Christian Scriptures. After developing the theme of justification through faith in Christ, Paul reaches the climax in chapters 9–11, the focus of this current book, in which he takes up the crucial issue of the relation of Judaism to the gospel. As a guide to this difficult Epistle of Paul, Roman Catholics can hardly offer a more qualified theologian than St. Thomas Aquinas, who commented on it at the height of his career, very likely in the last years of his life.

St. Thomas' most extensive treatment of the relation of Judaism to Christianity is to be found in his *Commentary on [St. Paul's] Epistle to the Romans*, especially in chapters 9–11. His approach is that of an exegete and theologian, not that of a social commentator. Yet, according to Steven Boguslawski, "Aquinas' interest in the Jews of his time pervades his commentary on Romans and represents more than merely a close reading of Paul's letter." In fact, his references to the Jews "are far more numerous than those which the Apostle himself supplies." Thomas finds here a positive role for Judaism in the future as well as in the present.

The *Commentary* has been little studied in itself, "and not at all in connection with this question of the role of the Jews." Among the few authors to study Aquinas and the Jews, John Y. B. Hood found Thomas to be a pragmatic defender of an ecclesial status quo, one who systematized the traditional theological and canonistic teaching of relative tolerance based on St. Augustine, rather than one who broke new ground. Jeremy Cohen, on the other hand, maintains that in contrast to earlier theologians, especially Augustine, "Aquinas taught that [the Jewish sages at the time of Jesus] knew that Jesus was the messiah and crucified him in spite of that knowledge. The disbelief of the Jews derived, therefore, not from ignorance, but from a deliberate defiance of the truth." Cohen finds there a connection with the anti-Jewish polemics of the thirteenth century.

According to Boguslawski, Cohen and others fail to recognize that Thomas does break new ground because they "incorrectly take Aquinas historically to represent the common trend of anti-Judaism, and theologically, to be a continuator of Augustinian supersessionism [the replacement of the church, the new Israel, for the old]." Countering their claims, Boguslawski demonstrates that in the *Commentary on the Romans,* correlated with the *Summa Theologiae,* Thomas frames the role of the Jews theologically by means of predestination and election. These concepts are the hermeneutical keys to explain and preserve the role of the Jews. Through them Aquinas interprets the relationship between Jew and Gentile in salvation history; he thus recognizes the historical and contemporary importance of the Jews. He departs from Paul's text to interject his own commentary with John 4:22: "Salvation is from the Jews."

Boguslawski has based his study on the soon-to-be published critical text of the *Commentary* and has prepared the first English translation. Through a thorough analysis of this source, neglected by previous historians, he has discerned the centrality of the concepts of election and predestination for St. Thomas in structuring the Jewish-Gentile question. His study argues convincingly that "since Aquinas' way of reading Romans sustains a positive theology of Judaism, he merits engagement by traditionalist and revisionist exegetes of Romans in the contemporary debate on Romans 9–11 and the status of the Jewish people." In view of Boguslawski's fresh and original treatment of this important source, *Thomas Aquinas on the Jews* is undoubtedly the most up-to-date on the subject and represents an outstanding, groundbreaking contribution to the theology and history of Jewish–Christian relations.

Rev. John E. Lynch, CSP, PhD
Professor Emeritus of Canon Law and History
The Catholic University of America

Preface

Exegesis of Paul's Letter to the Romans plays a crucial role in all Christian theology of the Jewish people. Paul, particularly in Romans 9–11, provides an eschatological trajectory that actually integrates competing truth claims: the enduring covenantal privilege of Israel as God's people, and the filial status of the peoples through faith in Christ.

Recognition of this seeming theological ambiguity is not new. Augustine of Hippo resolved the difficulty by supersessionism, relegating Israel's divinely ordained prerogatives to prefigurements of the Christian dispensation. In his day, Augustine acknowledged the de facto existence of Jews and Judaism in North Africa as one means to legitimate Christianity; theirs was a testamentary function at the service of the *verus Israel,* the Christian church.

By the Middle Ages, the Augustinian policy of testamentary tolerance of Jews and Judaism proved insufficient; new interpretive paradigms had to be forged to account for the ongoing presence and role of the Jewish people in medieval society. The Dominican theologian Thomas Aquinas (1224/5–1274), in his *Commentary on Romans* and his *Summa Theologiae,* located the ongoing role of the Jews and Judaism in salvation history under the rubric of divine providence, specifically, predestination and election. While Aquinas remained faithful to the apostle Paul's eschatological plot line as articulated in Romans 9–11, he also provided hermeneutical keys to resolving seemingly contradictory assertions without resorting to substitutionary theories or deconstructing the Jews' historical, covenantal privileges. Simultaneously, he preserved the corporate and individual aspects of salvation; justification of the individual by faith in Christ does not eclipse the corporate, eschatological outworking of salvation history enacted for Jew and Gentile alike. What is absent in Aquinas is the anti-Judaism characteristic of the High Middle Ages. While some commentators have used Romans 9–11 to justify supersessionism, Aquinas' exegesis asserted the inclusion of the Jews as integral to the culmination of salvation history.

If one reviews contemporary interpretation of Romans, one notices that the Reformation emphasis on the centrality of the doctrine of justification by faith tends to support a relatively negative view of Judaism in terms of traditional supersessionism. But this theological presupposition is precisely what theologians and exegetes are being encouraged to set aside in order to rediscover the centrality of chapters 9–11 in Paul's Letter to the Romans.

In this book I conclude that, perhaps unexpectedly, the pre-Reformation Aquinas offers a significant resource for the reading of Romans that can sustain a positive theological view of the Jewish people.

The distinctiveness of Aquinas' achievement emerges as all the more remarkable in the light of the theological tradition that he received as authoritative. In the Western theological tradition, it is crucial to see his work as both a development and a correction of Augustine. In addition, Aquinas' theology of the Jews is all the more impressive, considering the growing institutionalization of anti-Judaism in medieval culture. Therefore, it is not surprising that some contemporary commentators on Aquinas fail to discern his distinctiveness because they read him in the context of the anti-Judaism latent in the received theological tradition as well as that which emerges explicitly in the medieval church and society.

My thesis in this book is the following: Thomas Aquinas, in his *Commentary on Romans,* forges a positive theology of Judaism by correcting and developing the received tradition in order to emphasize that the Jewish people are predestined by God to benefit all humanity; they remain God's elect; theirs is the priority of salvation and faith; Jewish prerogatives (covenant, law, cult, circumcision, the patriarchs, etc.) are historical *realia* that testify to the Jews' dignity and intimate knowledge of God, and that it is into the faith of the Jews that the peoples are ingrafted. Aquinas' achievement emerges when one notes what he *does not say* about the Jews, given the specter of emerging anti-Judaism in thirteenth-century society as evidenced in forced conversions to Christianity, expropriation of Jewish properties, the confiscation and destruction of copies of the Talmud and other Jewish books, and the limitations imposed on Christians' converse with Jews.

Therefore, chapter 1 argues that the status and role of the Jewish people are central to Thomas' exegesis of Romans 9–11 and that he constructs his argument on the doctrines of predestination and the subsidiary theme of election. Chapter 2 analyzes the ecclesial policies regarding the Jews in order to ascertain the sociohistorical context in which Thomas found himself writing. Chapter 3 then undertakes an overview of Thomas' positions in the *Summa Theologiae* on significant policy questions of his time—namely, the status of Jewish belief, tolerance of Jewish rites, Christians' association with Jews, Jewish dominion over Christians, and coerced or forced baptism of Jews. Next, since Thomas' hermeneutical keys to Romans 9–11 are the doctrines of predestination and election, we must understand how these doctrines functioned for him. To accomplish this objective, chapter 4 first attends to the more systematic treatment of these controlling concepts in the *Summa Theologiae* and then compares Aquinas' reading of Romans with Augustine's in order to expose the similarities and differences between them. In light of these preparatory studies, chapter 5 analyzes Aquinas' exegesis of Romans 9–11. Finally, chapter 6 argues that since Aquinas' way of reading Romans sustains a positive theology of Judaism, he merits engagement by traditionalist and revisionist exegetes of Romans in the contemporary debate on Romans 9–11 and the status of the Jewish people.

1
Introduction to Thomas Aquinas' *Commentary on Romans*

INTRODUCTION

The achievement of Aquinas' *Commentary on Romans* emerges only when it is read in the light of a social phenomenon: the rise of anti-Judaism[1] in the thirteenth century. Jeremy Cohen, in his work *The Friars and the Jews: The Evolution of Medieval Anti-Judaism,*[2] ascribes the emergence of anti-Judaism to several factors that converged: the strength of the medieval papacy, an expanding middle class,[3] an undereducated secular clergy, the Fourth Lateran Council legislation concerning the Jews, and the rise of the Franciscan and Dominican friars, who "comprised the single most decisive element in molding the character of religious and cultural life in thirteenth-century Europe."[4] Based on "numerous sporadic incidents," Cohen asserts that

> the brunt of the friars' attack upon the Jews came not in...isolated occurrences but in concerted efforts usually undertaken with some degree of official sanction: in inquisitorial and missionary campaigns that expressed a basically new Christian polemical attitude toward medieval Jews and Judaism.[5]

The friars' condemnation of rabbinic Judaism, their ecclesially sanctioned inquisitorial activity, and their aggressive polemical and missionary tactics in response to "the exaggeration of Jewish support for Christian heretics" or to the Jews' consorting with "judaizing Christians" (*relapsi*) diminished the status and role of the Jews in medieval Europe.[6] Indeed, especially as participants in the Inquisition, wherever they could, the friars encroached upon the daily religious lives of the Jews. Burning or editing the books needed to sustain rabbinic tradition, invading the privacy and sanctity of the synagogue, and instilling fear through mob violence all pointed toward the same end: inducing the Jews to accept Christianity, thereby destroying the Jewish community in Christendom.[7]

Although Cohen refrains from explicitly linking Thomas Aquinas with such immediate, destructive activities against Jewish communities, he holds Aquinas among those responsible for developing strategies to convert unbelievers,[8] "rationalizing [Inquisitorial activity]...with ...accepted policy for [the] treatment of infidels"[9] and, most importantly, for imbuing Raymond Martini, OP, and other anti-Jewish polemicists with the "novel opinion that the rabbis of the first-century Jews" knowingly rejected and hated Jesus as a manifest "rejection of God, which radically altered the character of their Judaism from the divinely ordained, albeit imperfect, religion of the Old Testament to a wicked and heretical perversion thereof."[10] Furthermore, Cohen claims that

> in contrast to most Christian theologians in the West from Augustine through the end of the twelfth century, who castigated the Jewish sages at the time of Jesus for not recognizing him as the messiah when they should have, Aquinas taught that those sages knew that Jesus was the messiah and crucified him in spite of that knowledge. The disbelief of the Jews derived, therefore, not from ignorance, but from a deliberate defiance of the truth.[11]

Thomas, in effect, purportedly provides the theological reasons for the defective quality of Judaism, Jewish obstinacy, programmatic Christian conversionary efforts among the Jews, and their eventual disappearance as a people. Is this an accurate depiction of Aquinas' view of the Jews, considering the few texts of Thomas considered by Cohen?

The Significance of the Romans Commentary for Aquinas' View of the Jews

At the time of Aquinas, medieval ecclesiastical, political, and economic institutions demanded clarification of the role of the Jews in society. Aquinas never produced a tract entitled *Contra Iudaeos* or *Pro Iudaeis* in direct response to these societal disputes. There is the brief text commonly known as *De regimine Judaeorum ad Ducissam Brabantiae,* wherein Thomas attempts to circumscribe financial exploitation of Jews by secular rulers.[12] But his most sustained treatment of the Jews occurs in his *Super Epistolam ad Romanos,* especially in chapters 9–11.[13] Contrary to the anti-Jewish characterization of Thomas presented by Cohen, in the Romans commentary Aquinas does something theologically distinctive by placing the *ongoing* role of the Jews within the divine economy of salvation, specifically, under divine providence, predestination, and election. Aquinas takes Romans 8.29–30 ("For those whom he foreknew he also predestined to be conformed to the image of his Son, in order that he might be the first-born of many brethren. And those whom he predestined, he also called; and those whom he called he also justified; and those whom he justified he also glorified") as his starting point for *CRO* 9–11 and provides an extensive initial discussion of predestination;[14] he also concludes chapter 11 with a discussion of predestination and election.[15] These theological terms bracket the discussion of the relationship between Jews and the Peoples.

Cohen and other contemporary commentators on Aquinas fail to recognize the manner in which Thomas contextualizes the Jews' status and role by means of these theological categories.[16] Thomas does not articulate a theological rationale to eliminate the role of the Jewish people; quite to the contrary, Aquinas strives to preserve it.

Since Thomas never wrote a tract on the Jews, how do we know that the Jews, considered as a distinctive group within salvation history, were a serious concern for Aquinas? The brief "Letter on the Jews" is an inadequate basis for evaluation. The primary work in which Thomas Aquinas treats the question extensively is *CRO.* Surprisingly, the commentary has been little studied, and not at all in connection with the question of the role of the Jews.

John Y. B. Hood recognized this scholarly gap in Thomistic studies in his recent work *Aquinas and the Jews.*[17] Hood posits either a conservative, loyalist Thomism on the one hand, or medieval historians' deferral to specialist Jewish scholars on the other, in order to account for the investigative lacuna on Aquinas and the Jews. Hood states that "Aquinas wrote widely on both Judaism and the status of the Jews in Christian society,...[therefore, scholarly] neglect cannot be explained by a lack of source material."[18] Nevertheless, the texts that modern scholars characteristically cite are selectively culled from the Thomistic corpus without regard for literary genre or chronology. Both loyalist Thomists and specialist Jewish scholars misread Aquinas. Hood himself wrongly relegates Thomas' position on the Jews to that of a pragmatic defender of an ecclesial status quo. He contends that Thomas' "primary goal was to clarify and systematize traditional theological and canonistic teaching on the Jews *rather than to break new ground*."[19] Hood (and Cohen, as well) characterizes Aquinas as heir and proponent of Augustine's position on Judaism. While it is true that Thomas integrates the received tradition in which Augustine figures prominently, Hood's assessment is not accurate.[20] Aquinas is not an Augustinian tradent proposing a mere preservationist role for Jews as the Christians' "chest-keepers."[21] Thomas' commentary is not a refutation of Augustine or of the readers of Augustine, but *CRO* represents a correction and development which demonstrates that Thomas goes beyond the status quo. Thomas may not be a social commentator, but he does provide a positive understanding for the Jews that contextualizes what he says about their role even as they continue to observe the ceremonial law *post Christum natum*. He neither eliminates nor diminishes the historical and contemporary importance of the Jews in salvation history; they are not simply remote ancestral preservers of the old dispensation or ill-defined specters with an unspecified future.[22] Because Cohen, Hood, and others have read Aquinas in the context of the anti-Judaism latent in theological tradition, they fail to recognize the alternative reading of Paul's letter that he advances. In other words, because Cohen and others incorrectly take Aquinas historically to represent the common trend of anti-Judaism and, theologically, to be a continuator of Augustinian supersessionism, they fail to recognize that Thomas indeed "breaks new ground," and that he does so in the way he frames the role of the Jews theologically by means of predestination and election.[23]

One exception to this view is Hood, but his observations need to be extended and deepened by detailed attention to the texts of Thomas that give fullest attention to the role of the Jews in the plan of God, particularly *CRO* 9–11. Greater methodological precision is essential, namely, connecting the editorial strata of contemporaneous Thomistic works insofar as this is possible.[24] The careful correlation of *Summa Theologiae* with Thomas' *expositio* on Romans permits, theoretically, the integration of systematic considerations (preeminently the doctrines of predestination and election) with Thomas' *lectio continua* on Paul's letter. For example, confirmation of predestination and election as tied to Aquinas' understanding of the role of the Jews is also found outside the commentary: specifically in Ia. 23.aa.1–8 of the *Summa Theologiae*.[25] In these eight articles, which specifically deal with predestination, Romans is the predominant scriptural source of Thomas' theological argument.[26] More importantly, however, Aquinas incorporates material from, or at least demonstrates substantial correspondence with, Ia. 23 and his commentary on Romans 9–11.[27] These two works of Thomas advance and mutually reinforce his argument. Thus, intratextual (whether *CRO* or *ST,* for example) as well as intertextual attestations (*CRO* and *ST,* specifically) reveal predestination and election as essential theological concepts that Thomas employs to explain—and, as I shall argue, to preserve—the role of the Jews.

I contend that Aquinas' interest in the Jews of his time pervades his commentary on Romans and represents more than merely a close reading of Paul's letter. There are many references to the Jews in *CRO;* in fact, they are far more numerous than those that the apostle himself supplies.[28] Indeed, since chapters 9–11 of Romans are the parts of *CRO* in which Thomas' own position becomes clearest, they are the focus of my investigation.

Of course, Thomas approaches these chapters as an exegete and as a theologian, not as a social commentator.[29] His statements about the Jews and Judaism are shaped by his reading of Romans and by his theological concerns. Therefore, I shall demonstrate that Aquinas not only has a positive view of Judaism in the Pauline textual commentary, but also that he explains the status of the Jewish people by integrating discussions on the divine economy of salvation found in other works, specifically the *Summa Theologiae* and the *Sentences.*

Thomas' teachings regarding the Jews in *CRO* have both a doctrinal aspect and an apologetic function. The doctrinal aspect is preeminently the theology of predestination and election. The apologetic function is to clarify and preserve the role of the Jews in salvation history. There are several preliminary observations that make this a plausible interpretation of Aquinas. Concretely, from the beginning of *CRO,* Thomas' solicitude for the Jews in tandem with the issue of predestination is evident in his very conception of audience, author, and purpose of Paul's Letter to the Romans.

Audience and Paul's Authorial Intent in the *Commentary on Romans*

Thomas understands Paul to be addressing a mixed audience composed of Jews and Gentiles who are converts. He states:

> Paul specially received the apostolate to all peoples, so that through him what is said in Isa 49.6 might become clear....

Nevertheless the Jews were not being excluded from his apostolate, especially those who were living among the peoples....[30]

Aquinas explicitly posits that "in the first parts of this letter [Paul] had spoken to all the faithful living in Rome, whether they were from the Peoples or from the Jews" and later he would "direct his word to the converted Gentiles."[31] By so doing, Thomas describes Paul's apostolate as inclusive of his fellow Jews and rejects the notion of Gentile exclusivity or superiority.[32] While this may seem to be simply an obvious repetition of Paul, it again reminds one of Thomas' concern at the outset of the commentary not to exclude the Jews from a real function in salvation history.

Second, Aquinas correctly understands and explains Paul's rhetoric: self-identity and personal anguish elicit empathy from Paul's mixed audience and heighten the pathos of the Jew–Gentile relationship soon to be explored. Thomas portrays Paul himself as the prime analogue of salvation: he conjoins Paul's identifying with the Jews and their ongoing role in salvation history with his teaching on predestination. Thomas writes:

> Therefore, first [Paul] says: Not only am I not rejected, but God did not reject his people, the whole [people], which he foreknew, that is, predestined. Above 8.8: The ones whom he foreknew, these he also predestined. Ps 94.14: The Lord will not reject his people.[33]

Paul the Jew is not rejected; transferring this from the individual to the collective, the Jews as a whole are foreknown and are not rejected in virtue of God's predestinating will. Furthermore, Thomas prefaces the lengthy discussion of Israel's election and fall in chapter 9[34] with Paul's own sadness and pain—experienced as a result of the Jews' seeming plight. He repeats this rhetorical strategy at the outset of chapter 10.[35] The Apostle to the Gentiles remains an Israelite.

Third, while asserting that the purpose of Paul's letter is the instruction of Jews and Gentiles alike in the Roman Christian community (coalescence of these constituencies is what Aquinas understands to be the Pauline objective), Thomas insists that priority remains with the Jews. Indeed, it is significant that Thomas departs from Paul's text and punctuates his commentary with John 4.22: "Salvation is from the Jews."[36] This proof text functions nearly antiphonally, accomplishing both a rhetorical and a theological purpose. John 4.22 first appears in §101, where Thomas, commenting on 1.16b, writes:

> the gospel is for salvation as much to the Jews as to the Greeks. For God is not solely of the Jews, but also of the Peoples, below 3.29, and for that reason [Paul] adds to the Jew first and to the Greek....However, since below 10.10 it is said that there is no distinction between Jew and Greek, by what manner here is the Jew first?
>
> It must be said...that in as much as for pursuing the end of salvation, there is no distinction between them, for both attain an equal reward....However, *as far as the order of salvation the Jews are first, because promises were made to them, as below 3.2 and into their grace are the Peoples assumed, as though the branch of the wild olive tree were inserted into a good olive tree,* as below 11.24. Also from them our savior was born. John 4.22: Salvation is from the Jews. (emphasis mine)[37]

The priority of the Jews is maintained from the aspect of history; a history that has not yet reached its culmination.

Additional uses of John 4.22 demonstrate more developed argumentation about the role of the Jews. For example, Thomas declares that "Jew is an honorable [name]"[38] and that people so-called enjoy specific prerogatives;[39] among them, the lineal descent of Christ.[40] The use of John 4.22 in §881 reaffirms that the fall of the Jews is used to extend the preaching of the gospel to the Gentiles and the universal witness of their prophetic texts.[41] In §897 Thomas reproves Gentile boasting against seemingly excised Jews; rather salvation derives from the Jewish root.[42] Most importantly, John 4.22 buttresses the claim that all Israel shall be saved because "the savior...shall come, namely God made man for the purpose of saving us, out of Sion, that is from the people of the Jews, who are signified through Sion."[43] Thomas does not equivocate on the decisive revelation of God in Jesus nor on the fact that the Christ is the singular boast of the Jews.

Finally, Thomas exploits the equality of preceding guilt and the necessity of subsequent grace for Gentile and Jew alike—so essential to the resolution of Jewish–Gentile conflict in the letter.[44] Yet, while maintaining equality of Jew and Gentile in these ways, Thomas consistently reasserts the Jews' priority in salvation history. Moreover, he cautions non-Jews against smug self-confidence in the present and promises the future remedy of the Jews in the culmination of salvation history. Each of these components Thomas confirms by means of John 4.22 (and each will be considered more closely below).

From this brief overview, it is apparent that Aquinas recognizes a unique function for the Jewish people. Indeed, Thomas' understanding of audience, author, and authorial intent in Romans signals a significant part to be played by them. In the history of salvation, theirs is an ongoing role.

> [For even] they who shall fall totally, deceived by the Anti-Christ, will be restored to their pristine fervor by the converted Jews. And just as with the falling Jews the Gentiles were reconciled after hostilities, at this time, after the conversion of the Jews, imminently there is the end of the world. There will be the general resurrection, through which people shall return from the dead to life immortal.[45]

Whatever their apocalyptic role might be, their election is foreknown and predestined by God himself. The Jews' role and stature are not obliterated from the historical record nor so radically reinterpreted by Thomas as to be unrecognizable or nonessential in the future eschatological drama. It is my contention that, for Thomas, the role of the Jews is tied essentially to predestination and their election by God and that ignorance of these hermeneutical keys skews any scholar's assessment of Aquinas on this topic. Therefore, in order to understand how the Jews specifically continue within divine providence and function within Thomas' interpretation of Paul's eschatology, we must first investigate Aquinas' understanding of predestination and election *generally*. I will argue in subsequent chapters that, according to *CRO*, the ultimate destiny of Gentile humanity is integrally interwoven with the fate of the Jews.

Predestination: A Valid Hermeneutical Key to Interpret Romans 9–11?

προορίζω in Paul

The verb προορίζω means to foreordain or to predestinate; it is an intensified version of ὁρίζω.[46] Of the six uses in the New Testament, five occur in the Pauline corpus. In each instance God is the agent predestinating believers to existence (Eph 1.11), adoptive status (Eph 1.5), glory through wisdom (1 Cor 2.7), and conformity to the Son's image (Rom 8.30) in accord with his own purpose (Rom 8.29). Several attestations in Greek literature similarly link "divine agency" with the root verb ὁρίζω.[47] The first use of this word in Romans occurs in 1.4; interestingly, the Old

Latin and Vulgate support the strengthened form προο-.[48] "A feature of the eight ὁρίζ- passages in the NT (Heb 4.7; Acts 2.23; 10.42; 11.29; 17.26f; 17.31; Lk 22.22; and Rom 1.4) is that with the exception of [Acts] 11.29, they are all emphatically theological and christological; they describe the person and work of Jesus Christ."[49] *CRO* reflects this understanding; the predestination of Jesus is the prime analogue of the predestination of believers; that is, what the Son of God is by nature believers become by grace:

> Indeed it is clear that what is *per se* is the measure and norm of those things which are said [to be] through another and through participation. Hence the very predestination of Christ who is predestined that he should be Son of God by nature, is the measure and norm and therefore of our predestination, because we are predestined to adoptive filiation which is a certain participation and image of natural filiation, accordingly Romans 8.30: Those whom he foreknew and predestined to be conformed to the image of his Son.[50]

Predestination in *CRO*

The initial treatment of predestination by Aquinas analyzes Romans 1.4, specifically, that Christ was predestined[51] Son of God in power. In this exposition, Thomas lays down certain principles that will be applied to individuals in chapter 8, and to elect-Israel and the Gentiles in chapters 9–11.

In §43 Thomas defines predestination as "nothing other than to dispose from the heart ahead of time what ought to be done concerning a certain thing."[52] Predestination pertains to use or guidance, not to the constitution of a thing itself.[53] Nature with its intrinsic principles of motion is sufficient to account for some phenomena, and human intention, others; but divine providence functions as the overarching explanatory framework that accounts for arrangements that nature and human intentionality cannot achieve unaided. (Predestination, *quantum ad ipsum usum,* will be especially important in understanding God's use of Israel for a particular end: the inclusion of the Gentiles, as delineated in *CRO* chapter 11.) Infrarational creatures cannot properly be said to be predestined because they follow natural principles intrinsic to their constitution. "Predestination should be said properly only of those things which are above nature, in which the rational creature is ordered."[54] The human person as a rational creature is united to God through the grace of adoption;[55] Christ is united to God through the grace of union. Therefore, both adoptive filiation and the grace of union are included under predestination. Human persons are predestined to adoptive filiation, which is a certain participation and image of the Son's filiation, which he has by divine nature. Thomas explains that

> predestination is able to be attributed to the person of Christ accordingly as he subsists in human nature, although it cannot be attributed to him as he subsists in his divine nature.
>
> Whence...the Apostle set out beforehand that the Son of God [was] incarnate, and later attributed predestination to him so that it might be understood that he was predestined because he was made from the seed of David according to the flesh. And in this manner, from the Son of God, by explaining the mystery of the incarnation, he descended to the flesh, and by the flesh, according to predestination, ascended to the Son of God....[56]

As we have seen already, the theme of predestination recurs in Romans 8.29. Here, however, Thomas focuses on believers predestined by God from eternity who are called and sanctified in time, namely, those who were called [to be] saints according to his purpose. Predestination denotes divine purpose and mercy,[57] and although divine foreknowledge and predestination are one in God, they are distinct in human reason. Thus, "foreknowledge expresses only information of future things, but predestination expresses a certain causality in their respect," specifically, "concerning the goods of salvation" eternally willed by God.[58] However, this causality is not in response to a foreknowledge of those who would act well or believe in Christ, because to assert this "is nothing other than to posit grace to be given on account of our merits, and that the beginning of good works is from us, and the consummation...from God."[59] God did not predestine those whom he foreknew to be conformed to the image of Christ; conformity to Christ is the *goal* or *effect* of predestination, not its *ratio*. Conformity to Christ is understood by Thomas as adoptive filiation.[60] Aquinas expressly qualifies Romans 8.29. Paul says "the ones he foreknew he also predestined, not because all the ones foreknown he predestines, but because he was not able to predestine them unless he foreknew [them]."[61]

Throughout his analysis of the predestination of Christ in *CRO* chapter 1 and of individuals in *CRO* chapter 8, Thomas prepares for the corporate implications in *CRO* chapters 9–11. The election of some and the reprobation of others concretely express the proposition of predestination; as we shall see, Israel and the Gentiles are corporately used to manifest God's purpose: "to make known the riches of his glory for the vessels of mercy, which he has prepared beforehand for glory...whom he has called, not from the Jews only but also from the Gentiles" (9.23–24).[62] Here we have the implementation of divine foreknowledge and predestination articulated under the aspect of election, the *ratio* of which is mercy and whose goal is glory. R. Garrigou-Lagrange contextualizes the matter more broadly:

> Predestination is a part of providence. Now, providence...is the plan existing in the intellect directing the ordering of some things towards an end. But nothing is directed towards an end unless the will for that end already exists. Whence the predestination of some to eternal salvation presupposes, in the order of reason that God wills their salvation; and to this belong both election and love.[63]

In Romans 9, the election of Jacob and the reprobation of Esau, who function typologically in Paul's argument, illustrate predestination. The implications of divine election are deferred until Romans 11.

We see immediately that election and predestination are closely connected here. These are two hermeneutical keys that appear throughout Thomas' writings. Hood and others have not discerned the centrality of these controlling concepts in determining how they are used by Aquinas in structuring the Jewish–Gentile question. Because of the close connection between election and predestination, it is reasonable to examine carefully both of these themes in Thomas to see how they are developed and to use them in interpreting his position on the Jews. At the same time, we recognize that theological and exegetical readings always occur within specific social and historical situations, and that choices made in interpretation of texts, consciously or unconsciously, are informed by the historical context and have implications for life within it. Therefore a brief sketch of the ways some of Aquinas' predecessors and contemporaries treat the Jews (chapter 2), followed by an overview of Thomas' positions in the *ST* on significant policy questions of his time (chapter 3), and a fuller discussion of his understanding of predestination and election (chapter 4) will set the stage for my detailed analysis of his argument in *CRO* (chapter 5).

NOTES

1. W. D. Davies makes a useful distinction between anti-Semitism and anti-Judaism in "Paul and the People of Israel," *New Testament Studies* 24 (1977–78): 18. He states in response to the accusation that Paul's theology is, at its core, anti-Semitic that "it would serve the interests of accuracy if we dispensed with the use of the nineteenth-century term anti-Semitism, which has a genetic or racial reference, and used rather only 'anti-Judaism' in dealing with the New Testament, while fully recognising that all fanatical intolerance is evil and almost always cruel, whether religiously or racially founded." Whereas anti-Semitism is cultural and societal, anti-Judaism is also theological, circumscribing the role of the Jews in salvation history. To avoid possible anachronism, I will focus on the question regarding anti-Judaism.

2. Ithaca: Cornell University Press, 1982. See also Jeremy Cohen's *Living Letters of the Law: Ideas of the Jew in Medieval Christianity* (Berkeley and Los Angeles: University of California Press, 1999), wherein he adumbrates several of the aforementioned factors. Cohen's summary of "the doctrine of Jewish witness" (*Letters,* 23–65), particularly from the writings of Augustine, provides the theological backdrop for those elements contributing to the emergence of anti-Judaism. However, his proposed "ambiguities of Thomistic synthesis" (*Letters,* 365–89) fails to take into account the *Commentary on Romans* (citing it only once in this analysis) and its correlation with the *Summa Theologiae,* specifically Ia.23.aa.1–8.

3. "Since the friars represented the Christian middle classes both in their personal origins and in their religious program, their hostility toward the Jews may have derived...from anti-Jewish sentiments typically harbored by European merchants. By the thirteenth century, the Jews of Europe were engaged almost exclusively in commercial activities, especially lending of money; their success and influence in the marketplace set them among the chief competitors of the new Christian bourgeoisie" (Cohen, *Friars and the Jews,* 43).

4. Cohen, *Friars and the Jews,* 41. John Y. B. Hood, as we shall see below, rejects Cohen's contention that Aquinas was "part of a radical new trend; on the contrary his attitude toward Judaism and the Jews was essentially conservative....[And]...to the extent Aquinas was aware of new, anti-Jewish trends in theology or in mission activity, he was either skeptical or actively opposed to them." See Hood's *Aquinas and the Jews,* Middle Ages Series (Philadelphia: University of Pennsylvania Press, 1995), xi.

5. Cohen, *Friars and the Jews,* 44.
6. Ibid., 50.
7. Ibid., 85.
8. "...Raymond [of Penyafort] and Thomas Aquinas shared the same views on how best to convert the infidel, an affinity between the two men which allowed Raymond to solicit the composition of the *Summa contra gentiles*" (Ibid., 124).

9. Ibid., 47.
10. Ibid., 145.
11. Ibid., 124.
12. See Michael Lukens, "St. Thomas' Letter on the Jews," in *Conflict and Community: New Studies in Thomistic Thought*, ed. Michael B. Lukens (New York: Lang, 1992), 165–201. Lukens succinctly states: "the Letter is more complex than simply a literal theological application based on his systematic theology, that Thomas is employing in his response both his prior theological judgements and a particular political agenda toward the Jews. This thesis assumes that Thomas' response is set within a distinct political-economic conflict and contains a deeper meaning aimed at limiting secular power and at least indirectly at a supportive policy toward the Jews" (p. 169). This brief text of Thomas is popularly known as *De regimine Judaeorum ad Ducissam Brabantiae* although Leonard Boyle, OP ("Thomas Aquinas and the Duchess of Brabant," *Proceedings of the Patristic, Mediaeval, and Renaissance Conference* 8 [1983]: 25–35) contends that the addressee was Margaret of Constantinople. Boyle dates the letter between mid-1270 and early 1272. Therefore, this text is contemporaneous with Thomas' *expositio* on Romans during his second Parisian regency. Thomas does not consider the letter to be an exhaustive treatment of the Gentile–Jewish question. Indeed, seven of the eight questions posed consider matters financial. The eighth topic treats of a distinctive garb to be worn in public by Jews. These particular "practical" responses derive from the more speculative theological positions articulated in his Romans commentary and elsewhere.
13. Hereafter *CRO*. Translations have been made from the Marietti edition (1953) corrected by the Leonine Commission critical text (as yet unpublished). This text was available to me through the courtesy of John Aquinas Farren, OP, former *praeses* of the international commission and Louis Battailon, OP, former chair of the commission's Italian section, located at Grottaferrata, Italy. Through a generous fellowship provided by Yale University that enabled me to work with Fr. Battailon, I have completed an English translation of Aquinas' Romans commentary. Due to its length (600+ pages), only selected texts pertaining to the Jews (along with the corresponding critical Latin text) are included here. The numbering follows the Marietti edition.
14. See §§701–9.
15. §926.
16. Scholarly literature dealing with Aquinas and his perspective on Jewish–Christian relations in medieval society is scant indeed. See, for example, Marcel Dubois, "Thomas Aquinas on the Place of the Jews in the Divine Plan," *Immanuel* 24 (1990): 241–66. Dubois attributes Thomas' treatment of the Jews to "part of a theological reflection on the mystery of the divine plan...; [the vocation, permanence and destiny of the Jewish people]...only seemed explicable...within the development of the history of salvation" (p. 241). It is surprising that Dubois never considers the Romans commentary, simply the *Summa Contra Gentiles* and the *Summa Theologiae*.

The same lacuna is evidenced in six additional studies (see bibliography below) treating the topic of Aquinas and the Jews in *Aquinas and Problems of His Time*, ed. G. Verbeke and D. Verhelst (Leuven: Leuven University Press, 1976). Indeed, no scholar to date has produced a comprehensive analysis of the Romans commentary wherein Aquinas provides the most sustained treatment of the Jew–Gentile "problem." There is one study of the commentary as a whole, specifically dealing with Aquinas' exegetical method and Romans 5.12 as an illustration of the development of scholastic theology. See Thomas Domanyi, *Der Römerbriefkommentar des Thomas von Aquin: Ein Beitrag zur Untersuchung seiner Auslegungsmethoden* (Bern: Peter Lang, 1979).

The doctoral dissertation of Eugene F. Rogers, Jr., analyzes the "theological context of the natural knowledge of God in Thomas' commentary on Romans 1" and the cognitive processes of faith. Within this theological matrix he does assess Paul's assertion: "Iudaeo primo et Graeco" ("A Theological Procedure in the *Summa Theologiae*" [Ph.D. diss., Yale University, 1992]; see pp. 180–82).

17. See n. 4 above.

18. Hood, *Aquinas and the Jews*, x.

19. Ibid., xi (emphasis mine).

20. See chapters 4 and 5 below for a comparative analysis of Thomas and Augustine on Romans.

21. "We see and know that it is in order to bear this witness—which they involuntarily supply on our behalf by possessing and preserving these same books—that they themselves are scattered among all peoples, in whatever direction the Church of Christ expands" (Augustine, *De Civitate Dei,* 18.46, ed. George E. McCracken et al.; 7 vols., Loeb Classical Library [Cambridge, MA: Harvard University Press, 1957–60], 6:50–51).

22. Thomas, being faithful to the text of Paul, understands that the Jews are essential to the culmination of salvation history and cannot be supplanted. This would be a fruitful discussion for contemporary Jewish and Christian theologians to consider because Judaism per se is integral to ushering in the last days. This does not represent the elimination of Judaism, but reveals the internal intelligibility of Jewish faith and expectation.

23. Surprisingly προώρισεν (and its Vulgate equivalent *predestinatus est*) does not occur in the text of Romans 9–11 itself. Despite this absence, predestination functions as Thomas' controlling concept for the unit, taking his cue from Rom 8.28f. Of the thirty-nine instances of the word "predestination" and the twenty-three uses of "election" in Thomas' commentary, ten instances of "predestination" and eighteen instances of "election" are located in chapters 9–11. However, statistical analysis alone does not assure the decisive character of these concepts for understanding Thomas on the Jews.

24. I question the methodology employed by Hood, for example, who claims that in "juxtaposing texts which Aquinas wrote at different times there is little risk of doing violence to his thought" (*Aquinas and the Jews,* xiii). Additionally, Hood fails to distinguish between Thomistic texts controlled by the

scripture and those which he fashions independently that employ biblical texts as warrants for his position.

25. Sections of the first and third books of Thomas' commentary *Super Libros Sententiarum* (hereafter *Sent.*) are also relevant, particularly regarding the subsidiary theme of election. Translations are from the *Scriptum Super Libros Sententiarum,* 4 vols., ed. R. P. Mandonnet, OP, and M. F. Moos, OP (Paris: Lethielleux, 1926–47).

26. Rom 1.4: a.2. obj.2; Rom 8.28: a.7. resp.; Rom 8.29: a.5. obj.1; a.6. sed contra; Rom 8.30: a.1. sed contra; a.3. resp.; Rom 9.11–13: a.5. resp.; Rom 9.14: a.5. obj.3; Rom 9.15: a.5. obj.1; Rom 9.22: a.5. resp.; Rom 9.29: a.8. resp.; Rom 11.34: a.8. obj.2.

27. Question 23 having been written prior to the *CRO*. See below.

28. One hundred sixty-four paragraphs in *CRO* contain references to "Jew" or "Jews." Only chapters 6 and 13 contain no reference. By contrast, Paul makes just ten references to Jew(s) in Romans: 1.16; 2.9, 10, 28, 29; 3.1, 9, 29; 9.24; and 10.12. Most are clustered in chapters 1–3 and only two references occur in chapters 9 and 10.

29. Thomas' exegesis might be incorrectly characterized by some modern exegetes as eisegetical, attempting to impose systematic theological categories of discourse upon the Pauline text. To the contrary, however, as Magister in Sacra Pagina (1256–59), Thomas was known for having given a precise, literal meaning to texts. For Aquinas, the

> priority of the literal sense signifies...that it alone is suited to the necessities of the theological arguments, [and]...that all spiritual interpretations should be confirmed by a literal interpretation in order to avoid all risk of error. (*Summa Theologiae.* vol. 1, ed. Thomas Gilby [London: Blackfriars' McGraw Hill, 1967], Ia. 1.10. resp.; hereafter *ST.*)

Although the literal sense limned theology, the exegetical and the theological tasks were not discontinuous. Moreover, the use of an interpretive concept to explicate a text is not, in virtue of that fact, eisegetical.

30. Specialiter Paulus in omnes gentes apostolatum acceperat, ut ei competere possit quod dicitur Is. XLIX.6....Nec tamen ab eius apostolatu exclusi erant Iudaei, praesertim qui inter gentes habitabant... (§63).

What Thomas asserts so straightforwardly has proven to be a matter of debate for contemporary commentators. Some view Romans as a circular, magisterial letter serving as a compendium of the mature Paul's thought but not specifically intended for the mixed congregation in Rome. The omission of ἐν Ῥώμῃ in G and 1739^{mg} illustrates this generalizing tendency quite early. Scholarly disputes concerning the composition of the Roman community as predominantly Jewish Christian (e.g., Theodor Zahn, Franz-J. Leenhardt) or mainly Gentile Christian (e.g., Johannes Munck, Stanislas Lyonnet, C. K. Barrett) encounter a seemingly naïve historicism in Thomas' commentary.

31. [C]onsiderandum est, quod cum in superioribus huius epistolae partibus locutus fuerit omnibus fidelibus existentibus Romae, sive fuerint ex Gentibus, sive ex Iudaeis, nunc specialiter sermonem suum dirigit ad Gentiles conversos (§886).

32. In fact, Aquinas earlier (see §170 and §187) had identified an additional problem between Jews and Gentiles converted to the faith: the fact that they were judging each other regarding their prior state of life. Jews accused the Gentiles of idolatry; Gentiles castigated Jews because of their nonobservance of divine law. Paul, in correcting both groups, reveals one purpose of the letter: the cessation of internal community strife. Both groups are alike in sin; both groups require grace.

33. Dicit ego primo: Non solum ego non sum repulsus sed Deus non reppulit plebem suam totam, quam prescivit id est predestinavit. Supra VIII.8: Quos praescivit, hos et praedestinavit. Ps. XCIII.14: Non repellet Dominus plebem suam. Quod Apostolus hic exponit quantum ad praedestinatos (§863).

34. §§735ff.

35. §813.

36. §§101; 225; 746; 881; 897; 918.

37. ...evangelium sit in salutem, quia tam Iudaeis quam Gentibus. Non enim Iudaeorum tantum Deus imo et Gentium, infra III.29. Et ideo subdit Iudaeo primum et Graeco. Sed, cum infra X.10 dicatur non est distinctio Iudaei et Graeci, quomodo hic dicitur Iudaeo primum? Dicendum est ergo quod quantum ad finem salutis consequende non est distinctio inter eos. Aequalem enim mercedem consequuntur utrique....Sed quantum ad ordinem salutis Iudaei sunt primi, quia eis promissiones sunt factae, ut infra III.2, dicitur et in eorum gratia sunt Gentiles assumpti, ac si ramus oleastri insereretur in bonam olivam, ut infra XI.24. Ex his etiam Salvator natus est. Io. IV.22: Salus ex Iudaeis est.

38. Quantum autem ad gentem dicit Si autem tu cognominaris Iudaeus, quod est honorabile, secundum illud Ps 113.2: Facta est Iudae. Io. 4.22: Salus ex Iudaeis est (§225).

39. E.g., cum dicit Et requiescis in lege, ponit eorum praerogativam quantum ad legem....Et primo quidem, quantum ad ipsam legem....Secundo, quantum ad legislatorem, cum subdit et gloriaris in Deo, id est, in cultu et notitia Dei. Ier. 9.24: In hoc glorietur qui gloriatur, scire et nosse me (§226).

40. Ostendit dignitatem eorum ex prole cum dicit Ex quibus Christus est genitus secundum carne, sicut ipse dicit. Io. 4.22: Salus ex Iudaeis est (§746).

41 Dicit ergo primo Absit, ut scilicet inutiliter caderent, sed, magis, illorum scilicet Iudaeorum, delicto, salus Gentibus facta est occasionaliter unde et Dominus dicit Io. IV.22: Salus ex Iudaeis est.

...[Uno] modo potest intelligi de hoc quod suam impoenitentiam sunt in omnes Gentes dispersi. Christi Ecclesia ubique a libris Iudeorum testimonium habuit fidei christianae, ad convertendos Gentiles qui suspicari potuissent prophetias de Christo, quas praedicatores fidei inducebant, esse confictas, nisi probarentur testimonio Iudaeorum.

42 ...cum dicit Quod si gloriaris, etc., assignat rationem suae admonitio-

nis, quod si, non obstante hac admonitione, gloriaris—insultando Iudaeis stantibus vel excisis, hoc consideres, ad repressionem tuae gloriae, quod tu radicem non portas, sed radix te, id est Iudaea non accepit a Gentilitate salutem sed potius e converso. Io. IV.22: Salus ex Iudaeis est.

43. Primo Salvatoris adventum, veniet, Deus scilicet humanitus ad salvandum nos, ex Sion, id est ex populo Iudaeorum, qui significatur per Sion... (§918).

44. Illustrated, e.g., in §§299, 303, 313, 318, 320, 465, 644, 1154, and elsewhere.

45. ...qui totaliter cadent decepti ab Antichristo, Iudaeis conversis in pristinum fervorem restituentur. Et etiam sicut Iudaeis cadentibus, Gentiles post inimicitias sunt reconciliati, ita post conversionem Iudaeorum, imminente iam fine mundi, erit resurrectio generalis, per quam homines, ex mortuis ad vitam immortalem redibunt (§890).

46. See K. L. Schmidt, "προορίζω," *Theological Dictionary of the New Testament,* ed. Gerhard Kittel and Gerhard Friedrich, trans. Geoffrey W. Bromiley (Grand Rapids: Eerdmans, 1964–76), 5:452–56.

47. A few are Zeus and Dike in Sophocles, *Antigone,* 452; Euripides, *Fragments,* 218 (The Greek Fathers, 424); Epictetus, *Diss.,* 1.12.25; and Meleager in *Anthologia Palatina epigrammata amatoria,* 12,158. See Schmidt, "προορίζω," 452.

48. See Ignatius, *Eph.* 3.4, wherein bishops are similarly ὁρισθέντες.

49. Schmidt, "προορίζω," 453.

50. Manifestum autem quod id quod est per se est mensura et regula eorum quae dicuntur per aliud et per participationem. Unde praedestinatio Christi, qui est praedestinatus ut sit Filius Dei per naturam, est mensura et regula vitae et ita praedestinationis nostrae, quia praedestinamur in filiationem adoptivam, quae est quaedam participatio et imago naturalis filiationis, secundum illud Romans. VIII.30: Quos praescivit et praedestinavit conformes fieri imagini filii sui (§48).

51. The Greek genitive absolute τοῦ ὁρισθέντος is translated *qui praedestinatus est* in Thomas' text. This is found in Latin manuscripts C, W, S. The *Textus Latinus Novae Vulgatae Bibliorum Sacrorum Editioni* reads *qui constitutus est.* English versions translate the phrase variously and exegetes are divided.

52. [P]raedestinare nihil aliud est quam ante in corde disponere quid sit de re aliqua faciendum.

53. §44. He cites Augustine's definition of *use* in §45: "To use is to refer something to an end which is to be enjoyed."

54. [P]raedestinatio dicatur proprie eorum solum quae sunt supra naturam, in quae rationalis creature ordinatur (§45).

55. That is, through sanctifying grace; see below.

56. Nam praedestinatio potest attribui personae Christi secundum quod subsistit in humana natura, licet non attribuatur ei secundum quod subsistit in divina.

Unde...Apostolus prius Filium Dei incarnatum esse praemiserat, postea ei praedestinationem attribuit, ut intelligatur praedestinatus esse secundum quod factus est ex semine David secundum carnem. Et sic a Filio Dei, explicando incarnationis mysterium, descendit ad carnem, et a carne, secundum praedestinationem, ascendit ad Filium Dei... (§52).

57. Divine purpose and pity figure prominently in the election of Israel and reprobation of Esau in Rom 9.14ff., as we shall see.

58. [P]raescientia importat solam notitiam futurorum: sed praedestinatio importat causalitatem quamdam respectu eorum. Et ideo Deus habet praescientiam etiam de peccatis, sed praedestinatio est de bonis salutaribus (§702).

59. Unde ponere quod aliquod meritum ex parte nostra praesupponatur, cuius praescientia sit ratio praedestinationis, nihil est aliud quam gratiam ponere dari ex meritis nostris, et quod principium bonorum operum est ex nobis, et consummatio est ex Deo (§703).

60. This is a *communicated likeness;* see §704 and §706. Adoptive filiation bestows the rights of inheritance (Rom 8.17) and participation in his splendor.

In Thomas' commentary on Eph 1.5, he lists adoptive filiation among six aspects of predestination: "Then [Paul] adds the third blessing, that of predestination in the foreordained community of those who are good. Six characteristics of predestination are sketched here. First, it is an eternal act, he hath predestinated; secondly, it has a temporal object, us; thirdly, it offers a present privilege, the adoption of children through Jesus Christ; fourthly, the result is future, unto himself; fifthly, its manner of being realized is gratuitous, according to the purpose of his will; sixthly, it has a fitting effect, unto the praise of the glory of his grace" (*Commentary on Saint Paul's Epistle to the Ephesians,* trans. Matthew Lamb, OCSO [Albany: Magi Books, 1966], 46–47).

61. Dicit autem quos praescivit et praedestinavit, non quia omnes praescitos praedestinet, sed quia eos praedestinare non poterat, nisi praesciret (§705).

62. Thomas also states that the *vocatio Dei,* from the part of the saints, has an interior and an exterior aspect. The interior aspect is an instinct of mind that assents to faith and virtue; the exterior aspect of the call comes from the mouth of the preacher. For Aquinas, this partially explains Paul's attention to the preaching office in 10.14ff. See §706. In his earlier work, I *Sent.* d.41.2. ad 3 this basic distinction is found: "For this call is either interior through the infusion of grace, or exterior through the voice of the preacher. However the *interior call and the temporal election to grace are simultaneous*" (emphasis mine).

63. R. Garrigou-Lagrange provides brief studies of Thomas' precursors, as well as comparisons with other systematic theologians, in *Predestination,* trans. Dom Bede Rose, OSB (St. Louis: Herder & Herder, 1946), 202.

2
Medieval Church Policy toward the Jews

INTRODUCTION

Several topics in Thomas' writings mirror controversies in medieval society, namely, whether the Jews should be classed with unbelievers;[1] the association of Christians with Jews and other unbelievers;[2] the preservation of Jews' existing dominion over Christian believers;[3] maintenance of Jewish rites;[4] the contentious issue of forced baptism of Jewish children and adults, and miscellaneous accusations leveled against the Jews collectively and individually (for example, theft).[5] This chapter will provide an overview of ecclesial legislation and papal policies that affect the status and role of the Jews in medieval society. Of particular importance is the anti-Talmud controversy in Paris beginning in 1239 (in which Thomas' mentor, Albert the Great, took part). Moreover, demonstrable trends in Jewish polemical literature in response to rising anti-Judaism will further contextualize Thomas' thought concerning the "Jewish question"[6] in the thirteenth century.

THOMAS' PREDECESSORS AND CONTEMPORARIES: ECCLESIAL LEGISLATION AND PAPAL POLICY TOWARD THE JEWS

Many theological matters pertaining to the Jews are attested in ecclesiastical documents, especially papal bulls issued or reissued immediately prior to or during Thomas' lifetime. Some of these issues were addressed at the Fourth Lateran Council (1215) as well as at provincial[7] or diocesan councils (*synodus*).[8] Although conciliar documents and papal bulls carry the greatest authority, the policies articulated by regional and diocesan councils exhibit local implementation; these latter provide detailed information in reconstructing Christian–Jewish relations. Nevertheless, from the composite view of ecclesial documents a general policy toward the Jews emerges.[9] Jeremy Cohen contends that (in the thirteenth century)

> [f]or the first time in medieval Europe ecclesiastical authorities took concerted steps to proselytize among the Jews en masse, persecuting the Talmud ("that holds the Jews obstinate in their perfidy"...), exploiting inquisitorial jurisdiction to harass entire Jewish communities, invading synagogues to preach to Jewish worshipers, and coercing leading rabbis to participate in public, officially sanctioned disputations. The older *Adversus Judaeos* polemic had given way to a more serious threat, as the very legitimacy of the European Jewish community had been called into question.[10]

To a large degree, Cohen's characterization of the relationship between the church and the Jews is apt despite the traditional ecclesial policy of testamentary tolerance.

The "*Sicut*" Tradition

As a response to a request from Jews living in Rome,[11] Pope Innocent III issued (what became known as) his *Constitutio pro Judeis*[12] on September 15, 1199—twenty-five years prior to Thomas' birth. Solomon Grayzel has characterized the papal bull "as representative of the entire Christian attitude toward the Jews" of the day.[13] The text reads:

> Even as the Jews ought not have the freedom to dare do in their synagogues more than the law permits them, so ought they not suffer curtailment of those [privileges] which have been conceded them.
>
> This is why, although they prefer to persist in their obstinacy rather than acknowledge the words of the prophets and the eternal secrets of their own scriptures, thus arriving at an understanding of Christianity and salvation, nevertheless, in view of the fact that they have begged for our protection and our aid and in accordance with the clemency which Christian piety imposes, we, following in the footsteps of our

predecessors of happy memory..., grant their petition and offer them the shield of our protection.

We decree that no Christian shall use violence to force them into baptism while they are unwilling and refuse, but that [only] if anyone of them seeks refuge among the Christians of his own free will and by reason of faith, his willingness having become quite clear, shall he be made a Christian without subjecting himself to any opprobrium. For surely none can be believed to possess the true Christian faith if he is known to have come to Christian baptism unwillingly and even against his wishes.

Moreover, without the judgment of the authority of the land, no Christian shall presume to wound their persons, or kill them, or rob them of their money, or change the good customs which they have thus far enjoyed in the place of their habitation. Furthermore, while they celebrate their festivals, no one shall disturb them in any way by means of sticks and stones, nor exact forced service from any of them other than such as they have been accustomed to perform from ancient times. Opposing the wickedness and avarice of evil men in such matters, we decree that no one shall dare to desecrate or reduce a Jewish cemetery, or, with the object of extorting money, exhume bodies there interred.

Should anyone, being acquainted with the contents of this decree, nevertheless dare to act in defiance of it—which God forbid—he shall suffer loss of honor and office or be restrained by the penalty of excommunication, unless he make proper amends for his presumption. We desire, however, to place under the protection of this decree only those [Jews] who do not presume to plot against the Christian faith.

Given—[14]

Ecclesial policy (however longstanding) is often at odds with secular society. The commonplace threat of excommunication of an uncooperative prince or of Christians who refused to suspend socioeconomic interaction with Jews became known as the *judicium Judaeorum*.[15] As early as 591 Gregory the Great formulated the fundamental policy toward Jews (and other non-Christians) and the means of its implementation, recognizing the ineffectiveness of compulsory conversion of nonbelievers by church or state: "Hos enim qui a Christiana religione discordant, mansuetudine, benignitate, admonendo, suadendo ad unitatem fidei necesse est congregare."[16] During the First Crusade, Alexander II (ca. 1060) admonished the bishops of Spain to continue protecting the Jews from warriors

> who set out to war against the Saracens....In the same manner Saint Gregory also admonished those who agitated for annihilating them, indicating that it is impious to wish to annihilate those who are protected by the mercy of God, so that, with homeland and liberty lost, in everlasting penitence, damned by the guilt of their ancestors for spilling the blood of the Savior, they live dispersed throughout the various areas of the world.[17]

The Jews, dispersed as punishment for deicide, remain protected by God's mercy: so ought they be safeguarded by the episcopacy. Similarly, in 1146 Bernard of Clairvaux, while exhorting Christian princes to undertake the Second Crusade, included this *proviso* in his letter "to the people of England":

> [Y]our zeal needs the timely restraint of knowledge. The Jews are not to be persecuted, killed, or even put to flight....The Jews are for us the living words of Scripture, for they remind us always of what our Lord suffered. They are dispersed all over the world so that by expiating their crime they may be everywhere the living witnesses of our redemption. Hence the...Psalm..., "only let Thy power disperse them." And so it is: dispersed they are. Under Christian princes they endure a hard captivity, but "they only wait for the time of their deliverance." Finally we are told by the Apostle that when the time is ripe all Israel shall be saved. But those who die before will remain in death....If the Jews are utterly wiped out, what will become of our hope for their promised salvation, their eventual conversion?[18]

The dispersed and wandering Jews are to be protected because they signal accomplished redemption even as they expiate their culpability for Christ's passion and are oriented toward a decisive final conversion. For Bernard, Jews rightly suffer current captivity while awaiting the eschatological scenario charted by Paul in Romans 11.25-26. The theological justification for ecclesial protection of the Jews articulated by Alexander

II and Bernard of Clairvaux incorporates charges of deicide and approves their subjugated status as divinely inflicted expiatory punishment. Such begrudging protection of the Jewish people derived from a predominantly Augustinian view of their role in salvation history and simultaneously undermined their dignity and status as God's elect.[19] Ironically, Paul's authority as *Jew* and apostle was invoked through use of his letters to legitimate the Jews' servile function in early medieval Christendom.

In the thirteenth century, Innocent III confronted social issues with equally profound theological implications, for example, levirate marriage,[20] coerced baptism of Jews, and the risk of recidivism.[21] The Fourth Lateran Council, presided over by the same pope, likewise addressed issues of economics,[22] preferments in public office,[23] dress and public comportment,[24] and apostasy.[25] As the base text, Innocent III's *Constitutio* reaffirms the Jews' right to public worship, proscribes coerced baptism, robbery, and extortion, among other crimes.

Innocent's successors reissued *Sicut* with alterations and extensive additions demanded by time and social circumstance, but the theological substratum of papal policy remained essentially unchanged from the *Constitutio*.[26] Recourse to the papal court by Jews in Rome, France, Spain, and Germany accounts for the reissuance of the document both as a general instruction and as a "circumstantial" letter addressing particular concerns of the Jewish community in question.[27] The catalysts for subsequent emendations gleaned from the revised texts promulgated by Innocent's successors reveal an array of social trends that attest to the emergence of medieval anti-Judaism.[28] Urbanization, the establishment of universities, the new economic classes of skilled laborers and civil bureaucrats, as well as intensifying competition between ecclesial and secular leaders for exclusive societal jurisdiction, influenced Jews' self-definition and, by the fourteenth century, gradually reconfigured ecclesial policies of tolerance. The oft-repeated papal prohibitions and extension of protection in other correspondence attest "that the situation of the Jews by the end of the thirteenth century was...beyond any aid from the vague generalizations contained in the Bull *Sicut Judeis*."[29] Although no widespread ecclesial persecution of the Jews had yet been organized in the thirteenth century, their vulnerability as a religious minority increased. Indeed, there is a subtle yet important shift from the earlier bulls, which condescended to respect the Jewish rites and traditions, to Clement IV's bull, *Turbato Corde*.[30]

For Innocent III, as with the inception of the *Sicut* tradition, the *perfidia Judeorum* is deliberate obstinacy; nonetheless, toleration of the Jews is warranted "quia tamen per eos fides nostra veraciter comprobatur."[31]

One detects among other elements undergirding papal toleration and papal protection in the bull the Augustinian preservationist[32] role of the Jews as the Christians' "chest-keepers."[33] Indeed, Innocent's prefatory remarks repeat the rationale as well as one *locus classicus* of the Augustinian doctrine of testamentary toleration of the Jews, namely, Psalm 59.10–12: "Ne occideris eos ne quando obliviscantur legis tue."[34]

Although papal protection of person and property remains, toleration of Jewish religious practices and writings becomes increasingly circumscribed during subsequent pontificates. Papal policy and Christian polemic suggest a progressive drift from the Jews' validation to an outright condemnation of Judaism in the Talmud controversies and, ultimately, to the explicit conversionary efforts of the fourteenth century.[35] Cohen states that Pope Gregory IX, in his condemnation of Talmud in 1239,

> could not have foreseen that he had sanctioned the commencement of an ideological trend that would justify attempts to eliminate the Jewish presence in Christendom, a radical shift from the Augustinian position that the ["biblical"] Jews occupied a rightful and necessary place in Christian society.[36]

The long-standing Augustinian substratum of testamentary tolerance gave way in the Talmud controversy to intolerance.[37] Gregory IX's involvement with the Jewish communities in France is particularly illustrative of the trajectory of ecclesial policy.

Early in his pontificate, Gregory IX continued the policy of testamentary tolerance toward the Jews. Specifically, on April 6, 1233, he issued a bull to end the beatings, torture, despoiling, and unjust imprisonment of certain Jews, which practices were sanctioned by local civil authorities of the French kingdom. Gregory predicated social protection upon theological convictions:

> Although the perfidy of the Jews is to be condemned, nevertheless their relation with Christians is useful and, in a way, necessary; for they bear the image of our Savior, and were created by the Creator of all....They are therefore not to be destroyed, God forbid, by His own Creatures, especially by believers in Christ, for no matter how perverse their midway position may be, their fathers were made friends of God, and also their remnant shall be saved.[38]

Furthermore, Diaspora Jews are likened to Christians living in pagan lands, who similarly deserve just treatment. Papal intervention and supervision are warranted, not only because the Jews are useful but also because of their vestigial prerogatives and future promissory role.

The Talmud Controversy

Unfortunately, the utility and historic privileges of the Jews receded in the Talmud controversy of 1239.[39] It began when Pope Gregory IX wrote a letter of recommendation for Nicholas Donin to William of Auvergne, archbishop of Paris, on June 9, 1239, as well as a circular letter to "venerabilis Fratribus Archiepiscopis, et karissimis filiis..., Francie, Anglie, Aragonie, Navarre, Castelle, ac Legionum, et Portugallie Regibus illustribus"[40] instructing them to seize copies of the Talmud and Hebrew books in the possession of Jews in their respective districts on "the first Saturday of Lent," March 3, 1240.[41] Only King Louis IX of France fulfilled the papal directive. Public examination of selected passages of Talmud took place in the infamous Paris disputation between Nicholas Donin, a Christian convert from Judaism, and Rabbi Yehiel ben Joseph in June 1240 (of which a Hebrew and an "official" Latin account exist). That same month, a court presided over by Eudes de Chateauroux (chancellor of the University of Paris) questioned Rabbi Yehiel and Rabbi Judah ben David of Melun about Talmudic texts. In each proceeding the charges against Talmud and, by implication, its Jewish adherents were made known and sustained. Seemingly, the Jews had forgotten the Law of Moses in preference for the Talmudic teachings. Gregory IX directed the prior of the Dominicans and the minister of the Franciscan Friars in Paris to burn those books of the Jews found to contain error, to silence opponents by use of ecclesiastical censure, and to report faithfully the results of their investigations.[42] "[P]erhaps after further official inquiry twenty or twenty-four wagonloads of manuscripts—probably ten to twelve thousand volumes—were burned in Paris...over the course of one and one-half days in 1242."[43]

Innocent IV intensified the anti-Talmudic campaign in a bull (May 9, 1244) delivered to the king of France directing that the Talmud "condemned by [the] doctors, as well as their commentaries (*cum glossis suis*) which have been examined and condemned by them, should...be burned in fire wherever they can be found throughout [the] kingdom."[44] Although Innocent cites substantially similar caricatures of Talmud as those stated by Gregory IX, his rhetoric effectively eviscerates the papal policy of testamentary tolerance. Allusions to 2 Corinthians 3.15 and Romans 11.8–9 "justify" Innocent's assertions that

> [t]he wicked perfidy of the Jews, from whose hearts our Redeemer has not removed the veil of blindness because of the enormity of their crime, but has so far permitted to remain in blindness such as in a measure covers Israel, does not heed, as it should, the fact that Christian piety received them and *patiently allows them to live among them through pity only.* ...For, ungrateful to the Lord Jesus Christ, who, in the abundance of his kindliness, patiently expects their conversion, they, displaying no shame for their guilt nor reverence for the honor of the Christian Faith, *throw away and despise the law of Moses and the prophets, and follow some tradition of their elders.*[45]

Jews not only dishonor the Christian faith but have turned from and despised the Law of Moses. The Jews' guilt perpetuates their collective blindness. The pity of the church is unacknowledged by them. The kindly forbearance of Christ awaits their conversion.

Innocent continues the bull with a list of alleged blasphemies concerning Mary and Christ contained in the Talmud and its glosses. The common Testament seemingly had been eclipsed by the traditions, fables, errors, and blasphemies of Talmud. Questions that Innocent did not address explicitly became painfully apparent to Jewish and Christian adversaries in the theological dispute: If the Jews had turned from the Law of Moses, how could they continue to function as the "chestkeepers" of the Christians or be the "living words of scripture"? Moreover, how could the papal policy of toleration of the Jews be maintained if the common Testament has been eclipsed by the tradition of their elders? Despite papal rhetoric regarding the Jews' testamentary function, it was the theological controversies concerning Talmud that threatened the continuity of Jewish life and, arguably, the Jews' very existence among Christians.

A renewed investigation of Talmud and ancillary commentaries was undertaken by the papal legate to France, Odo, bishop of Tusculum, who was instructed (ca. 1247) by Innocent IV to return to the Jewish communities those Hebrew books that posed no threat or could be tolerated. Innocent IV altered his prior mandate after "the Jewish masters of... [France]...asserted...that without that book which in Hebrew is called 'Talmut,' they cannot understand the Bible and their other statutes and laws in accordance with their faith...."[46] Odo reprised the earlier papal directives to various ecclesial and secular authorities and vigorously protested the new papal policy contending that

> it would...be most disgraceful, and a cause of shame for the Apostolic Throne, if books that had been so solemnly and so justly burned in the presence of the scholars, and of the clergy, and of the populace of Paris, were to be given back to the masters of the Jews at the order of the Pope—for such tolerance would seem to mean approval.[47]

Nonetheless, Odo begrudgingly complied with the new directive, reexamining Hebrew books seized or submitted by Jewish masters, and (not surprisingly) condemning them anew because they were "full of innumerable errors, abuses, blasphemies and wickedness"; these "in the name of God cannot be tolerated...without injury to the Christian faith."[48] Odo's edict, issued formally in May 1247, listed the names of forty-four ecclesiastical personages, "men of discretion, expert in these matters, God-fearing, and zealous for the Christian faith."[49] Among the names listed is that of Albertus Magnus, who, less than one year later, would be Thomas' primary Dominican mentor in Cologne.

Throughout the Talmud controversies and the evolution of medieval anti-Judaism, the Jewish communities were not inactive participants as disputants or victims.[50] Throughout western Europe the interaction of Jews with the *ummoth ha-'olam* (nations of the world) demanded by economic and political interests simultaneously heightened Jewish self-consciousness, social definition, theological traditions, and the anti-Christian polemic of Jewish intellectuals. Religious dissociation from the dominant Christian culture was desirable and actively sought by Jews.[51] While radical group exclusivity was a practical impossibility, religious separation and the curtailment of social interaction with non-Jews was a realizable goal. Theologically considered, the separateness of Jews originated in their election as God's people, in contradistinction to the surrounding nations. The Hebrew Bible and Talmudic tradition legitimated ethnic and religious boundaries. Historically, the acceptance of the Torah indelibly marked Israel as superior to all the surrounding nations that had been unwilling to assume God's yoke. Consequently, Israel was the nation nearest to God;[52] submission to the 613 commandments and exclusive study of Torah was Israel's singular boast and highest virtue;[53] Israel was endowed with a qualitatively different kind of prophecy,[54] and the *Shekhinah* graced elect-Israel, accompanied Diaspora-Israel, and would be the renewed boast of redeemed-Israel.⁵⁵ The Talmud represents the development of the Oral Torah as divine revelation given at Sinai. Jewish law, ethics, and theological speculation preserved continuity amid changed social circumstances. These and other elements of Jewish self-identity were assaulted during the rise of anti-Judaism in the thirteenth century, sometimes by the same ecclesiastical authorities who repeated the Augustinian policy of testamentary tolerance. As we have seen, theory and praxis were not infrequently at odds.

CONCLUSION

The gradual erosion of the *Sicut* tradition and the ongoing disputes concerning Talmud reflect the ecclesial intellectual environment surrounding Judaism when Aquinas entered the Dominican novitiate in Paris in 1245.⁵⁶ He remained there for his initial philosophical and theological studies until his formal training by Albert the Great in Cologne from the summer of 1248 until the fall of 1252.⁵⁷ It is difficult to imagine that Thomas had no knowledge of the condemnation of the Talmud and other Hebrew books while residing in Paris, since his Dominican brethren (along with the Franciscan Friars) were deputed to execute the papal policy of Gregory IX in 1239 (a mandate that Odo reiterated in his *responsum* to Innocent IV in 1247). Admittedly, we have no direct evidence of Thomas' knowledge of the seizure and disposition of copies of the Talmud (and other Jewish works) in Paris. It seems likelier than not, however, that he was aware of the persecution of Talmud and the impact on the resident Jewish community, given that his mentor in Cologne, Albert the Great, was one of the experts appointed to implement the papal policy.

The treatment of the Jews by Thomas' ecclesial predecessors and contemporaries establishes the context in which Thomas writes *CRO*. However, since each of Aquinas' scriptural commentaries is, to a large degree, constrained by the biblical control text, we require additional confirmation apart from the commentary tradition that Thomas, at the very least, is not anti-Jewish. The *Summa Theologiae* provides one means of discerning his theological views because in it scriptural texts (as well as ecclesial authorities and customary law) are selectively employed in the service of the *sacra doctrina*. Although biblical texts employed in the *ST* continue to norm theological discourse, these scriptural texts do not determine Thomas' architectonic plan of the work. In the *Summa Theologiae* Aquinas is not constrained by a *lectio continua*. By carefully examining Thomas' treatment of Jews in seemingly disparate questions of the *ST* we can determine the degree to which such theological positions are properly his own and/or reflect the ecclesial and secular governmental trends.

The following overview of Thomas' positions in the *ST* on significant policy questions of his time will set the stage for my detailed analysis of Thomas' argument in *CRO*. Specifically, after examining selected issues pertaining to the Jews in Aquinas' *ST*, I shall propose predestination (chapter 4) and election (chapter 5) as key hermeneutical tools that he employs in order to exegete Romans 9–11 generally, and to determine the role of the Jews in particular. I also shall argue that Aquinas' theological treatment of the Jews in *CRO*, while reflecting the Augustinian tradition, advances his own distinctive exegetical contribution to the commentary tradition without deconstructing the Jewish people's historical prerogatives or resorting to theological supersessionism.

NOTES

1. *ST* IIa IIae. 10.6–8.
2. *ST* IIa IIae. 10.9.
3. *ST* IIa IIae. 10.10.
4. *ST* IIa IIae. 10.11.
5. *ST* Ia IIae. 94.5. ad 2; 100.8. ad 3; IIa IIae. 66.5. ad 1; and 104.5. ad 2. These and other topics are integrated into Thomas' *lectio continua* on Romans, as we shall see.
6. As Solomon Grayzel characterizes it (*The Church and the Jews in the XIIIth Century,* vol. 1 [1933; rev. ed. New York: Hermon, 1966], 2).
7. For example, the Provincial Council of Beziers (April 19, 1246) legislated restrictions on Jews regarding usury, the employment of Christian servants or nurses, the marketing of meat slaughtered at home, and appearance in public during Holy Week, and mandated the wearing of an identifying badge, monetary support of churches, and the excommunication of Christians who entrust themselves to Jews during illness. See Grayzel, *Church and the Jews,* 1:333 §37.
8. For example, the diocesan synod of Worcester (July 26, 1240) forbade consultation of Jewish fortune-tellers, nursing of Jewish children by Christian women, or lodging of Jews, as well as receiving Jewish money, safeguarding it in churches, or entrusting money to Jewish money lenders. "In other matters too,...the decrees of the Councils with regard to the Jews, [were to] be strictly observed." See Grayzel, *Church and the Jews,* 1:34, 31.
9. Ibid., 6–9.
10. Jeremy Cohen, "Towards a Functional Classification of Jewish anti-

Christian Polemic in the High Middle Ages," in *Religionsgespräche im Mittelalter,* ed. Bernard Lewis and Friedrich Niewöhner (Wiesbaden: Harrassowitz, 1992), 104.

11. Solomon Grayzel provides a comprehensive analysis of the bull's central ideas, culled from other documents dating from the sixth century in "The Papal Bull *Sicut Judeis,*" in *Studies and Essays in Honor of Abraham A. Neuman,* ed. Meir Ben-Horin, B. D. Weinryb, and S. Zeitlin (Leiden: E. J. Brill, 1962), 243–80, esp. 243–44.

12. Sometimes referred to by a subsection of the bull that begins "*Sicut ergo Judeis*" or abbreviated in the scholarly literature as the "*Sicut* tradition." This phrase has a lengthy history, dating from a letter of Gregory I (590–604) to the bishop of Palermo in 598 that begins "*Sicut Judaeis....*" See the concise summary of the *Sicut* tradition by Grayzel, "Popes, Jews, and Inquisition: From 'Sicut' to 'Turbato,'" in *Essays on the Occasion of the Seventieth Anniversary of the Dropsie University,* ed. A. I. Katsh and L. Nemoy (Philadelphia: Dropsie University, 1979), 151–88, esp. 152–57. See also Grayzel's "Changes in Papal Policy Toward the Jews in the Middle Ages," in *Proceedings of the Fifth World Congress of Jewish Studies,* vol. 2, ed. Pinchas Peli (Jerusalem: Hacohen, 1972), 43–54, esp. 48, where Grayzel argues that Innocent subscribed to an Augustinian view of the Jews: "In this spirit he wrote to Philip Augustus of France in 1205, that it pleased God for Jews to serve Christian rulers." In his letter of the same year to the archbishop of Sens (see below) and the bishop of Paris, Innocent accused the Jews of insolence and ingratitude, since they were condemned to perpetual servitude for the crime of the crucifixion. In his letter to the count of Nevers in 1208, he likened the Jews to Cain and repeated "the...theological reason for their survival, although they really deserved death."

13. Grayzel, *Church and the Jews,* 1:92 §4. The generic addressee ("To all the Christian faithful") in Innocent's prefatory remarks accounts for the bull's elevated status as a "constitution," as opposed to particular correspondence arising from isolated circumstance in a local church.

14. Grayzel, *Church and the Jews,* 1:92–93 §5.

15. Although the boundaries of ecclesiastical and secular jurisdictions during the Middle Ages were not always clearly delineated, the church articulated the fundamental social policy regarding the Jewish communities of Europe. Nevertheless, the early medieval church relied heavily on the secular arm to implement ecclesial policy; papal letters repeatedly attest to the popes' urging Christian princes and lords to pursue a desired course of action in matters concerning the Jews even though the popes themselves were powerless to require it of them except by occasional threat of excommunication. See Grayzel, "Popes, Jews, and Inquisition," 168.

16. Gregory I, *Monumenta Germaniae Historica,* I, 34, March 16, 591.

17. Robert Chazan, ed., *Church, State, and Jew in the Middle Ages,* Library of Jewish Studies (New York: Behrman House, 1980), 100. Chazan provides a convenient collection of pertinent documents of ecclesial persons and corporate entities.

18. Ibid., 103.

19. For the moment, I shall defer analysis of Augustine's influence (see chapters 4 and 5 below). However, what Gedaliahu G. Stroumsa wrote concerning religious identity as expressed in polemical literature in late antiquity is equally true of the medieval ecclesial documents concerning Judaism: "In religious polemics, as in other kinds of polemics, one does not speak to each other, but rather to oneself about the other, the demonized other.... Suffice it here to say that these texts often seem to border on the incantatory rather than any rational pondering of arguments. Their goal is not to convince, but to strengthen already existing conviction" ("Religious Contacts in Byzantine Palestine," *Numen* 36 [1989]: 89).

20. "[A]lthough they are accustomed to have marital relations with a brother's widow, nevertheless, lest on this account they give up their good intentions...since certain ones among them do not want to adopt the Faith unless we permitted them to retain the widows of their brothers..." (Grayzel, *Church and the Jews*, 1:101 §11).

21. Ibid., 100 and 102 §12.

22. Specifically, usury and the censures to be implemented against Jews extorting "heavy and immoderate amounts from Christians" and those Christians who maintain commerce with them. See Grayzel, *Church and the Jews*, 1:307 §9, 313 §13.

23. Demanding the removal of Jews appointed and the censures to be enacted against the Christians responsible for their preferment. See Grayzel, *Church and the Jews*, 1:311 §11.

24. See ibid., 309 §10.

25. Declaring: "For there is less evil in not recognizing the way of the Lord than in backsliding after having recognized it" (Grayzel, *Church and the Jews*, 1:311).

26. This bull was reissued more than any other papal document concerning the Jews. Including Innocent III, six popes issued *Sicut* in the twelfth century, ten popes in the thirteenth century (Honorius III on November 7, 1217; Gregory IX on May 3, 1235; Innocent IV on October 22, 1246 and July 9, 1247; Alexander IV on September 22, 1255; Urban IV on April 26, 1262; Gregory X on October 7, 1272 and perhaps on September 10, 1274; Nicholas III on August 2, 1278; Martin IV on August 2, 1281; and Honorius IV [1285–1287] and Nicholas IV [1288–1292], whose dates of issuance are unknown), four in the fourteenth century (including one anti-pope, John XXII), and three popes in the fifteenth century. The multiple promulgations of *Sicut* apparently respond to the growth of anti-Judaism during Aquinas' lifetime. See Grayzel, "*Sicut Judeis*," 243–44, 253–54, and 263–74.

27. Grayzel speculates that the Jewish community of Rome was the intermediary primarily responsible for pressing reissuance of the bull for other Jewish communities. Proximity to the papal court and chancery argues in favor of their role. The generic address (*Universis Christifidelibus*) allowed anonymity to the Jewish community requesting the bull and, at the same time, the inclusion

of additional papal protections needed by the petitioners. "This may also explain...why two...popes...are credited with two issues of the *Sicut Judeis,* though in each case one of the issues contains additional protection" (Grayzel, "*Sicut Judeis,*" 255).

28. For example, two popes reigning during the lifetime of Aquinas, specifically, Innocent IV (July 9, 1247; see Grayzel, *Church and the Jews,* 1:275–76 §118) and Gregory X (October 7, 1272; see Solomon Grayzel, *The Church and the Jews in the XIIIth Century,* vol. 2, *1254–1314,* edited and arranged, with additional notes by Kenneth R. Stow [Detroit: Wayne State University Press, 1989], 116–17 §31), reissued an emended *Sicut* to reiterate papal protection of the Jews and partially to refute the charge of ritual murder committed by Jews against Christian children. Six years after Thomas' death, on August 2, 1281 (see Grayzel, *Church and the Jews,* 2:147–48 §45), Martin IV promulgated the bull to curtail the needless incursion of inquisitors into the Jewish communities and to severely penalize false witness against Jews in court. Clement VI (1348) reissued the bull in order to defend the Jews from the charge of having caused the Black Death by poisoning the water supply. The catalysts for reaffirming papal protection derive from complex social interaction and disinformation regarding disparate Jewish communities. See Grayzel, "Popes, Jews, and Inquisition," 156–58, and "*Sicut Judeis,*" 256–63.

29. Grayzel, "*Sicut Judeis,*" 262.

30. *Turbato Corde,* issued on July 27, 1267, is the charge given to Dominican and Franciscan inquisitors by Clement IV (see Grayzel, *Church and the Jews,* 2:103 §26). This papal letter effectively broadened the jurisdiction of "inquisitors of heresy" to include "four categories of persons over whom the Inquisition...was given authority: born Jews who had been baptized and the Jews who presumably helped them to return to Judaism, and born Christians who were attracted to Judaism and the Jews who allegedly lured them into the Jewish religion" (Grayzel, "Popes, Jews, and Inquisition," 175). Nonetheless, while the competency of the Inquisition was increased, no Jewish pogrom was envisioned nor immediately generated.

31. Grayzel, *Church and the Jews,* 1:92 §5.

32. This is much more commonly called the "doctrine of Jewish witness" in the contemporary literature of Jewish–Christian dialogue. While my later treatment of Augustine is intentionally confined to those tributary elements reflected in Aquinas' synthesis, I recommend Jeremy Cohen's comprehensive analysis of the Augustinian foundations of the "witness tradition" (*Living Letters of the Law: Ideas of the Jew in Medieval Christianity* [Berkeley and Los Angeles: University of California Press, 1999], 23–65).

33. Augustine, *Ennarr. In Ps.,* LXVI,9: "Codicem portat Judeus, unde credat Christianus. Librarii nostri facti sunt...." See also "Thus the Prophet says, 'Thou shalt not kill them, lest at any time they forget they law,' or more clearly stated, thou shalt not destroy *the Jews completely* [*omnino*], so that the Christians should never by any chance be able to forget Thy Law, which, though they them-

selves fail to understand it, they display in their book to those who do understand" (Grayzel, *Church and the Jews,* 1:93 §5).

34. See Grayzel, *Church and the Jews,* 1:93 §5, as well as Augustine, *City of God* 18.46.

35. See Cohen, "Towards a Functional Classification," 113.

36. Cohen, *The Friars and the Jews: The Evolution of Medieval Anti-Judaism* (Ithaca: Cornell University Press, 1982), 242.

37. As we shall see in subsequent chapters, Thomas, while addressing specific sociotheological issues, articulates a comparatively stronger theological rationale than the Augustinian tradition of testamentary tolerance that he inherited. While establishing the Jews' status and role by means of predestination and election, he also asserts their historical prerogatives, their rights within society, and the Jews' eschatological function.

38. Grayzel, *Church and the Jews,* 1:201 §70.

39. Similar assaults upon Talmud and the Jews' patrimony occurred in the Barcelona disputation of 1263 and again in the Tortosa Disputation, 1413–14. Varying accounts of these *disputationes* are translated and edited by Hyam Maccoby in *Judaism on Trial: Jewish-Christian Disputation in the Middle Ages* (London and Toronto: Associated University Presses, 1982).

40. Grayzel, *Church and the Jews,* 1:240 §95.

41. Ibid., 241 §96:

> If what is said about the Jews of France and of the other lands is true, no punishment would be sufficiently great or sufficiently worthy of their crime. For they, so we have heard, are not content with the Old Law which God gave to Moses in writing: they even ignore it completely, and affirm that God gave another Law which is called "Talmud," that is, "Teaching," handed down to Moses orally. Falsely they allege that it was implanted within their minds and, unwritten, was there preserved until certain men came, whom they call "Sages" and "Scribes," who, fearing that this Law may be lost from the minds of men through forgetfulness, reduced it to writing, and the volume of this by far exceeds the text of the Bible. In this is contained matter so abusive and so unspeakable that it arouses shame in those who mention it and horror in those who hear it.
>
> Wherefore, since this is said to be the chief cause that holds the Jews obstinate in their perfidy, we thought that Your Fraternity should be warned and urged, and we herewith order you by Apostolic Letters, that on the first Saturday of the Lent to come, in the morning, while the Jews are gathered in the synagogues, you shall, by our order, seize all the books of the Jews who live in your districts, and have these books carefully guarded in the possession of the Dominican and Franciscan Friars. For this purpose you may invoke, if need be, the help of the secular arm; and you may also promulgate the sentence of excommunication against all those

subject to your jurisdiction, whether clergy or laity, who refuse to give up Hebrew books which they have in their possession despite your warning given generally in the churches or individually.

Copies of the letter were amended to accord with the ecclesial or secular role of the recipient.

42. Grayzel, *Church and the Jews,* 1:243 §98. This letter is dated June 20, 1239, five days prior to the convocation of the examining board at which Rabbi Yehiel (June 25–26) and Rabbi Judah were asked to defend Talmud. Two others were summoned before Eudes' examiners: Samuel ben Solomon of Chateau-Thierry and Moses ben Jacob of Coucy. After the appearance of Yehiel and Judah it was deemed unnecessary to question the others. See Cohen, *Friars and the Jews,* 62–63, esp. n. 22.

43. Cohen, *Friars and the Jews,* 63.

44. Grayzel, *Church and the Jews,* 1:253 §104.

45. Ibid. (emphasis mine).

46. Ibid., 275 §119. This motivation is acknowledged in a letter to the king of France on August 12, 1247; the letter forwarded originally to Odo is lost, although the bishop's written response and inquisitorial activities are known. See below.

47. See Grayzel, *Church and the Jews,* 1:275–78 n. 3, esp. 278.

48. Chazan, *Church, State, and Jew in the Middle Ages,* 237.

49. Grayzel, *Church and the Jews,* 1:279 n. 3.

50. D. J. Lasker provides an analysis of the anti-Christian polemical literature and the types of argumentation used by Jewish disputants, namely, exegetical, historical, and rational (*Jewish Philosophical Polemics against Christianity in the Middle Ages* [New York: KTAV, 1977]). See also Cohen, "Towards a Functional Classification." Cohen offers a fluid, fourfold classification of polemical literature based on the function of the texts (polemic for the community of the faithful; guidebooks for direct confrontation; defending the faith, and condemnation of the aggressor). He also provides a succinct review of previous systems of classification of polemical literature beginning with Joseph ben Shem Tov ibn Shem Tov (fifteenth century) and including Amos Funkenstein's "landmark essay" of 1968 ("Changes in the Patterns of Christian Anti-Jewish Polemic in the Twelfth Century" [in Hebrew], *Sion* n.s. 33 [1968], which appeared in an abridged form in English in 1971, "Basic Types of Christian Polemic in the Later Middle Ages," *Viator* 2 [1971]: 373–82). Each of these works amply demonstrates the categories and characteristics of Jewish controversy literature known as *vicuah* or *nizzuah/nizzahon*. They also disprove the notion of Jewish passivity in these sociotheological disputes with secular or ecclesial authorities and institutions. "Like the evolving Christian attack on Judaism during the same period, Jewish anti-Christian polemic utilized variegated means to denigrate its opponent. In fact, the development of the Jewish attack on Christianity parallels that of medieval Christian anti-Jewish polemic" (Cohen, 112).

51. See the important work of Jacob Katz (*Exclusiveness and Tolerance* [London: Oxford University Press, 1961]), in which the author analyzes the evolution of Jewish exclusivity and openness in the Middle Ages.

52. See, e.g., Rashi on Exod 19.5.

53. See Rashi on Ruth 1.16 and Lev 19.33, respectively.

54. See Rashi on Exod 33.16–17 and Num 22.5–8.

55. See Rashi on Deut 30.3; Katz, *Exclusiveness and Tolerance,* 15–16.

56. Thomas received the Dominican habit in April 1244; however, he was forcibly detained by his family at Roccasecca until fall of 1245. See Jean-Pierre Torrell, *Saint Thomas Aquinas,* vol. 1, *The Person and His Work,* trans. Robert Royal (Washington, DC: Catholic University Press, 1996), 24.

57. "[H]e could have studied the liberal arts [in Paris] either at the faculty of arts or in the priory. But nothing would have prevented him from studying theology in some courses with Albert at Saint-Jacques during the same time. He recopied Albert's *De caelesti hierarchia* in a manuscript that gives testimony to the Parisian system of 'pieces'" (Torrell, *Saint Thomas Aquinas,* 1:24).

3
The Jews in the *Summa Theologiae*

INTRODUCTION:
A BASIC THEOLOGICAL PERSPECTIVE

Thomas does not conceive of the Jews as an undifferentiated social group. With regard to responsibility for the crucifixion, for example, he distinguishes subgroups within Judaism, absolving the majority common folk and blaming the leadership.[1] Thomas' identification of the Jews (in a pejorative sense) with the leaders of the Jewish people is clear in *ST* IIIa. 47.5. resp., wherein he differentiates the elders (*majores*) from the common people (*minores*). He asserts that the leaders knew that Jesus was the Christ but were ignorant of the "mystery of the Godhead." Nevertheless, theirs was an *affected* ignorance.[2] The persecution and crucifixion of Christ were not excusable insofar as the leaders "saw manifest signs of his Divinity,...[which] they perverted out of hatred and envy for Christ; and they were unwilling to believe the words whereby he declared himself to be the Son of God." Common people, namely

> the uneducated, unacquainted with the mysteries of the Scriptures, did not fully recognize Christ either as the Messiah or Son of God. Although some of them did believe in him, the greater number did not. If they occasionally wondered whether he was not the Messiah, because of his many signs and the power of his teaching, they were nevertheless so misled by their leaders that they did not believe him to be either Son of God, or the Messiah. Hence Peter said to them I know that you acted in ignorance, as did also your rulers (Acts 3.17).[3]

In addition, Thomas reprises the substance of this argument in the following article (a. 6) and makes it abundantly clear that Jesus' prayer of forgiveness on the cross (Luke 23.34) "is not to be referred to the rulers among the Jews, but to the common people."[4] The tension between Jewish exclusivity and Christian social tolerance stems from Israel's perpetually elect status. Thomas theorized that the privilege of Torah was given to the Jews because they were unlike the surrounding nations, which practiced idolatry;[5] theirs was a superior status engendered by closer union with God. "[T]he more the Jewish people were dedicated to the worship of God the more they surpassed other peoples." Aquinas cites Deuteronomy 4.8 to illustrate his point: "For what other nation is there so renowned that has ceremonies and just judgments and the Law in its entirety?"[6] As demonstrated previously, Thomas believed that

> it was solely as a result of a gratuitous act of election that the fathers received the promise and the people descended from them received the Law....But any further inquiry as to why he chose this people and not another for Christ to be born from may suitably be met by the reply of Augustine [*Tract. super Joan. XXVI.* On *John* 6.44] *Do not seek to determine why he draws one and not another to himself if you wish to avoid error.*[7]

Aquinas insists that "the Jewish people...was specially appointed to the worship of God"; this people (and in particular its priests) were marked by "special features befitting divine worship, whether spiritual or bodily."[8] The election and role of Israel are inextricably rooted in salvation history; indeed, Thomas' exegetical interpretations of prefigurement radically depend on historical, not metaphorical, Israel.[9] Indeed, "[t]he carnal election of Israel is intimately related to the historicity of Judaism."[10] Therefore, entry into the worshiping people of Israel, the regulation of matters pertaining to Jews' divine worship, and the prevention or removal of impediments to corporate or individual worship have rational causes (*rationabiles causas*), possessed of *both* literal and figurative dimensions.[11]

Moreover, "[a]mong the Jewish people from whom Christ was to be born, not only words, but also deeds were prophetic....Therefore it is lawful to apply these deeds to our instruction," all the while recognizing that not every event ordered by divine providence functions as a predictive sign or as a harbinger of future events.[12] For Thomas, the carnal descent of Christ from Israel qualifies each prerogative of Jewish history. Salvation, after all, is from the Jews.

Unlike the preparatory privileges that have come to fruition (the

Law, the patriarchal promises, and the like), elect Israel's role remains incomplete because of its anticipated eschatological function. The Christian contention that Israel's faith was incomplete or that the Jews' role in salvation history is incomplete is not intrinsically anti-Jewish nor does it necessarily abet later anti-Semitism. On the contrary, Thomas likens the preparatory function of the Mosaic Law for the Jewish people to the gradual exploitation of natural inclinations in the young because

> one who attempts to induce someone to observe precepts has to begin by exploiting those inclinations which are already present in him in order to move him in the required direction. ...[I]n its function of preparing [people] for Christ the Old Law was, as it were, something imperfect preparing for what was perfect. Hence it was given to a people who, *measured by the perfection which was to be achieved through Christ,* were still imperfect. This is why that people is compared to a child whose life was directed by a tutor [Gal 3.24]....[I]t is a characteristic of [people] who are still imperfect that they do desire temporal benefits, *though always subject to God.* The mark of perverse [people], on the other hand, is that they make temporal benefits an end in themselves.[13]

This understanding of the Law and the pedagogy of the Jews is neither harsh nor negative (but Pauline); the Law led imperfect people to God through the temporal things to which they are intrinsically inclined.

Aquinas' theological position does not reflect a dualistic teleology. The Jews are not an alien group because Christianity derives from them and depends on the Jewish people for historical witness and eschatological fulfillment.[14] However, Judaism has no necessary relation to Christianity for its self-identity, nor (from the Jewish perspective) for its corporate fulfillment.[15] Thomas' formulation of the church's origin and eschatology did not permit him to articulate a theological doctrine of Christian exclusiveness: the role of the Jews must be taken into the account.

Selected Sociotheological Issues in the *Summa Theologiae*

The Status of Jewish Belief

In IIa IIae. 10, Thomas distinguishes various types of *infidelitas*[16] based on their relationship to the virtue of faith.[17] Those who oppose the faith may do so in two ways: either before faith has been accepted, or after the faith has been accepted, either in figure or in revelation of the truth. Therefore, *infidelitas* is of three sorts: the unbelief of the pagans and heathens who resist prior to accepting the faith; the unbelief of the Jews who oppose the faith, having received it *in figura;* and the unbelief of heretics who, having received the faith, reject the revelation of the truth.

In a. 6. resp. Thomas ranks the gravity of unbelief. Unbelief is fundamentally a privation[18] and

> in this respect [the one] who denies the faith after accepting it sins more grievously than [one] who denies it without ever having accepted it....Thus the infidelity of those who in effect attack by corrupting the Gospel faith they profess is more serious than that of the Jews who have never embraced it...[and the Jews'] unbelief is more grievous than that of heathens who have not accepted the Gospel faith in any way at all.

The vice of unbelief manifest in rejecting the faith is more serious than unbelief shown by corrupting particular elements of the faith or holding erroneous doctrines concerning it. For Thomas, "infidelity has the character of fault more because it resists faith than because it does not hold the truths of faith....And so...the unbelief of heretics is the very worst (*est pessima*)."[19] So serious is this sin of heretical infidelity that, after due process, heretics may even warrant the penalty of death.[20]

For Thomas, the Jews occupy a midpoint of faith and infidelity alike. The Jews are possessors of faith *in figura;* their resistance to the fullness of the Christian faith is attributable to wrongly (*male*) interpreting the Old Law. The Jews occupy an intermediate position between Christians and pagans precisely because they prefigure the truth. Therefore, comparatively speaking, it is better to be a confessing Jew than a heretical Christian.

The Tolerance of Jewish Rites in the Divine Economy

Similarly, Thomas confirms the tolerance of Jewish rites, arguing that a good comes (*bonum provenit*) from their observance, namely, a witness to the Christian faith set forth *in figura.* In *ST* IIa IIae. 10.11. resp., Aquinas argues predominantly from the Augustinian stance of testamentary tolerance. He also cites "Gregory on the Jews" in the *sed contra:* "Let them have free permission to observe all their feasts, just as hitherto they and their fathers have for ages observed them."[21] Historically considered, even heretical or pagan rites have been intermittently tolerated by the church in order to avoid some potential evil (*vitandum scandalum vel dissidium*). Nevertheless, these "bear no truth or profit [and] are not to be tolerated in the same way" as those rites of the Jews. There is a qualitative difference between Jewish rites and the rites of other unbelievers, consistent with the Jews' mediate position. That Thomas confirms certain elements of the ecclesial policy regarding the Jews is not surprising. What is significant is his rejection of the commentary tradition that argues that the rites of the Jews are equivalent to idolatry: "Be not held again under the yoke of bondage [Gal 5.1], a gloss comments, *The bondage of that law was not lighter than that of idolatry.*"[22] For Thomas, Jewish rites are not an evil to be suffered, nor are they idolatrous or to be curtailed aggressively; rather, Jews and Christians derive useful benefit from their observance.

Association with Jews

Aquinas differs from the traditional ecclesial policies concerning social intercourse with Jews, arguing a position consistent with the principles articulated above. The degree to which Aquinas preserves the mutual association of Christians with Jews emerges through comparison with prior church legislation. For example, Gratian's *Decretum* (ca. 1145), citing the Sixth Toledan Council and the Council of Agde,[23] forbade association with Jews, especially with reference to table fellowship. The Jews' Kashrut laws provoked an apparent retaliatory prohibition:

> For those foods which we eat with the Apostle's permission are judged impure by them. Thus Christians will begin to be inferior to Jews if we use those foods which are offered by them, while they disdain foods offered by us....[24]

Furthermore, Christians could not reside with Jews, bathe with Jews, nor solicit medicinal assistance from them when ill; were "anyone to do so—if he is a cleric, he should be deposed; if he is a layman, he should be excommunicated."[25] The *Decretum, Decretales,* and the *Summa de Poenitentia et Matrimonio* stress the removal of Christians from Jewish company or commerce; violators of the policy are subject to ecclesial sanctions, especially excommunication.[26] Concomitant with maintaining an official policy of protection of the Jews, the legislative collections promoted Christian exclusivity and eroded the longstanding theological foundations of mutual tolerance through lamentable rhetoric.[27] From the

Fourth Lateran Council (1215) Jews were mandated (by implementation of the secular arm, if need be) to wear a badge marking them as a distinct subgroup within medieval society.[28]

The medieval rabbinate likewise sought to implement rules of separation and to establish legitimate bases to define the limits of economic and sociopolitical engagement with non-Jews. The lessening of mutual tolerance and the refinement of group boundaries resulted from the common fear that those admitted to intimate family events, redolent with religious significance, might be converted. In point of fact, frequent contact did not effect social integration of Jews and Christians, but rather the opposite occurred.[29] Although a casuistic distinction arose between the nations of old who were idolaters ("nations restricted by the ways of religion") and contemporaneous Christian-Gentiles ("nations not restricted by the ways of religion"), dietary prohibitions regarding table fellowship with non-Jews perdured (even with the esteemed rabbi Menachem Ha-Me'iri).[30] The Jewish dietary precepts, which effectively eliminated table fellowship with Christians, symbolized (for some) the Jews' impugning of the Christian religion; the regulations reinforced mutual exclusion and the adherent's identification with the group.

Aquinas distinguishes, however, "according to the various conditions of persons, affairs, and times."[31] The church, he contends, legitimately prohibits association with heretics and apostates and imposes the sentence of excommunication as a sanction upon those Christians who violate these norms. Those strong in their faith, however, are not forbidden to mix with pagans and Jews, as necessity arises; such contact may be salutary insofar as social intercourse encourages conversion to the Christian faith. Interestingly, Aquinas also examines the question from biblical history as well, citing Deuteronomy 7.23 and the Gloss on Leviticus 15.22, demonstrating the risk that the Jews faced entering into the territory of non-Jews. Because the "Jews were prone to idolatry,...it was to be feared lest through long living with these people they would be estranged from the faith;...the text goes on, For she will turn away thy son from following me."[32] He does not explicitly nor implicitly condemn Jewish exclusivity, having contextualized the historical separateness of the Jews as a divine mandate. Rather, Thomas recognizes the shared prospect of conversion and counsels forbidding only those who are feeble in faith "to have intercourse with unbelievers, and especially to be on very familiar terms with them or join in with them without need."[33] Thus, it is the particular circumstances of persons, occasions, and affairs that determine association with non-Christians; Thomas clearly disagreed on this matter with his elder brother in religion, Raymond of Penyafort, as well as with the collected ecclesial legislation.

Jewish Dominion over Christians

Another equally contentious issue was whether unbelievers should be allowed authority or dominion over believers. Three categories of dominion are of particular concern in the *Decretum* and the *Decretales:* Jewish masters and Christian (or soon to be baptized) slaves,[34] Jews in public office,[35] and Jewish employers hiring Christian laborers.[36] Succinctly summarizing the legislation: Jews are to set Christian slaves free; they are forbidden to sell any *baptizandi* to a fellow Jew; they are not to hold public office lest their position afford them the opportunity to inflict harm upon Christians, nor are they to employ Christian nurses, midwives, or servants. A freed slave of a Jewish master, however, may opt to remain as a farmhand or sharecropper to satisfy outstanding debts to him.[37] Civil or personal jurisdiction of Jews over Christians is forbidden because the subservient status of these Christians precludes safeguarding their spiritual or temporal well-being.

Theoretically, Aquinas agrees concerning newly inaugurated roles of dominance and subservience since "subjects are easily influenced by their superiors to fall in with their will, unless the subjects be strong characters."[38] However, dominion of unbelievers over believers also risks that the former group "would despise the faith by coming to know the failures of believers."[39] Thomas shows himself a realist. Human law according to reason is not eliminated by divine law; nor is preexisting dominion, which is a human institution, always supplanted by the ecclesial legislation. "Consequently the distinction between the faithful and infidels, considered in itself, does not cancel the dominion or authority of infidels over the faithful."[40] Civil or personal jurisdiction of Jews and unbelievers is not universally prohibited because "unbelief in itself is not inconsistent with dominion, since [dominion] was brought in by the *Jus Gentium,* which is human law."[41] So, for example, even Christian laborers may be hired to work on land belonging to Jews.[42]

Coerced or Forced Baptism of Jews

Thomas unequivocally opposes the baptism of Jewish children or *aliorum infidelium* when the child's parents do not consent.[43] By arguing from biological generation and parental protection *sicut sub quodam spirituali utero,* Thomas asserts that

> it would be contrary to natural justice for [the child] to be taken away from the care of the parents or have any arrangements made for him against their wishes. As soon, however, as [the child] begins to have the use of freewill, then he begins to be his own master and to provide for himself in matters of divine and natural rights. Then he may be brought to the faith, not by compulsion but by persuasion; he can even consent to the faith and be baptized, but not before [the child] enjoys the use of reason.
>
> Accordingly we read that the children of the patriarchs were saved *in the faith of their parents*....[44]

Moreover, this avoids one practical danger: children without the use of reason could easily turn from the Christian faith and bring it into disrepute.

What makes Aquinas distinctive regarding forced baptism is that he bases his argument primarily on the natural right of parents and only secondarily on the incapacity of children without the use of reason to will this or any other act requiring informed consent. For Thomas, the authority and custom of the church regarding baptism of unbelievers' children supersede the authority of any theologian, whether an "Augustine or Jerome or of any other divine whomsoever."[45]

As for adult unbelievers (i.e., *sicut gentiles et Judaei*), "[t]hese are by no means to be compelled for belief is voluntary."[46] Belief must remain voluntary even for subject, conquered, or captive peoples. Heretics and apostates (including recidivist Jews) may be compelled to embrace the faith anew, since "the acceptance of faith is a matter of freewill yet keeping it when once it has been received is a matter of obligation."[47] Compelling apostates and heretics to resume the obligation of the faith freely undertaken previously differs in essence from compulsory baptism.

Solomon Grayzel claims that only Innocent IV "hints" that Jewish children who have been forcibly baptized perhaps should be restored to their parents.[48] His predecessor, Innocent III, taught that the permissibility of a convert's reversion to Judaism depended on the degree of volition exercised by the adult at the moment of duress or force.[49] Only those Jews who kept objecting to baptism could be permitted to return to Judaism; those who remained silent had given implicit consent and "were to be compelled to remain Christians. It is obvious...that few indeed of the former would survive that moment."[50] Of those who did endure coerced baptism as adults the risk of apostasy was understandable, especially when secular princes desired the unencumbered resources of their former moneylenders; violation of an individual's will and mutual economic benefit urged resuming one's former religious convictions and social role. The reversion of adults to their former way of life prompted the Fourth Lateran Council to decree

> that such people shall in every possible manner be restrained by the prelates of the churches, from observing their old rites, so that those whom their free will brought to the Christian religion shall be held to its observance by compulsion, that they may be saved. For there is less evil in not recognizing the way of the Lord than in backsliding after having recognized it.[51]

For Aquinas however, violence and compulsion render an act involuntary because they are principles extrinsic to the will imposed upon the subject. No Jews, whether children or adults, may be forced by ecclesial or secular authorities to accept baptism; this is profoundly rooted in Aquinas' anthropology and psychology of human acts.[52] Theoretically, coerced baptism was proscribed by one provision of the *Constitutio* decreeing that "no Christian shall use violence to force them to be baptized so long as they are unwilling and refuse."[53] But Innocent III himself, at the dawn of the thirteenth century, grappled with the issue of consent and volition of Jews whose baptism, if not forced, had been coerced. Similarly, Grayzel cites the papal policy of Nicholas III in 1277 (a few years after Thomas' death) "in answer to a Dominican Inquisitor,...that Jews baptized while in fear of death and later reverting to Judaism and refusing to live as Christians even after prolonged imprisonment, must be treated as ordinary heretics, i.e. burned at the stake."[54] Sadly, Aquinas' social and theological positions concerning coerced baptism of Jews were not heeded by popes or even by his own brethren in the Order of Preachers.

CONCLUSION

Thomas may well have witnessed the assault on Talmud and other Hebrew books in Paris at the inception of his Dominican religious life. His primary mentor, Albertus Magnus, was an active participant in the crisis that resulted in the selective destruction of the Jews' patrimony. Nonetheless, Thomas in his *ST* does not disparage the privileges of Israel (that which is already accomplished through them). Nor does he deny their eschatological role (that which is yet to be accomplished through them).

Aquinas posits that through the privilege of the Mosaic Law, the Jews possessed the gospel *in figura* and therefore they occupy a mediate position of faith and unbelief; although their belief is imperfect, the Jews are subject to God. Thomas understands that Jews were not an undifferentiated group in either his own time or the time of Jesus. He argues that Jewish rites ought to be tolerated, not as an evil suffered but for the good derived. Aquinas asserts that Christians retain the right of association with Jews (respecting persons, affairs, and times) and that Jews may even employ Christians. Although the Jews are not to impede the exercise of the Christian faith, any formerly established dominion of Jews over Christians is not automatically supplanted by ecclesial jurisdiction: tolerance must be mutual. Additionally, Thomas is unalterably opposed to the baptizing of Jewish children without the consent of their parents. This protection of Jewish children is based primarily not on papal policy, church custom, or social contract but rather on natural justice. He also maintains that adult Jews should suffer no violence nor be compelled to submit to an involuntary baptism: free will is essential to belief and remains an inviolable criterion for Christian faith.[55]

Thomas' sociotheological positions concerning the Jews, which are located throughout the *ST,* should not be viewed in isolation from Thomas' ecclesial predecessors or his contemporaries. Furthermore, his view of the Jews in *ST* should not be read apart from the sustained treatment and privileged status that he accords the Jews in *CRO* 9–11, because the *prima pars* and Aquinas' first lecture series on Romans are contemporaneous labors. Indeed, as intertextual congruency will demonstrate, *ST* Ia. 23 informs these three chapters of Aquinas' commentary and serves as the essential point of access for his interpretation of Romans 9–11. For Thomas, predestination provides the fundamental theological framework for understanding Paul's eschatological plot line and the ongoing role of the Jews. Because of God's predestination and election of Israel, certain privileges and functions should be safeguarded for them.[56] Aquinas argues to his positions in *CRO* from biblical history, ecclesiastical custom, and theological authorities, just as he does in *ST*. (Augustine is one authority from the received tradition whom Thomas cites and whose doctrine of predestination and election he corrects and develops to frame the argument on the Jews in *CRO*.) However, he does not merely synthesize these three components: he forthrightly critiques them, reminding his audience that the Jews' privileges in salvation history perdure because salvation comes from the Jews (John 4.22) in accord with

God's predestinating will. Thomas did not suffer from an inner theological contradiction[57] either within the *ST* itself or between his exegetical *CRO* and the *ST:* his theological analysis of predestination and election preclude this from happening.

In the next chapter, I shall proceed in the following way: since predestination and election are Thomas' hermeneutical keys to Romans 9–11, we must understand how these doctrines functioned for him. In order to accomplish this objective, first I will demonstrate substantial and material congruency between *CRO* and *ST* (this is a hermeneutical issue to which critics of Aquinas insufficiently attend). Because of the contemporaneous production of Ia. 23. aa.1–6 and his first lectures on Romans as evidenced by textual agreement, it is legitimate to interpret sections of *CRO* that treat of predestination and election in light of the texts from *ST*. (The issue is not simply the correspondence between the works; after all, they could be wrong in their agreement about something!) Next, by an immediate comparison of Thomas' constructive proposal on the Jewish people with Augustine's position on predestination, election, and the Jews in his Romans commentaries (chapters 4 and 5), we shall see not only how it is that Thomas amends and develops Augustine's views, but how he advances his own unique position.

NOTES

1. We also discover in his *Lectura Super Ioannem* (hereafter *CJn*) an attempt to specify the seemingly pejorative use of the generic term *Jew(s)* in the Fourth Gospel by specifying those Jews who exhibited a characteristic opposition to Jesus (e.g., the Pharisees; see *CJn* 7.5 §1109 and 1.13 §241). Thomas recognized the "encoded sense" employed by the Fourth Evangelist (see Raymond Brown, *The Gospel According to John: Introduction, Translation, and Notes,* 2 vols.; Anchor Bible 29, 29A [Garden City, NY: Doubleday, 1966, 1970], 1:LXXI). For example, in *CJn* 7.3 §1052 Aquinas writes:

> They were amazed at the power he had which kept [Jesus] from being apprehended. So they said: Is he not the man they, i.e., their leaders, want? This agrees with what was said before: "For reasons like this the Jews began to persecute Jesus, because he performed such works on the sabbath" (above 5.16); "*Evil has come out of the elders of the people, who ruled them*" (Dn 13.5). This also shows that Christ spoke the truth, while what their leaders said was false. For above, when our Lord asked them: Why do you want to kill me? They denied it and said: You have a demon within you! Who wants to kill you? But here, what their leaders had denied, these others

admit when they say, Is he not the man they want to kill? Accordingly, they are amazed, considering the evil intentions of their leaders.

2. "Affected ignorance aggravates rather than excuses a fault, for it indicates that a man is so intent on sinning that he wants to be ignorant of anything that would deter him from it. And thus did the Jews sin, in crucifying Christ not only as man, but also as God" (*ST* IIIa. 47.5. ad 3).

3. *ST* IIIa. 47.5. resp. Mark 15.10 attributes to envy the handing over of Jesus to Pilate by the chief priests, elders, and scribes. Is not (what is sometimes described as) anti-Jewish commentary embedded in the New Testament texts by first-century Jewish-Christian authors themselves?

4. *ST* IIIa. 47.6. ad 1. However, Jeremy Cohen ("Jews as Killers of Christ," *Traditio* 39 [1983]: 21) fails to give due attention to the fact that the ignorance of the *majores* is affected, as opposed to the *minores,* who are misled by them. To ascribe "the intentionality of the Jews' misdeed" in the crucifixion of Christ to an undifferentiated Judaism misreads the *ST* texts and *CRO*. Although Cohen's article provides a concise collection of patristic and medieval texts in attempting to trace the trajectory of Jewish culpability in Jesus' death and the rise of anti-Judaism, he overstates the case with reference to Aquinas. For example, Cohen contends that thirteenth-century friars taught that "European Jews...no longer fulfilled the function that warranted their toleration in Christendom; a properly oriented Church should not stop short of persecuting their heresy, converting them *en masse* to Christianity and banishing the recalcitrant who refused to follow the truth" (p. 24). We shall see below that Aquinas explicitly opposes identifying the Jews as heretics, converting Jews *en masse,* or banishing them from society. With reference to Thomas, Cohen is unquestionably incorrect. Moreover, one must question whether *Judaism* is synonymous with the Jewish *majores* any more than the term *church* is identical with *hierarchical leadership*.

One may also call into question Cohen's methodology in *Living Letters of the Law: Ideas of the Jew in Medieval Christianity* (Berkeley and Los Angeles: University of California Press, 1999), 372–75, where he, by his own admission, blends "the results of...like-minded Thomistic discussions" effectively to conclude to an undifferentiated Judaism. For example, Cohen speaks of "the Jewish sin against Jesus," "the Jews'" actions toward Jesus, and the "deicide of the Jews," while ostensibly investigating the role of "the Jewish sages." Although rhetorically understandable, Cohen obscures the distinctions that Aquinas explicitly makes. See further discussion below.

5. *ST* Ia IIae. 98.4. resp.
6. *ST* Ia IIae. 98.5. ad 2.
7. *ST* Ia IIae. 98.4. resp.
8. *ST* Ia IIae. 102.6. resp.
9. *ST* in Ia IIae. 102.6. resp., Aquinas cites 1 Cor 10.11 to demonstrate that "the worship prescribed in the Law prefigured the mystery of Christ....

Consequently, two sets of reasons may be assigned for these observances: one, according to their appropriateness to divine worship; the other, according as they prefigure some element of the Christian life."

10. Michael Wyschogrod, *The Body of Faith: Judaism as Corporeal Election* (Minneapolis: Seabury, 1983), 177.

11. See *ST* Ia IIae. 102.5. An exhaustive discussion of Thomas' understanding of the judicial and ceremonial precepts of the Mosaic Law is well beyond the scope of the current study. What is essential to the present discussion, however, is the superior status and role of the Jews considered historically and exegetically by Aquinas.

For an innovative approach to the literal and spiritual senses in Aquinas that warrants further investigation, see Cohen, *Letters*, 378–89. While Cohen's argument initially appears compelling, close analysis reveals it to be selective, methodologically considered. He marshals "evidence" mostly by inference without regard to the chronology of Thomas' corpus or the theological integrity of individual works. Most notably Cohen cites only one instance of Aquinas' *CRO* (5.6) and is apparently unaware of its correlation with *ST,* which properly contextualizes Thomas' argument.

12. *ST* IIa IIae. 96.3. ad 3. Hyam Maccoby analyzes the shift of emphasis in Jewish exegetical method in the wake of anti-Talmudic campaigns and public disputations (*Judaism on Trial: Jewish-Christian Disputation in the Middle Ages* [London and Toronto: Associated University Presses, 1982], 46). He contends that Jewish–Christian controversy intensified the quest for *pshat* (i.e., the literal meaning of scripture) rather than *drash* (i.e., the symbolic meaning). Aquinas exhibits a similar quest for the rational-literal cause of Torah observances in preference to allegory, or prior to rational-prefiguring causes oriented to Christ. Jacob Katz recognizes an analogous hermeneutic in the literature of the Jewish counterdialectic (*Exclusiveness and Tolerance* [London: Oxford University Press, 1961]). Rabbi Samuel ben Meir (Rashbam) sought to "attribute dietary laws to hygienic considerations...[which he]...intended as a refutation of Christian arguments against the reasonableness of these precepts" (p. 18). Thomas could readily accede to the interpretative maxim: "a biblical text never loses its literal meaning" (*b. Shabb.* 63a)—even if it points toward the Messiah.

13. *ST* Ia IIae. 99.6. resp. (emphasis mine).

14. Even in *CJn* §605–6, expositing on John 4.22, Thomas reasserts the intrinsic bond with the Jews:

> Salvation comes from the Jews in three ways. First in their teaching of the truth, for all other peoples were in error, while the Jews held fast to the truth, according to Romans (3.2)....Secondly, in their spiritual gifts: for prophecy and the other gifts of the Spirit were given to them first, and from them they reached the others: You, i.e., the Gentiles, a wild olive branch, are ingrafted on them, i.e., the Jews; If the Gentiles have become sharers in their spiritual goods, they ought to help the Jews as to earthly goods. Thirdly, since the very

author of salvation is from the Jews, since Christ came from them in the flesh (Rom 9.5).

Note Thomas' use of texts from Romans to support his position.

15. Indeed, Judaism's prerogative of membership through carnal descent demands a nearly exclusivist self-definition and occasions dilemmas concerning the degree of Jewish social interaction permissible in an increasingly urban and predominantly Gentile society. Not until the teaching of R. Menachem Ha-Me'iri (late fourteenth century) was a broader policy of religious toleration of Christians and Muslims by Jews articulated. See the discussion below concerning the Jews' right of association.

16. Unbelief may be taken either *secundum puram negationem*, namely, to describe one who possesses no faith (a.1), or to describe opposition to the faith (*consistat in renitendo fidei*), as below in a.5. If taken "according to a pure negation" it has the character of penalty (*poenae*) rather than fault (*non habet rationem peccati*), particularly in those who have never heard the gospel or about the Christian faith. The Jews' *infidelitas* is of the latter sort, which implies a degree of culpability; see a.1 ad 2. This position, of course, accords well with Rom 10.18: But, I say, have they not heard?

17. In a.10.5. resp. Thomas sketches a general theory of virtue to explain the theological virtue of faith and how it may be opposed. Since "virtue consists in attaining some norm of human knowledge or conduct," the diversity of vices may be considered under the aspect of its relationship to the virtue or regarding the constituent elements of that virtue. Therefore, considered under the first rubric "there are several infidelities determinate in number and kind," but, regarding the corruption of constituent elements of faith, "there are not distinctive kinds of unbelief, for errors can be multiplied indefinitely."

18. "[T]he sin of infidelity, or indeed any grave sin, is in privative, not purely negative, opposition to God's grace. A lack of, *carentia*, from *careo*, to be wanting of what should be present" (T. Gilby, OP, *ST*, vol. 32; n. a, p. 49).

19. *ST* IIa IIae. 10.6. resp.

20. See *ST* IIa IIae. 11.3. resp.

21. See *Decretum* I, 45, 3.

22. *ST* IIa IIae. 10.11. obj.2, citing Interlinear. Lombard (*Patrologia cursus completus: Series Latina* [= PL], ed. J.-P. Migne, 221 vols. [Paris: J.-P. Migne, 1844–91], 192:152). From Augustine, *Contra Faustum* 9.18 (PL 42:358).

23. See II. Causa XXVII, Questio I, Canon XIII and Canon XIV, respectively. Further, Robert Chazan provides a translation of pertinent legislation in *Church, State, and Jew in the Middle Ages,* Library of Jewish Studies (New York: Behrman House, 1980), esp. 20–26.

24. Ibid.

25. Ibid. Related written papal policies were compiled and organized chronologically by Raymond of Penyafort in the *Decretales*; the work was completed nearly a century after Gratian's *Decretum* and was promulgated by Gregory IX in 1234. Another relevant synthetic, topical organization of ecclesial

policy, was produced by Raymond, entitled *Summa de Poenitentia et Matrimonio*. He devotes one subsection to "Jews, Saracens, and their slaves." This subdivision is found also in the *Decretales*. See Chazan, *Church, State, and Jew in the Middle Ages,* 28 and 38.

26. Raymond's *De Poenitentia et Matrimonio* contains the following prohibition: "Christians...should not eat with Jews nor live with Jews nor accept them at their social functions, as in the *Decretum*. However, we may eat with Saracens, as in the *Decretum*. The reason for the distinction is because Jews through the abuse of Scriptures and their contempt for our food impugn more deeply our faith. Others say indiscriminately and more properly that, just as a Christian should not do the aforesaid with a Jew, so too should he not do so with a Saracen, *since Saracens also regularly Judaize*, whence the same reason for the prohibition and the same danger" (Chazan, *Church, State, and Jew in the Middle Ages,* 39; emphasis mine).

27. One of the most appalling examples found in the *Decretales* is the letter of Innocent III to the archbishop of Sens and the bishop of Paris, which, in part, states: "because of their [the Jews'] perfidy, even the Saracens who persecute the Catholic faith and do not believe in the Christ whom the Jews crucified cannot tolerate them and have even expelled them from their territory, vehemently rebuking us for tolerating those by whom...our Redeemer was condemned to the cross. Therefore the Jews ought not be ungrateful to us, requiting Christian favor with contumely and intimacy with contempt. Yet, mercifully admitted into our intimacy, they threaten us with that retribution which, according to the common proverb, the mouse in a pocket, the snake around one's loins, and the fire in one's bosom are accustomed to exhibit to their hosts." See Solomon Grayzel, *The Church and the Jews in the XIIIth Century,* vol. 1 (New York: Hermon, 1966), 115 §18.

28. Ibid., 10, 309 §68. Grayzel contends that "French Jews as a whole had never worn the Badge as a distinguishing mark [because] they yet fell into the category mentioned in the edict of IV Lateran Council, i.e., 'In nonnullis provinciis a Christianis Judeos...habitus distinguit diversitas.'" Later, in 1268, after the near expulsion of the Jews from the Kingdom, the wearing of the badge was required of the Jews by Louis IX (probably at the instigation of Pablo Christiani). See ibid., 65–66, n. 112.

29. See Katz, *Exclusiveness and Tolerance*, 56. Although economic or political interests might bring Jews and Christians together, these were transitory and sometimes competitive in nature.

30. See ibid., 115–16. The distinction permitted specific Talmudic precepts to be reinterpreted in light of Maimonides' philosophical thinking.

31. *ST* IIa IIae. 9.10. resp. Thomas denies ecclesial jurisdiction over Jews and other nonbelievers in exercising spiritual judgment or punishment "who in nowise received the Christian faith [*qui nullo modo fidem christianam receperunt*]...." The exercise of temporal judgment over Jews and pagans derives from some infraction of law committed while dwelling among Christians, and usually

depends on the secular arm for implementation of sanctions. See also ad 2., which restates his rationale.
  32. *ST* IIa IIae. 9.10. ad 4.
  33. *ST* IIa IIae. 9.10. resp.
  34. *Decretum* I, LIV, Canon XIII; Canon XV–XVIII. *Decretales* VI, I–II; VI, V; VI, XIX.
  35. *Decretum* I, LIV, Canon XIV. *Decretales* VI, XVI.
  36. *Decretales* VI, VIII; VI, XIII.
  37. *Decretales* VI, II.
  38. *ST* IIa IIae. 10.10. resp.
  39. *ST* IIa IIae. 10.10. resp.
  40. *ST* IIa IIae. 10.10. resp. However, the church has the power to take away this right, "which it sometimes does and sometimes not." Therefore one born into slavery (*vernaculus*) is to be freed when that slave becomes a Christian or, if purchased, the slave is to be sold within three months. Thomas preserves the authority of ecclesial law over unbelievers who are in its temporal jurisdiction because the church acts as do "secular princes in making laws for subjects in favor of liberty." Although ecclesial jurisdiction theoretically could extend to those who are not temporal subjects or church members, no equivalent law exists to demand the forfeiture or sale of slaves. The self-restraint of the church in these matters aims to avoid scandal. Thomas circumscribes ecclesial competency just as he limited the jurisdiction of secular authorities in seizing property or income derived from usury as in *De regimine Judaeorum ad Ducissam Brabantiae*.
  41. *ST* IIa IIae. 12.2. resp., which deals with the forfeiture of dominion by an apostate ruler. Thomas reasserts that the difference between believers and unbelievers derives from divine law, which "does not annul human law." The church retains the right to punish those civil rulers who once received the faith and have renounced it subsequently, by absolving the apostate's subjects from personal and civil allegiance. However, the church cannot "penalize the unbelief in those who have never received the faith."
  42. *ST* IIa IIae. 10.10. ad 3.
  43. *ST* IIa IIae. 10.12. resp.
  44. Ibid.
  45. Ibid.
  46. *ST* IIa IIae. 10.8. resp.
  47. *ST* IIa IIae. 10.8. ad 3. What Aquinas argues here must be viewed in the context of "the voluntary" (*voluntarium*) and enemies of the voluntary, for example, violence, compulsion, fear, ignorance, and so on. In Ia IIae. 6.6. ad 1, he makes clear that compulsion vitiates the voluntary aspect of any act; fear, by contrast, permits a mitigated voluntariness in an act considered absolutely (although it may be viewed as involuntary when abstracted from concrete circumstances). If the "imperated activity" of the will (as distinguished from the intrinsic elicited act of the will) is due to violence, then "it is here that violence

makes an act involuntary" (Ia IIae. 6.5. ad 1). The applicability to forced baptism of unbelievers (whether Jews or non-Jews) is apparent.

Alexander of Hales, an older contemporary of Aquinas, provides an illuminating comparison to the principles that Thomas utilizes. In his *Summa Theologiae,* Alexander synthesizes legislation derived from the *Decretum* and *Decretales,* with the legitimacy of imperfect volition in coerced baptism. He agrees that those who have never believed are not to be compelled; apostates, however, are to be compelled to "serve the faith or return to it." He asserts:

> One who has never believed should never be compelled by absolute force. In this way the authorities who speak of this should be understood, for in this way faith is not gained nor is the nature of baptism imprinted, as noted in the *Decretales*. If the force is conditional, such as through threats or lashes, then in this way faith and the imprint of baptism are received, since there is volition. In this way some have been compelled "to hold the faith which they accepted under duress, 'lest the name of the Lord be brought to disrepute' and the faith which they accepted be held vile and contemptible," as noted in the *Decretum*.

See Chazan, *Church, State, and Jew in the Middle Ages,* 49.

48. "You [i.e., the king of Navarre] shall do all in your power to prevent any violence from being committed against [the Jews] in the matter of baptizing their children, for this should be a voluntary offering, not a forced one" (Grayzel, *Church and the Jews,* 1:261 §110).

49. Ibid., 103 §12:

> Some there are who say that, since sacraments yield their effects through themselves, as for example Baptism,...their impress, if not their aim, remains...even upon the unwilling and the objectors. Thus not only do children, who do not consent, receive the sacrament but even dissimulators, who, if not by word, dissent at least at heart. ...[T]hose who are immersed even though reluctant, do belong to ecclesiastical jurisdiction at least by reason of the sacrament, and might therefore be reasonably compelled to observe the rules of the Christian Faith. It is, to be sure, contrary to the Christian Faith that anyone who is unwilling and wholly opposed to it should be compelled to adopt and observe Christianity. For this reason a valid distinction is made by some between kinds of unwilling ones and kinds of compelled ones. Thus one who is drawn to Christianity *by violence, through fear and through torture*, and receives the sacrament of Baptism in order to avoid loss, he (like one who comes to Baptism in dissimulation) *does receive the impress of Christianity*, and may be forced to observe the Christian Faith as one who expressed a conditional willingness though, absolutely speaking, he was unwilling....He, however, who never consented, but wholly objected,

accepted neither the impress nor the purpose of the Sacrament, for it is better expressly to object, than to give the least consent.... (emphasis mine)

50. Grayzel, *Church and the Jews,* 1:15.
51. Ibid., 311 §12.
52. See *ST* Ia IIae. 6–17.
53. Grayzel, *Church and the Jews,* 1:93 §5.
54. Ibid., 15 n. 15. This policy was reasserted by Nicholas IV. See also n. 16 regarding a decision of a cardinal legate in 1217 not to return baptized children to their Jewish parents in Toulouse.
55. John Y. B. Hood reaches similar conclusions. He writes: "the connection between Aquinas and novel manifestations of hostility toward Jews is tenuous. Aquinas was firmly opposed to mob violence and forced conversions, and he lent no support to paranoid myths about Jews; at most, his ideas may have contributed to a cultural and theological milieu that made 'innovative missionizing' and treating Jews as heretics possible" (*Aquinas and the Jews,* Middle Ages Series [Philadelphia: University of Pennsylvania Press, 1995], 108).
56. Contra Cohen's concluding paragraph (*Letters*, 388–89).
57. Whereas papal policy, according to Grayzel, did. He writes that the popes' "attitude suffered from an inner contradiction: you could not, sometimes in one and the same pronouncement, call the Jews dangerous to religion and society and yet expect your plea for toleration and protection to find a willing ear" ("The Papal Bull *Sicut Judeis,*" in *Studies and Essays in Honor of Abraham A. Neuman,* ed. Meir Ben-Horin, B. D. Weinryb, and S. Zeitlin [Leiden: E. J. Brill, 1962], 54).

4
Predestination and Election in Aquinas and Thomas' Received Tradition

INTRODUCTION

To date, no study has located Thomas' understanding of the role of the Jews within the theological framework of predestination and election, and no contemporary studies analyze the connection between *ST* Ia. 23 and *CRO* 9–11 and the role of Jews.[1]

Study of selected texts from Thomas' *ST*, *Sent.*, and *CRO* demonstrates what the theological significance is for Aquinas. For Thomas, the role of the Jewish people may be understood only within the larger theological context of divine providence and the doctrines of predestination and election. Aquinas does not envision a discontinuity between systematic determinations of a given topic and a biblical commentary wherein the same subject matter arises. For Thomas, there is a unity of theological and exegetical inquiry because the object under consideration, *sacra doctrina,* is one and the same. There is little surprise, therefore, that substantial agreement exists between the *ST* Ia. 23 and *CRO* on the doctrine of predestination, as well as *I Sent.* d.41 and *CRO* on the doctrine of divine election, especially in chapters 9–11.[2] These passages from *Sent.* and *ST* (in particular) contain controlling concepts or hermeneutical keys that govern Thomas' exegesis and inform Thomas' teaching concerning the ongoing role of the Jewish people in salvation history. Therefore, the more comprehensive and systematic determinations of *ST* and *Sent.* provide the broader conceptual framework for Thomas' comments on these three chapters of his scriptural commentary and contextualize his discussion of the relationship between Jews and Gentiles. In this chapter, first I shall attend to the general contribution that *ST* Ia. 23 makes to Aquinas' use of the doctrine of predestination in

CRO. Afterward, I shall undertake a similar analysis of the doctrine of election in *I Sent.* and in his Romans commentary. Finally, before proceeding to a detailed analysis of *CRO* 9 and 11 in chapter 5, we must delineate the distinctiveness of Aquinas' use of these doctrines by contrasting them with the most important theological treatment of these issues in the doctrinal tradition that Thomas received from Augustine.

PREDESTINATION IN AQUINAS' *ST* AND *CRO*

Thomas wrote *ST* and the first edition of *CRO* contemporaneously, and, not surprisingly, there are a variety of ways in which *ST* and *CRO* agree. In the *prima pars* Thomas locates his discussion of predestination within an analysis of God's knowledge and will, specifically under the aspect of God's providence (Ia. 22.1–4).[3] In Ia. 23. resp., he explicitly states that "everything falls under his Providence, [and] also that the function of providence is to arrange things to an end." (Interestingly, Romans informs Aquinas' argument since he adduces Romans 8.30 in the *sed contra* of q. 23.) God's will orders the individual to an end that is above the natural capacities of the rational creature: the end that is God himself. A similar care to establish the broader context of predestination within divine providence surfaces in *CRO* §§699ff.,"because as it is said in Proverbs 8.17: I love the ones loving me; to love is to will the good for the beloved; however for God *to will is to work*. For all things whatever he wished, he did, as it is said in Ps 135.6."[4] Immediately, in *CRO* §700, Aquinas attributes predestination to God's eternal will

> who first predestined believers from eternity; secondly he calls them in time; thirdly he sanctifies...so that the purpose may be referred to predestination, which according to Augustine is the purpose of the one having pity, Eph 1.1: Ones predestined according to his purpose.[5]

From the outset of his commentary, even the definition of predestination that Thomas utilizes in *CRO* mirrors that found in *ST* Ia. 23.1: to predestine is to send. In *CRO* §43 he writes: "Indeed destination is taken in two ways. Sometimes on behalf of a mission: for the ones who are sent for something are said [to be] destined...." Thomas' second definition derives from the first: "to predestine is nothing other than to dispose from the heart beforehand what is to be done concerning a certain thing."[6]

Additionally, Thomas is careful to note that predestination is not to be equated with the natural dispositions of a thing's constitution,[7] but properly said only of those creatures which are rational and ordered to the things that are above nature.[8] Of further significance in *ST* and *CRO* is the concern to place predestination within God as an immanent activity that has its effect in the object of his activity, namely, individual human beings. This can also be applied by extension to corporate entities (such as Israel) by the use of the hermeneutics often employed by Thomas.

Another element found in both texts involves the temporal aspect of an individual's salvation. We have seen above that in *CRO* §700 Thomas explains how God predestines the believer from eternity, but calls and sanctifies the individual in time. In *ST* Ia. 23. a.2, Thomas writes:

> predestination is like the plan, existing in God's mind, for the ordering of some persons to salvation. The carrying out of this is passively as it were in the persons predestined, though actively in God. When considered executively in this sense, predestination is spoken of as a "calling" and a "glorifying," thus St. Paul says, whom he predestinated, them also he called and glorified.[9]

Another textual congruence is evidenced regarding the concept of reprobation. In the *sed contra* of Ia. 23.3, Thomas cites Malachi 1.2–3 ("Jacob I loved, but Esau I hated"); this is a verse that receives extensive treatment in the Romans commentary. In Ia. 23.3 and in *CRO* §764, Thomas carefully distinguishes between those whom God ordains to be saved and those whom he permits to fall away from grace:

> [A]s predestination includes the will to confer grace and glory, so reprobation includes the will to permit someone to fall into fault and to inflict the penalty of damnation in consequence.[10]

> as predestination is the preparation for glory, so reprobation is the preparation of punishment.[11]

Furthermore, in ad 2 he explains that rejection and punishment derive from one's free decision, and he cites Hosea 13.9 ("Your destruction is from yourself, O Israel...") as scriptural warrant. The same text is employed in *CRO* §764.

The clearest example of the common use of the hermeneutical tools of predestination and election occurs in *CRO* §763 and *ST* Ia. 23. In the former, Thomas reprises the argument advanced in Ia. 23.4. resp., which defines predestination, election, and love, as well as the order of these in God and in us. The texts of *ST* and *CRO*, respectively, read:

> The predestination of some to eternal salvation means that God wills their salvation. This is where special and chosen loving come in. Special because God wills this blessing of eternal salvation to some...for...loving is willing a person good, chosen loving (*electio*) because he wills this to some and not to others for,...some he rejects.
>
> Election and dilection operate (*ordinatur*) differently in us and in God. When we love things our will does not cause them to be good; it is because they are good already that we are roused to love them; therefore we choose someone to love, and our choice precedes our loving. With God the converse is true. For when he chooses to love another and thereby wills him good, his will is the cause of the other being singled out and so endowed. Clearly, then, the notion of God's special loving precedes that of his choosing, and that of his choosing that of his predestining. Therefore all the predestined are picked loves (*electi et dilecti*).

> [E]lection and love are ordered differently in God and in man. For in man election precedes love, for the will of man is moved to loving from the good which he considers in the thing loved, by reason of which he chooses this thing before another, and is the cause of every good which is in the creature. And in this manner, the good by reason of which one creature is preferred to another through the mode of election follows upon the will of God, for the good of that man, which pertains to the notion of love. Whence it is not on account of a good he may choose in a man that God loves him, but more from the fact that he loves him, he prefers him to others by electing him.[12]

Finally, Ia. 23.5. asks whether foreknowledge of merits is the cause of predestination. This concern is substantially echoed in several sections of *CRO*, most of which occur in chapters 9–11. Indeed, the argument advanced in the third objection, citing Romans 9.14, is substantially reproduced in §773:

> For it is manifest that distributive justice has a place in the things which are owed from what is due; consider (for example), if some merit a wage, so that greater wages may be given to those laboring more. However it does not have a place in the things which one gives freely and mercifully....
>
> Since therefore all people on account of the sin of the first parents are born liable to damnation, God through his grace liberates them, by mercy only he frees [them]. And thus to certain ones whom he frees he is merciful; to certain ones he is just, whom he does not free; he is wicked to neither however.
>
> And in this manner the Apostle solves the question through the authority which ascribes everything to divine mercy.[13]

Thomas had provided the rationale for *CRO* §773 earlier in Ia. 23.5. ad 3:

> God wills to manifest his goodness in men, in those whom he predestines in the manner of mercy by sparing them, in those whom he reprobates in the manner of justice by punishing them. This provides a key to the problem why God chooses some and rejects others; it is offered by St. Paul, What if God, desiring to show his wrath...and to make known the riches of his glory for the vessels of mercy, which he hath prepared beforehand for glory....Why does he choose some to glory while others he rejects? His so willing is the sole ground.... We cannot complain if God prepares unequal lots for equals. This would be repugnant to divine justice as such were the effect of predestination a due to be rendered, not a favor. He who grants by grace can give freely as he wills, be it more be it less, without prejudice to justice, provided he deprives no one of what is owing. In the householder's words of the parable, Take what is thine and go thy way. Is it not lawful for me to do what I will with my own?[14]

Indeed several common components emerge in comparing these texts: concern to locate election within the ambit of divine mercy, and correlatively, reprobation within divine justice; the assertion that divine volition orders all things and persons providentially; the *exempla* employed to illustrate the principle; and most importantly (because the effect of predestination is granted gratuitously, not from an owed debt), the denial of the infringement of justice. Divine mercy and providence account for the election of certain individuals and the reprobation of others; as we shall see, they also account for the hardening of some for the benefit of others considered corporately. In all this, God does not act unjustly: a determination that finds extensive treatment in *CRQ* §§766–74.

For Thomas the certitude of predestination (a.6) finds scriptural expression in Romans 8.29, regarding which "the Gloss comments, [that] Predestination is the foreknowledge of and the preparation for God's benefits, whereby those who are liberated most certainly are."[15] Foreknowledge and a certain eternal causality with respect to the benefits of salvation are ascribed to God in *CRO* §702 also; again, the material congruence is striking. Aquinas uses the core of this argument to deal with the impugning of divine justice in Romans 9.14, an issue raised by Paul himself. That is, on the conceptual level, by making remote the causality of God he preserves God from the taint of injustice. For, although divine providence is certain, it also functions through contingent causes "according to the condition of the proximate causes providentially appointed them" (Ia 23. 6. resp.). Therefore predestination considered as an effect in individuals does not obliterate human free will from which it contingently issues. In brief, God's knowledge and will do not dispense with contingent causality in the material world nor in the exercise of free will.[16] At the same time, God owes nothing to creatures, and divine predestination is prior to the enactment of free choice and the graces that enable it. Like *ST*, so too in the manner of argumentation in *CRO*, Thomas moves from primary to secondary causality and the role of human willing.

Most important in Ia 23. 6, however, is the principle expressed in ad 1, a principle that is at the heart of *CRO* chapters 9–11. Thomas writes:

> A person may wear the crown on two titles, from divine predestination, and thus no one loses it, and from the merit of grace, for what we merit is in a sense ours, and thus we can lose it by subsequent mortal sin. Another, who is substituted in his place, gains the lost crown. *God does not allow some to fall without raising others in their place* according to the text in Job. He will shatter mighty men without number, and set others to stand in their stead. Accordingly human beings took the place of the fallen angels, *and Gentiles that of the Jews.* (emphasis mine)

Thomas, commenting on Romans 11.11 in *CRO* §879, writes:

> Therefore he says, moving the question, have they stumbled such that they fall? This can be understood in a two-fold way. By one mode, thus: Did God permit them to stumble solely such that they fall, that is, for no other use from that following afterward, except only wishing them to fall? That indeed would be against the divine goodness, which is such that...he would never permit anything evil to be done except for the sake of the good which he elicits from the evil. Wherefore also in Job 34.24 it is said: He will crush the many and innumerable men, and he will make others to stand for them. And Rev 2.11: Hold fast to what you have, lest another should take your crown, because namely God permits certain ones to fall thus, so that the fall of some may be the occasion of the salvation of others.[17]

The material correspondence between *ST* Ia. 23. 6. ad 3 and §879 is apparent. How it is that the Gentiles may be said to "take the place of the Jews" without necessitating a supersessionist stance vis-à-vis the Jews, we shall see in the later analysis of Romans 9–11.

The seventh and eighth articles of Ia. 23 also cite Romans 8.28 and 11.29, respectively. The number of the predestined is fixed: "not only by reason of his knowledge...but also by reason of his own defining decision and choice."[18] This concern substantially appears in *CRO* §§915ff., where Thomas discusses what constitutes the "fullness of the Gentiles" (*plenitudo Gentium intraret*), as well as the salvation of "all Israel" (*omnis Israel salvus fiet*). The identity of the predestined is determined and foreknown by God, and those reprobated are such for the benefit of the elect—a tenet applicable to Jews and Gentiles alike.

What these passages demonstrate, at the very least, is the consistency of Thomas' thought on predestination and election between the writing of the *prima pars* in 1268 and the *CRO expositio* of 1272. These texts, especially *ST* Ia. 23.1–7, also elucidate Thomas' Romans commentary. The fuller theology of predestination in *ST* contextualizes Thomas' understanding of the status and role of the Jewish people. The phenomenon of textual congruity demonstrated in these fundamental principles of predestination will be evidenced similarly in Thomas' understanding of the doctrine of election in *I Sent.* and *CRO*.

ELECTION IN AQUINAS' *I SENT.* AND *CRO*

The doctrine of election is closely allied to Thomas' understanding of predestination.[19] This association should not surprise us in *CRO* insofar as Paul links the two concepts in Romans 8.29–33. However, we must ask whether the doctrine of election warrants the prominence given it by Aquinas in *CRO*.[20] Is Aquinas' consideration of election, with reference to the Jews, simply dictated by the Pauline text or (as with predestination) does the topic enjoy a certain prominence in Aquinas' thought independent of his *lectio continua* on Romans?

Although Paul rarely uses election (ἐκλογή) and its cognate forms, significantly, more than half of the Pauline uses occur in Romans (8.33; 9.11; 11.5, 7, 28; and 16.13). In these texts, we see that the purpose (κατὰ πρόθεσιν) of God is manifest in predestination (προορίζω, 8.29, 30) and, "so that his purpose might remain" steadfast, in accordance with divine election (κατ' ἐκλογήν, 9.11). Indeed, election serves to bracket chapters 9–11, commencing with 9.11 and culminating in 11.28. The "purpose of God" is explained by predestination and election as associated concepts that receive greater specificity in the intervening material. "[T]he Latin terms *predestinatio* and *predestinare* include the election idea, but go further by pointing to a foreordination, thus referring primarily to God's foreordaining our salvation (ἡ κατ' ἐκλογὴν πρόθεσις)."[21] All Israel remains beloved κατὰ...τὴν ἐκλογήν on account of their fathers, despite the hardening that has come upon a portion of it (11.28).[22] Nevertheless, there is also an elect part of Israel (ἡ...ἐκλογή, 11.7), identifiable with a remnant (λεῖμμα) according to the election of grace (κατ' ἐκλογὴν χάριτος, 11.5). Corporate Israel is elect; a faithful remnant is elect; individuals are elect (see 16.13 in addition to 9.11). Paul (in the non-Pauline pastoral epistles) endures for the sake of the elect (2 Tim 2.10) and is a servant apostle κατὰ πίστιν ἐκλεκτῶν θεοῦ (Titus 1.1). God's activity of choosing bestows a titular status on those selected. In all of this, there seems to be a certain elasticity in Paul's application of the term ἐκλογη.

In Romans 8.33 Paul explicitly asserts that no one may lay a charge against or condemn God's elect. Furthermore, he states that elect Israel perdures, beloved by God (ἀγαπητοί),[23] while being ("according to the gospel") simultaneously enemies (ἐχθροί) for the sake of the Gentiles (11.28): "for the gifts and the calling of God are irrevocable" (11.29). Yet how can all these claims be true? And what is Thomas' position on

Paul's plot line, especially with reference to the doctrine of Israel's irrevocable election?

As we shall see, Thomas teaches in *CRO* that God pre-elects Jacob over Esau, not because the former was holy but so that he might become holy; Aquinas explicitly states that "this is the proposition of predestination, concerning which it is said: Predestined according to his purpose."[24] Some preliminary questions must be asked: Does Thomas' understanding of election in *CRO* replicate or refine certain aspects of predestination? And, regarding election, are there material borrowings from or substantial correspondence with works prior to or contemporaneous with *CRO*?

It should not surprise us that the subsidiary theme of election appears in tandem with Aquinas' understanding of predestination in *CRO* since they are linked by Paul. That Thomas has observed the linkage in Romans is not wholly attributable to his careful reading of the apostle, however. Indeed, the two theological concepts are intertwined from the beginning of Thomas' teaching career in Paris: in his first and third commentaries on the *Libri Sententiarum*[25] (as well as in *ST* 1a. 23.4 as we have seen above[26]). The interrelation is made explicit in *I Sent.* d.41.1.2.[27] In *distinctio* 41, Thomas defines election as a "certain segregation" which

> in one mode is eternal, [and] by another mode temporal. For if it may be understood according to which the proposition is of God himself, thus it is eternal, because from eternity he willed to segregate the good from the evil in glory. But if it may be understood accordingly as it is in the execution of a work, thus it is temporal; just as when someone is segregated from original or actual fault in grace, or from common status in a prelate's office, and so on concerning the other things which, by divine gift, are especially conferred to certain ones.[28]

Predestination adds something to the concept of election "just as providence adds [something] above [the concept of] a disposition."[29] Aquinas succinctly defines election as "the divine ordination itself, by which certain ones are preferred to others for the attaining of beatitude."[30] Predestination, additionally, signifies the preparation of the goods of grace and the goods of glory for the elect by means of which they are conformed to that end. These basic theological distinctions and definitions, culled from the *I* and *III Sentences*, recur not only in *ST*, but also in *CRO* with specific application to Jews and Gentiles alike. For example, commenting on Romans 9.24, Thomas writes:

> After the Apostle shows that the grace of God is given to people from divine election, through which people are called to grace, here he shows that the aforementioned election or call belongs not only to the Jews (such that they may be able to boast on account of that which is said in Dt 4.37: I loved your fathers and chose their seed after them) but also to the Peoples.[31]

Those who are predestined, called, justified, and glorified (Rom 8.30) have a certain assurance rooted in God's election.

> [Paul] shows that no accusation is able to be injurious to the saints of God: and this by reason of divine election. For he who chooses a certain one, in virtue of this is seen to approve him. However the saints were chosen by God. Eph 1.4: He chose us in himself before the constitution of the world, so that we should be holy. Nevertheless he who accuses, reproves him whom he accuses. However the accusation of someone has no force against the approbation of God. And for that reason he says who shall accuse, namely efficaciously, against the elect of God, that is against the ones God chooses so that they may be holy? Whence it is said Rev 12.10: The accuser of our brothers is cast out.[32]

Thomas proposes Paul as an example of God's elect from the outset of *CRO*, a status signified by his name[33] and by his task, which is distinct from that of the other disciples.[34] A more explicit argument is advanced by Thomas regarding Paul's status as a Jew, chosen and predestined by God, who instantiates God's fidelity to his people:

> Then, when he says Far be it, etc., he solves the question showing that God did not reject totally the people of the Jews. And this is what he says Far be it, such that the people of the Jews be rejected totally by God. And this indeed, first, he proves as far as his own person, saying For I too, who am living in the faith of Christ, am an Israelite, namely with the people; 2 Cor 11.22: They are Israelites and so am I.[35]

For Jews and Gentiles alike, Aquinas makes it eminently clear that election is from the grace of God, not from preceding works.[36] God is the agent whose purpose (i.e., considered as an end or final cause) is to manifest in them the "abundance of his goodness" by means of election and compassion; God recalls the elect from evil, draws them toward justice, and ultimately, leads them to glory.[37] Indeed, being children of God derives from election as does the dignity of the Jews.[38]

The seeming ambiguity evidenced in Aquinas' doctrine of predestination is similarly apparent in his doctrine of election. The election of some from among the Jews and of some from among the Gentiles (as opposed to others) is attributable to the "absolute will of God."[39] Divine *predilectio* results in the election of particular individuals.[40] Since neither one mode of divine activity nor one creature could manifest adequately the divine goodness, God's mercy is manifest in those freed by his grace, and God's justice, likewise, is manifest in those whom he punishes for sin, that is, reprobates. As Thomas writes:

> However the excellence of such things is from the divine goodness which is not able to exist neither by one mode nor to be manifested sufficiently in one creature. And for this reason he produced diverse creatures, in whom by diverse modes it is manifested. However, especially in rational creatures (in whom his justice is manifested as far as those whom he punishes for their merits), certainly his mercy is in those whom he frees by his grace. And in this manner so that both would be manifested in people, he freed some mercifully, but not all.[41]

The application of these principles is most complex regarding the Jews. Thomas, following Paul, must articulate a resolution that preserves the elect status of corporate Israel (on the one hand), while simultaneously seeing the distillation of a remnant and the incorporation of some Gentiles (on the other hand) as not being a betrayal of the divine promise—or worse yet, seeing God as the perpetrator of a grave injustice. How may each assertion be true? For example, in §863 we read:

> Therefore first he says: Not only am I not rejected, but God did not reject his people, the whole [people], which he foreknew, that is, predestined. Above 8.8: The ones whom he foreknew, these he also predestined. Ps 93.14: The Lord will not reject his people. That the Apostle here expounds as far as concerns the ones predestined.[42]

But previously in §802 he commented:

> It was said because Hosea spoke for the Gentiles, Isaiah cries out, that is, he speaks openly for the conversion of Israel. Isa 58.1: Cry out do not cease, as though your voice [be] a trumpet.
> However in this first authority firstly, he posits the paucity of those converted from out of Israel, saying Though the number of the sons of Israel shall be as the sand of the sea, that is, innumerable in advance of the multitude. Gen 22.17: I shall multiply your seed...etc. 3 Kgs 4.20: Judah and Israel are innumerable as the sand of the sea.—A remnant shall be saved, that is, not all, nor the major part, but a certain few who are left from the fall of others....Below 11.5: The remnant, according to the election of grace, were saved.[43]

Thus, in §802 the predestination of Israel reduces to the predestination of a remnant, but later in §863, Thomas asserts that the whole people shall be saved. Can these competing claims be reconciled simply by appeal to God's antecedent and consequent will in predestinating and electing?[44]

For Aquinas, God loves the elect more because he wills more good for them, and these chosen are taken from among Jews and Gentiles alike. Divine election effectively relativizes the status of Jew and Gentile, making them equal in their present call, justification, and glorification. At the same time, however, Thomas preserves the Jews' dignity and their privileged status, not only historically, but as essential to the outworking of election in time. The gift of God and the call are temporal.

> Because it must be said that the gift here is taken for a promise which is made in accordance with the foreknowledge and predestination of God. However, the call is taken for election, because on account of the certitude of both, what God promises, now by a certain mode he calls. Nevertheless also the very gift of God is temporal and the call temporal; it is not made void through a change of God as though of one repenting, but through the change of man, who rejects the grace of God.[45]

The status of corporate Israel, the role of the remnant, and the election of the individuals are integrally preserved. Since this is so, there is a necessity and a responsibility incumbent upon the Christian church to preserve the role of the Jews in the temporal outworking of salvation history. Thomas accomplishes this objective theologically by attributing that temporal process to God's eternal predestinating will and election; these principles are the hermeneutical key to understanding *CRO* chapters 9–11. Election is a "certain segregation" seen in the separation of Israel from the nations and the isolation of a remnant from among the Jews and the Gentiles. The former establishes the fundamental prerogative of Israel, which the distillation of the remnant does not abrogate. If there is a seeming ambiguity in Aquinas' exposition, it is one that reflects the enactment of divine providence among Jews and Gentiles alike—a temporal tension that Paul himself recognizes. We see, in particular, this dynamic tension in *CRO* chapters 9 and 11.

Since Aquinas has a consistent understanding of the historical nature of divine activity and the principles of predestination and election are equally applicable in Paul's or Thomas' own day, I argue that Aquinas' exegesis in *CRO* concerning the role of the Jews is uniquely tied to these theological concepts. However, some scholars hold the position that Thomas simply inherits and transmits an Augustinian interpretation concerning the relationship between the Jews and Gentiles.[46] I will now consider Augustine's *Propositions from the Epistle to the Romans* and his *Unfinished Commentary on the Epistle to the Romans*[47] to compare the topics of predestination, election, and the role of the Jews in order to demonstrate that Aquinas' exegesis is not simply derivative. From a comparison of Aquinas' hermeneutics with those of Augustine, I will show that Thomas does not merely transmit the received Augustinian tradition but frames the Jew–Gentile problem in a unique manner. Finally, through analysis of *CRO* in light of Augustine's commentaries on Romans, we will see whether Aquinas should be characterized as a supersessionist, that is, one who puts eschatological Israel, the church, in opposition to empirical Israel, the Jewish people.[48]

AUGUSTINE AND THE JEWS: THOMAS' RECEIVED TRADITION

Several contemporary scholars attribute Aquinas' tolerant position concerning the Jews, in part, to Augustinian tradition. John Y. B. Hood says that Aquinas "on most...issues...was representative of an older tradition, a tradition rooted in *Sicut Iudaeis*, Gregory the Great, Augustine, and ultimately Paul. But by the late thirteenth century this tradition was largely out of touch with the forces of social change."[49] Jeremy Cohen claims that "during the early Middle Ages, the Roman Church's attitude toward the Jews emanated from what may be termed an Augustinian theology of Judaism."[50] Thomas, as a medieval theologian, is variously characterized as an inheritor, a transmitter, or a synthesizer of received traditions, be these of patristic or legal provenance. However, no assessment of Aquinas' *possible* debt to Augustine on the topic of the Jews identifies Thomas' theological framework (namely, predestination and election) as one that allows for the ongoing rights and role of the Jews in the divine economy. It is important to look at the legacy of Augustine, which was shaped and transformed by Aquinas. Apart from the work of Paula Fredriksen, there has been no text-critical or analytical study of Augustine on Romans and, consequently, no comparison made with Thomas' *CRO* 9–11.

Analysis of *PER* and *CER* would partially determine the extent of Augustine's potential to influence Aquinas' understanding of the Jews and would suggest areas that are Thomas' innovations. For example, in *PER* §60,11 Augustine, commenting on Romans 9.13 ("Jacob I loved, but Esau I hated"), states:

> God did not elect anyone's works (which he himself will grant) by foreknowledge, but rather by foreknowledge he chose faith, so that he chooses precisely him whom *he foreknew would believe in him;* and to him he gives the Holy Spirit so that by doing good works he will as well attain eternal life.[51]

Yet Thomas explicitly refutes this early position of Augustine[52] in *CRO* §703:

> Concerning the order of preknowledge and predestination some say that preknowledge of the merits of the good and of the evil is the *ratio* of predestination and of reprobation, so that namely, it may be understood that God may predestine certain ones, because he knows beforehand *those who shall act well and those who shall believe in Christ.*
>
> ...[T]o posit that a certain merit on our part may be presupposed, the preknowledge of which may be the reason of predestination, is nothing other that to posit grace to be given on account of our merits, and that the beginning of good works is from us, and the consummation from God.[53]

The question arises, therefore: Do other significant differences exist between Augustine and Thomas in their Romans commentaries, particularly with respect to their understanding of the role of the Jews in salvation history? Before additional textual comparisons may be undertaken concerning Romans 9–11, however, prior investigation of two topics in *PER* and *CER* are necessary: Augustine's portrayal of the Jews and his understanding of predestination.[54]

Augustine's View of the Jews

Augustine's fundamental perspective on the Jews is supersessionist; they have been supplanted by Christians, whether Jewish or Gentile believers in Christ. "L'Ancien Testament est la promesse, le Nouveau est l'accomplissement"[55]—a principle Augustine consistently applied to all Jewish prerogatives. Indeed there is no unifying theological concept that accounts for the present status or informs the ongoing role of the Jews in salvation history *except* that their blindness and dispersion have effected (unwittingly) the spread and endorsement of Christianity.

> It is a great confirmation of our faith that such important testimony is borne by enemies. The believing Gentiles cannot suppose these testimonies to Christ to be recent forgeries; for they find them in books held sacred for so many ages by those who crucified Christ, still venerated by those who daily blaspheme Him....The unbelief of the Jews has been made of signal benefit to us so that those who do not receive these truths in their heart for their own good nonetheless carry in their hands, for our benefit, the writings in which these truths are contained. And the unbelief of the Jews increases rather than lessens the authority of these books, for this blindness is itself foretold. They testify to the truth by their not understanding it.[56]

The Jews are little more than the Christians' *scriniaria*[57] and "chest-keepers."[58] It must also be admitted, however, that Augustine's reading of Romans sometimes proffers familiar themes that soften his supersessionist tendencies (albeit evidenced in a fragmentary way in *PER* and *CER*).[59] For example, according to Augustine, Jews and Gentiles alike are indicted by Paul[60] and neither group has the right to be proud or haughty.[61] The warnings of Augustine accord with those of the apostle:

Paul does not say that the Jews have not fallen, but that their fall was not in vain, since it profited the Gentiles by salvation....Thereafter he even begins to praise the Jewish people for this fall of unfaithfulness, so that the Gentiles might not be proud, since this fall of the Jews was so precious for their salvation. Rather, the Gentiles ought to take heed all the more lest, when they grow proud, they likewise fall.[62]

Therefore, how is it that Jews and Gentiles alike enter into salvation?

An analysis of Augustine's references to the Jews in the *PER* and *CER* (ca. mid-390s[63]) calls into question the tolerant attitude toward the Jews frequently ascribed to him.[64] Nor does Augustine's *Tractatus Adversos Iudaeos,* written ca. 425,[65] persuade an inquirer differently.[66] (Even Blumenkranz provides a compendium of Augustine's anti-Jewish polemics.[67]) In fact, one discovers *in nuce* in the early Augustine's Romans commentaries theological positions evidenced late in Augustine's career.[68] Not surprisingly, some of his comments in *PER* and *CER* derive from a close reading of Paul's letter, while others are theological inferences that he makes about the Jews. Primarily, these latter observations expose Augustine's case (or lack thereof) for the Jews. Blumenkranz and others have long claimed that Augustine forged his theological position concerning the Jews in response to contemporaneous Jewish proselytizing efforts in North Africa.[69] Paula Fredriksen (among others) has challenged this assumption "for the simple reason that we have little evidence for actual Jewish missions in antiquity generally.... By Augustine's period...such activities would have long been illegal."[70] Rather, she contends that Augustine's position on the Jews and Judaism emerges not from the threat of Jewish proselytism but "from a biblical hermeneutic that he develops during the 390's" that derives from an anti-Manichean reading of Paul, although not exclusively so.[71] Fredriksen's reconstrual of the factors motivating Augustine represents not only a departure from the dominant position of Blumenkranz but also a significant paradigm shift in interpreting Augustine's post-390 writings. This change from a sociological to a theological model of interpretation (broadly construed) also locates *PER* and *CER* at the pivotal point of transition in the bishop's career.[72] Augustine's view of the Jews and Judaism derives not from the exterior threat of competition but from measured, theological analysis of the relationship between grace and free will.[73]

The Jews in *PER* and *CER*

Augustine understands Paul's primary purpose in Romans to be the exclusion of meritorious works as the preceding warrant for evangelical grace, that is, the gift of the gospel. A subsidiary concern of Paul, in Augustine's estimation, is the resolution of conflict between Jewish Christians and Gentile converts in the Roman congregation.[74] In *CER* §1,1 Augustine states that Romans poses the question "whether the Gospel...came to the Jews alone because of their merits through the works of the Law; or whether the justification of faith which is in Christ Jesus came to all nations, without any preceding merits for works."[75] He identifies the catalyst for the letter as "some...Jewish believers [who] had begun to agitate against the Gentiles and particularly against the apostle Paul, because he admitted the uncircumcised...to the grace of the Gospel...."[76] The purpose and audience established, Augustine further qualifies these:

> But clearly Paul teaches this with such moderation that he permits neither the Jews to be proud because of the merits of the Law, nor the Gentiles to be haughty towards the Jews because of the merit of their faith in accepting Christ, *whom the Jews crucified*....Paul unites in Christ through the bond of grace peoples from among the Jews and Gentiles both, taking away from both all pride because of merit, and bringing both together to be justified by the discipline of humility.[77]

From the opening sections of *CER*, Augustine identifies Jews as intolerant, agitating, Christ-killers[78] whose synagogues have fallen into desuetude.[79] Furthermore, Augustine describes Paul himself as set apart from the Jews and allied with the Gentiles "into whose ranks as believers in Christ he had been called"[80]—a stark contrast to Paul's self-description in Romans 11.1 ("I myself am an Israelite, a descendant of Abraham, a member of the tribe of Benjamin"). He later presents the Jews as ignorant of Christ's preeminence,[81] hostile to the Holy Spirit[82] (or at least ignorant of it[83]), unfaithful, malevolent slanderers,[84] blasphemous,[85] murmurers,[86] and deniers of God by their deeds.[87]

In *PER* the Jews have not understood the purpose of the Law; what was a peculiar Jewish prerogative has been reduced by Augustine primarily to the role of a moral informant.[88] The Law was the source of "the numerous and multitudinous rites which had oppressed the Jewish people."[89] The Jews, by means of the same, misunderstood Law...sought to judge the Gentiles; therefore, Paul justifiably indicts *them*.[90] Jews are prideful, glorying in their works:[91] a trait that certain Jewish Christians continued to demonstrate.[92] Further, citing Titus 1.10–12[93] for support, such Jewish "Christians" are characterized as self-serving opportunists.[94]

The Jews in the *Tractatus Adversus Iudaeos*

Lest it be thought that the preceding ascriptions to the Jews are peculiar to Augustine's early career, we witness similar attributions in *Tractatus Adversus Iudaeos* toward the end of his career.[95] The bishop repeats and develops themes evidenced in *PER* and *CER*, among these that the Jews crucified Christ;[96] they are "stationary in useless antiquity";[97] their root, the patriarchs and prophets, has died;[98] convicted by the Law which they mistakenly perceived as their boast,[99] they have been replaced by their younger brother Jacob, the Christian people.[100] Indeed, Augustine applies Isa 65.1 and 6.10 to the Jews[101] with unrelenting verve:

> If you truly want to say: "We are the house of Jacob," then say it when you hear: "Blind the heart of this people, and make their ears heavy, and shut their eyes." Then say: "We are they," when you hear: "I have spread forth my hands all the day to an unbelieving and contradicting people." Say "We are they," when you hear: "Let their eyes be darkened that they see not; and their back bend thou down always." In these and other prophetic words of this kind say: "We are they." Without any doubt you are, but you are so blind that you say you are what you are not, and do not recognize yourselves for what you really are.[102]

PRELIMINARY CONCLUSIONS

What operative principles from Augustine's *PER* and *CER* may be drawn before continuing our comparison with Thomas' *CRO* 9–11 and the subsidiary theme of election? Clearly, Augustine employs a language of culpability and merit in *PER* and *CER*: God elects those of faith and reprobates the obdurate. Second, early in Augustine's career he understands that the foreseen fundamental option for or against faith elicits the divine "response." And although he will retract this position and refashion his doctrine of grace and human volition in subsequent stages of his career, at this juncture he makes no provision for the rehabilitation of the seemingly reprobate in the trajectory of salvation history. That is, if individuals are essentially responsible for their status as elect or reprobate, so too are members of corporate entities such as Israel or the Gentiles. Therefore, it is perfectly consistent (and necessary) to deny the rehabilitation of the corporate entity Israel *in se* at the culmination of sacred history according to the categories of strict justice that Augustine employs. God does not extend mercy to the obdurate, because this would violate God's own nature by transgressing divine justice. Hence, when Augustine speaks of Israel in *PER* §69, it is in a qualified sense, specifically, "the Jews will be reckoned as descendants who have believed in the Lord. This is why [Paul] says...'a remnant will be saved.'"[103] Once corporate Israel has been redefined as the remnant Israel who believed in the Lord, historical Israel is replaced by a metaphorical, not an eschatological, Israel of Jews observing covenantal obligations.[104] In turn, there is no need to preserve historical Israel except as an indirect or unwitting witness to the truths of Christianity. Therefore, when Paul states in Romans 11.26 that "all Israel will be saved," Augustine must reconfigure who constitutes Israel in order to maintain a doctrine of election, reprobation, and, ultimately, divine salvation in accord with divine justice as he construes it. Paul's teaching on these matters is thereby (consciously or unconsciously) subordinated to that of Augustine. However tolerant Augustine is alleged to be, he significantly denigrates the Jews' function and dignity as articulated by Paul in Romans 9–11. At the very least, one may say that Augustine is consistent in the outworking of his theological principles.

Closer analysis of the process of election and reprobation—even in the various *retractiones* we have considered—confirms this theological diminution of the Jews. In *Ad Simpl.*, as we shall see in the next chapter, God bestows mercy on those called and given faith for belief unto justification, which results in election because of the actualizing of good works by the *de facto* believer graced by the gift of the Holy Spirit. The *divine ratio* for God's initial choice is "most hidden" and beyond the grasp of the human intellect.[105] But since Augustine fails to contextualize the rationale and process within the category of divine providence, there exists no way for him to account for the eschatological inclusion of Israel that would not simultaneously violate divine justice. Augustine, in *PER*, merely hints that the fall of the Jews is purposive insofar as it is most precious to the Gentiles and permits their inclusion—this could be construed as providential only in an attenuated sense. Logical consistency urges him to assert the reprobation of individuals as a *positive* act of the divine will and makes Augustine vulnerable to the charge of double predestination.[106]

Next I shall argue that Aquinas' understanding of the doctrine of election of Jacob in *CRO* 9 is exhibited corporately in the election and predestination of Israel in *CRO* 11. Second, I shall argue that Augustine's conception of election, whether enacted by a preexisting merit of works or a merit of faith (or even divine mercy), does not avoid the charge of divine arbitrariness, exhibited in God's election and reprobation of individuals. The difference between Aquinas' conceptual framework in *CRO* and that of Augustine in *CER, PER*, and *Ad Simpl.*, will be demonstrated by giving particular attention to their respective theological views in three important *exempla*, namely, Jacob, Esau, and Pharaoh (and a subsidiary consideration of reprobation). Summary conclusions will assess the anti-Judaism latent in Augustine's Romans commentaries and how Thomas corrects and transforms the received tradition by means of the doctrines of predestination and election. Thomas does not refute Augustine, but by shaping his legacy, develops the role and status of the Jewish people *theologically*, beyond the status quo of mere "testamentary tolerance."

NOTES

1. In fact, apart from R. Garrigou-Lagrange's work on predestination fifty years ago, little has been written on the topic of predestination and election in Aquinas in contemporary studies. Representative studies that treat of predestination in Thomas include Lee H. Yearley, "St. Thomas Aquinas on Providence and Predestination," *Anglican Theological Review* 49 (1967): 409–23; and Charles Partee, "Predestination in Aquinas and Calvin," *Reformed Review* 32 (1978): 14–22. The former correlates Thomas' teaching on predestination within the broader framework of divine providence. The latter study assesses common and distinctive features of Catholic and Reformed theology. J. J. Macintosh ("Aquinas and Ockham on Time, Predestination and the Unexpected Examination," *Franciscan Studies* 55 [1998]: 181–220) provides a succinct analysis of future contingents in tandem with some consideration of Thomas' teaching on the doctrine of predestination (pp. 182–220). In addition, Thomas M. Tomasic ("Natural Moral Law and Predestination in St. Thomas Aquinas: An Incurable Contradiction?" in *The Medieval Tradition of Natural Law,* ed. Harold J. Johnson [Kalamazoo, MI: Medieval Institute Publications, Western Michigan University, 1987], 179–89) explores whether Thomas' natural law theory contradicts human autonomy and causation delineated in *De Veritate* I.2 and *ST* Ia IIae. 92.2.

2. Since the *prima pars* was written between 1266 and November 1268, it is possible that there is a material borrowing from *ST* in *CRO*. Pierre Mandonnet ("Chronologie des écrits scripturaires de saint Thomas d'Aquin," *Revue Thomiste* 11 [1928]: 27–46, 116–55, 211–45; 12 [1929]: 53–69, 132–45, 489–519) disagrees. He claims that Aquinas lectured on Romans to 1 Corinthians during his stay in Naples (1272–1273) and that he never lectured on the mate-

rial in Paris. Palémon Glorieux ("Essai sur les commentaires scripturaires de saint Thomas et leur chronologie," *Recherches de théologie ancienne et médiévale* 17 [1950]: 254–58) refutes this assertion, claiming that Aquinas would have had insufficient time to edit the entire Romans commentary in Naples (because he ceased all writing on December 6, 1273) and that Mandonnet's chronology ignores the attestations of Bernardo Gui (*Legenda*, chap. 16) and William of Tocco (*Hystoria*, chap. 17) that Aquinas lectured on Paul in Paris. In addition, Glorieux claims that there was a lost commentary on Romans originally delivered in the Roman Province between 1259 and 1265. James A. Weisheipl delineates five "heterogeneous pieces" that comprise Aquinas' *Expositio et lectura super Epistolas Pauli Apostoli,* the first of which is the edited text written or dictated by Thomas (*expositio*). And furthermore "Thomas did not lecture on Paul at Naples, but rather at Paris during his second regency" (*Friar Thomas D'Aquino: His Life, Thought, and Work* [Garden City, NY: Doubleday, 1974], 373). This chronology is important when considering Aquinas' perspective on the Jews in Romans because his regency follows the bitter Christian–Jewish disputes that resulted in the confiscation and public burning of Talmud in Paris in 1242. More to the point, it permits us to compare *CRO* in the form edited by Thomas himself with the *prima pars* completed earlier in 1268.

3. See also *I Sent.* d.39.2.

4. [Q]uis, ut dicitur Prov. VIII.17: Ego diligentes me diligo; diligere est bonum velle dilecto; Dei autem velle est operari. Omnia enim quaecumque voluit fecit, ut in Ps CXXXIV.6 dicitur (emphasis mine).

5. ...qui primo fideles ab aeterno praedestinavit; secundo ex tempore vocat; tertio sanctificat...ut propositum referatur ad praedestinationem, quae, secundum Augustinum, est propositum miserendi, Eph I.11: Praedestinati secundum propositum eius.

6. Destinatio autem dupliciter sumitur. Quandoque pro missione: dicuntur enim destinati qui ad aliquid mittuntur....[S]ecunda significatio a prima derivari videtur....Secundum hoc igitur praedestinare nihil aliud est quam ante in corde disponere quid sit de re aliqua faciendum.

7. See, for example, §45: "sicut non dicimus proprie quod homo est praedestinatus habere manus."

8. See §45.

9. The themes of *vocatio Dei* and the glorification of persons so elected recur throughout *CRO* 10 and 11. See below.

10. Ia. 23.3. resp.

11. §764.

12. Electio autem et dilectio aliter ordinantur in Deo et in homine. In homine enim electio praecedit dilectionem. Voluntas enim hominis movetur ad amandum ex bono quod in re amata considerat, ratione cuius ipsam praeelegit alteri et praeelectae suum amorem impendit. Sed voluntas Dei est causa omnis boni quod est in creatura. Et ideo bonum per quod una creatura praefertur alteri per modum electionis, consequitur voluntatem Dei, quae est de bono illius, quae

pertinet ad rationem dilectionis. Unde non propter bonum quod in homine eligat Deus eum diligit, sed potius eo quod ipsum diligit, praefert eum aliis eligendo (§763).

Garrigou-Lagrange states the general principle succinctly: "no created being would be better than another unless it were loved more by God [I. 20.3]. St. Thomas makes [predilection] the keystone of his treatise on predestination" (*Predestination,* trans. Dom Bede Rose, OSB [St. Louis: Herder, 1946], 78).

13. Manifestum est enim quod iustitia distributiva locum habet in his quae debentur ex debito, puta si aliqui meruerunt mercedem, ut plus laborantibus maior merces donetur. Non autem habet locum in his quae sponte et misericorditer aliquis dat....

Cum igitur omnes homines propter peccatum primi parentis nascantur damnationi obnoxii, quos Deus per gratiam suam liberat, sola misericordia liberat. Et sic quibusdam est misericors, quos liberat, quibusdam autem iustus, quos non liberat, neutris autem iniquus.

Et ideo Apostolus quaestionem solvit per auctoritatem, quae omnia divinae misericordiae adscribit.

14. Also in this article, Thomas refutes theological positions taken by Origen and Pelagius; the former claimed that souls were allotted bodies on the basis of preexisting merit; the latter, that the impetus for doing well begins with the human person and the consummation from God. In each case preexisting merit elicits divine election. Thomas cites Romans 9.11–12 to refute the former and 2 Cor 3.5 to refute the latter. Again, each of these concerns is replicated in *CRO* §§758 and 767, as well as §§771 and 772.

15. *Sed contra.*

16. "Precisely as transcendent universal cause of the being and activity of creatures, God's providential governance of the universe makes our free activity possible....God's causality embraces and empowers the diverse sorts of causality in the universe by making it possible for each created agent to act according to its nature; determined, physical agents acting necessarily according to pre-established patterns, and intelligent, deliberative human and angelic agents acting freely....In his goodness, God shares the dignity of being a real cause with creaturely agents" (J. Augustine DiNoia, OP, "Providence," in *Our Sunday Visitor's Encyclopedia of Catholic Doctrine,* ed. Russell Shaw [Huntington, IN: Our Sunday Visitor, 1997], 548).

17. Quod potest dupliciter intelligi. Uno modo sic: numquid Deus permisit eos offendere solum ut caderent, id est propter nullam aliam utilitatem inde consequentem, sed solum volens eos cadere? Quod quidem esset contra bonitatem divinam...quod numquam permitteret aliquid mali fieri nisi propter bonum, quo ex malo elicit, unde et Iob XXXIV.24 dicitur: Conteret multos et innumerabiles, et stare faciet alios pro eis. Apoc. II.11 dicitur: Tene quod habes, ne alius accipiat coronam tuam, quia scilicet Deus aliquos sic permittit cadere, ut quorumdam casus sit aliorum salutis occasio.

18. Ia. 23. 7. resp.

19. Est autem...considerandum, quod tria posuit in Deo pertinentia ad sanctos, videlicet electionem per quam intelligitur predestinatio, et dilectio. Que quidem realiter sunt idem in Deo, sed differunt ratione (§763).

20. Aquinas' use of *elect/election* occurs in eighteen paragraphs in chapters 9–11 and in five additional paragraphs in the remainder of the letter. By contrast, Paul uses *election* four times in Romans 9–11, specifically, 9.11; 11.5, 7, and 28. He speaks of the "elect" in 8.33 and 16.13.

21. Erich Dinkler, "The Historical and the Eschatological Israel in Romans Chapters 9–11: A Contribution to the Problem of Predestination and Individual Responsibility," *Journal of Religion* 33 (1956): 120.

22. See *ST* I.21.4. ad 4., where Thomas writes that "God's justice and mercy appear both in the conversion of the Jews and of the Gentiles. But an aspect of justice appears in the conversion of the Jews which is not seen in the conversion of the Gentiles; inasmuch as the Jews were saved on account of the promises made to the fathers." In *CRO* Aquinas does not identify the "beloved Jews" specifically as converts.

23. See also 1 Thess 1.4, wherein Paul addresses the brothers as "beloved by God" and immediately acknowledges their election (εἰδότες...τὴν ἐκλογὴν ὑμῶν). Also cf. Col 3.12: ὡς ἐκλεκτοὶ τοῦ θεοῦ ἅγιοι καὶ ἠγαπημένοι.

24. Hoc autem est propositum praedestinationis, de quo ibidem dicitur: Praedestinati secundum propositum eius (§759).

25. See *I Sent.* d.40.1. ad 4. ("Quod sit praedestinatio...") and especially d.41.aa.1,2. The four books of *Sentences* were completed between 1252 and 1256, prior to Thomas' first lectures on Paul in Italy.

26. Cf. *I Sent.* d.41.1.2.ad 1 for the order of election and predestination, and *III Sent.* d.32.2. resp., which specifies *dilectio amicitiae* as the cause of election. Aspects of these two *distinctiones* are seen in *ST* Ia. 23.4 (e.g., compare ad 3 with d.32. resp.) and are substantially developed in *CRO*.

27. There is no article exclusively dedicated to the question of election in *ST*, although it enjoys a certain prominence in Ia. 23.4. Therefore, I have chosen Thomas' earlier discrete treatment of the subject in *I Sent.* for analysis and comparison with *CRO*.

28. *I Sent.* d.41.1.2. resp.

29. Ibid.

30. Ibid. Thomas uses Dionysius' comparison of divine goodness and the sun found in *I Sent.* d.41.1. ad 2. in *ST* Ia. 23 4. obj.1. In ad 2, however, he writes: "Speaking more precisely...of the sharing of this or that good, then God does not grant without choice (*non absque electione*), for some blessings he gives to some and not to others. Hence there is choice (*electio*) of those he brings together in grace and glory."

31. Postquam Apostolus ostendit quod Dei gratia datur hominibus ex divina electione, per quam homines ad gratiam vocantur, hic ostendit quod praedicta electio sive vocatio non solum pertinet ad Iudaeos ut ipsi poterant gloriari,

propter hoc quod dicitur Deut. IV.37: Dilexi patres tuos et eligi semen eorum post eos sed etiam ad Gentes (§796).

32. [O]stendit quod nulla accusatio possit esse sanctis Dei nociva: et hoc ratione divinae electionis. Qui enim aliquem elegit, ex hoc ipso eum approbare videtur. Sancti autem sunt electi a Deo. Eph I.4: Elegit nos in ipso ante mundi constitutionem, ut essemus sancti. Qui autem accusat, improbat eum quem accusat. Non autem valet alicuius accusatio contra Dei approbationem. Et ideo dicit quis accusabit, scilicet efficaciter, adversus electos, id est adversus quos Deus elegit ut sint sancti? Unde dicitur Apoc XII.10: Proiectus est accusator fratrum nostrorum (§716).

33. "...insofar as it is from the Hebrew it is the same as 'wonderful' or 'elect' (*mirabilis vel electus*)....And these indeed fit him. In fact he was elect with respect to grace (*electus...fuit quantum ad gratiam*), hence Acts 9.15: This one is to me as a vessel of election" (§17). Also see §64.

34. "Set apart...either through conversion from unbelievers...or...whether set apart by election (*segregatus per electionem*) from the other disciples, accordingly Acts 13.2: Set apart for me Saul and Barnabas, etc." (§23).

35. Deinde, cum dicit, Absit, etc., solvit quaestionem ostendens quod Deus non totaliter reppulerat populum Iudaeorum. Et hoc est quod dicit Absit, ut scilicet populus Iudaeorum sit totaliter a Deo repulsus. Et hoc quidem, primo, probat quantum ad personam suam, dicens: Nam et ego, qui in fide Christi existens, Israëlitae sum, scilicet gente; II Cor XI.22: Israëlitae sunt et ego (§861).

36. See §796. But in §735 the *origin of grace* derives from the "sole election of God," not from any merit from "preceding works."

37. Finis enim electionis et miserationis bonorum est, ut manifestet in eis abundantiam bonitatis suae, revocando eos a malo, et ad iustitiam eos trahendo, et finaliter eos perducendo in gloriam (§794).

38. Postquam posuit dignitatem Iudaeorum, ostendit quod ista dignitas non pertineat ad eos qui processerunt ex antiquis patribus carnaliter sed ad spirituale semen quod est a Deo electum. Et primo ostendit, quod huiusmodi dignitas proveniat ex electione divina; secundo ostendit, quod hac electio pertinet communiter et ad Iudaeos et ad Gentiles... (§748).

39. "[O]n what account he may wish to have mercy on this one and that one or to harden him...is not able to be assigned except the absolute (*simplex Dei voluntas*) will of God."

Thomas continues illustrating the principle from the builder's craft selecting equal stones for varying locations in a wall; "but why one may place these stones in the summit and those at the base has not a certain reason, except that the craftsman willed it" (§788).

40. Cf. §763, as above. Garrigou-Lagrange (*Predestination,* 80) posits that "Thomas expresses what is the foundation for the principle of predilection, in the fine distinction he draws between the antecedent will, which is the principle of sufficient grace, and the consequent will, which is the principle of effi-

cacious grace. On this point he says: 'Whatever God simply wills takes place; although what he wills antecedently may not take place.' [cf., I. 19.6 ad 1.]." This distinction becomes particularly relevant to Romans 11.26. See below.

41. Tanta est autem divinae bonitatis excellentia, quod non potest nec uno modo nec in una creatura sufficienter manifestari. Et ideo diversas creaturas condidit, in quibus diversimode manifestatur, praecipue autem in creaturis rationalibus, in quibus eius iustitiam manifestatur quantum ad illos quos pro eorum meritis punit, misericordia vero in illis quos ex sua gratia liberat. Et ideo ut utrumque in hominibus manifestaretur, quosdam misericorditer liberavit, sed non omnes (§792).

42. Dicit ergo primo: Non solum ego non sum repulsus sed Deus non reppulit plebem suam, totam, quam prescivit, id est praedestinavit, supra VIII.8: Quos praescivit, hos et praedestinavit. Ps XCIII.14: Non repellet Dominus plebem suam. Quod Apostolus hic exponit quantum ad praedestinatos.

43. Dictum est quod Oseam loquitur pro Gentibus, Isaias clamat, id est aperte loquitur pro conversione Israel. Is LVIII.1: Clama, ne cesses, quasi tuba vocem tuam.

In hac autem prima auctoritate, primo, ponit paucitatem conversorum ex Israel, dicens si fuerit numerus filiorum Israël tamquam arena maris, id est innumerabiles prae multitudine. Gen. XXII.17: Multiplicabo semen tuum velut arenam que est etc. III Reg IV.20: Iuda et Israël innumerabiles quasi arena maris. Reliquiae salvae fient, id est non omnes, nec maior pars, sed aliqui pauci qui relinquenter ex excidio aliorum....Infra XI.5: Reliquiae secundum electionem gratiae salvae factae sunt (§802).

44. Thomas' commentary in §932 seems to imply this distinction: ut omnium misereatur, id est ut in omni genere hominum sua misericordia locum habeat...quod quidem non est extendum ad daemones...nec etiam quantum ad omnes homines sigillatim, sed ad omnia genera hominum. Fit enim hoc distributio pro generibus singulorum et non pro singulis generum.

45. Sed dicendum est quod donum hic accipitur pro promissione, quae fit secundum Dei praescientiam vel praedestinationem. Vocatio autem hic accipitur pro electione, quia propter certitudinem utriusque, quod Deus promittit, iam quodammodo dat et quos elegit, iam quodammodo vocat. Et tamen ipsum temporale Dei donum et temporalis vocatio, non irritatur per mutationem Dei quasi poenitentis sed propter mutationem hominis, qui gratiam Dei abiicit... (§926).

46. See, e.g., John Y. B. Hood, *Aquinas and the Jews,* Middle Ages Series (Philadelphia: University of Pennsylvania Press, 1995), 10, 18, and 109–10.

47. Hereafter, *PER* and *CER* respectively. I use the critical text and translations of Paula Fredriksen Landes (*Augustine on Romans: Propositions from the Epistle to the Romans, Unfinished Commentary on the Epistle to the Romans,* Society of Biblical Literature Texts and Translations 23, Early Christian Literature 6 [Atlanta: Society of Biblical Literature, 1982]) for the *PER* and *CER* alike.

48. As do contemporary exegetes such as Erich Dinkler; see, e.g., his "Historical and the Eschatological Israel," 109–27.

49. Hood, *Aquinas and the Jews*, 111.

50. Jeremy Cohen, *The Friars and Jews: The Evolution of Medieval Anti-Judaism* (Ithaca: Cornell University Press, 1982), 19.

51. Fredriksen, *Augustine on Romans*, 33 (emphasis mine).

52. Augustine later rejected the position articulated in *PER* §60 in his *Retractiones* 22,2: "I had not yet sought diligently enough or discovered up to this time what is the nature of the 'election of grace'....This certainly is not grace if any merits precede it; indeed then, what is given not according to grace, but according to debt, is given for merits rather than bestowed. Hence I should not have written what I said immediately afterwards: 'In fact, the same Apostle says, "The same God who works all things in all"; but it has not been said anywhere "God believes all things in all"'; and then I added: 'What we believe, therefore is ours; but what we do well is His who gives the Spirit to those who believe'" (Augustine, *Retractiones* [trans. M. I. Bogan; Fathers of the Church 60; Washington, DC: Catholic University of America Press, 1968], 99).

We shall analyze more fully the ways in which Augustine modifies his understanding of Romans 9 in *Ad Simplicanum* I,2,3–22 (*De Diversis Quaestionibus ad Simplicianum* [*Aurelii Augustini Opera* XLIV, pars xiii,i]; Turnholt: Brepols, 1970). For a concise study of Augustine's evolving thought on election, Jews, and Judaism see Fredriksen's (Landes), "Excaecati Occulta Jusitia Dei," *Journal of Early Christian Studies* 3 (1995): 299-324. As we shall see, however, neither Augustine's original theological positions on election and predestination in *PER* and *CER* nor his subsequent modifications fully accord with Aquinas' own exposition in *CRO* 9 and 11. These fundamental differences account for their divergent understanding of the role of Jews.

53. Circa ordinem autem praescientiae et praedestinationis dicunt quidam quod praescientia meritorum bonorum et malorum est ratio praedestinationis et reprobationis, ut scilicet intelligatur quod Deus praedestinet aliquos, quia praescit eos bene operaturos, et in Christum credituros.

...Unde ponere quod aliquod meritum ex parte nostra praesupponatur, cuius praescientia sit ratio praedestinationis, nihil est aliud quam gratiam ponere dari ex meritis nostris, et quod principium bonorum operum est ex nobis, et consummatio est ex Deo (emphasis mine).

54. The latter study must also assess the subsidiary theme of election and the *vocatio Dei*. Other Augustinian works will be employed selectively.

55. Thus Bernhard Blumenkranz ("Augustin et les juifs: Augustine et le judaïsme," *Recherches Augustiniennes* 1 [1958]: 227ff.) summarizes Augustine's biblical hermeneutic: "quandamodo in veteri novum lateat, et in novo vetus pateat" (*Quaest. in Heptateuch*, II, 73 and 103).

56. 16.21 (*Corpus Scriptorum Ecclesiasticorum Latinorum* [CSEL] [Vienna, 1887–], 25.1.463). Translation is based on Richard Stother, *Nicene and Post-Nicene Fathers*, first series, ed. Philip Schaff (repr., Peabody, MA: Hendrickson, 1994), 4:155–345.

57. Quid est enim aliud hodieque gens ipsa nisi quaedam scriniaria Chris-

tianorum, baiulans legem et Prophetas ad testimonium assertionis Ecclesiae, ut nos honoremus per sacramentum quod nuntiat illa per literram? (CSEL 25.1.351).

58. Codicem portat Judeus, unde credat Christianus. Librarii nostri facti sunt, quomodo solent servi post domino codices ferre, ut illi portando deficiant, illi legendo proficiant (*Ennarr. in Ps.* 66.9. Jeremy Cohen summarizes the "witness doctrine" in the Augustinian corpus in this way: "Augustine explained, repeatedly and pointedly: The Jews preserve the literal sense [of scripture], they represent it, and they actually embody it—as bookbearers, librarians, living signposts, and desks, who validate a Christological interpretation of the Old Testament" (*Living Letters of the Law: Ideas of the Jew in Medieval Christianity* [Berkeley and Los Angeles: University of California Press, 1999], 59). His treatment of Augustine is comprehensive, respecting the chronology of texts and the developing thought of the author (see table 1, "Elements of the Augustinian Doctrine of Jewish Witness: A Chronology of Noteworthy Texts," 41). A similar methodological treatment of Aquinas by Cohen would be a welcome contribution to the discussion. Cohen's current analysis undergirding a proposed "Thomistic synthesis" is not compelling because it does not respect the difference between developing systematic thought (and the internal principles of intelligibility) of the medieval theologians from the patristic, specifically, Augustinian sort of commentary that Aquinas and others employ. In sum, Cohen's arguments appear to some to be tendentious and akin to "proof-texting." For my part, I do not think that Cohen sufficiently distinguishes between the two theological genres of patristic commentary and systematic theology. He relies on the historical chronology of Augustine's works to demonstrate developing thought clustered around specific themes, for example, the witness doctrine. By contrast, he does not accord Aquinas the same careful chronological analysis, but uses different kinds of Thomistic works without regard for genre or development.

59. For example, a real Jew is one who is so inwardly (*PER* §12); the Law and circumcision are spiritual, not literal (*PER* §11). These themes derive from a careful reading of Romans and Paul's listing of Jewish prerogatives, not necessarily from Augustine's desire for Jewish inclusivity.

60. *PER* §7–8.

61. *CER* §1; *PER* §66.

62. *PER* §70,1,3.

63. Fredriksen, *Augustine on Romans*, ix.

64. See, e.g., Fredriksen, "Excaecati," 1: "Augustine's vision of the Jews as a living witness to Christian truth was both original and, compared with his attitude toward pagans and non-Catholic Christians, uncharacteristically tolerant." Bernhard Blumenkranz had earlier contextualized Augustine's position regarding the Jews within the phenomena of Jewish proselytism and "des sectes hérétiques....Tandis qu'Augustin s'efforce de démontrer aux Juifs le progrès accompli par le Nouveau Testament sur l'Ancien, il découvre ainsi son flanc

aux attaques des Manichées qui refusent toute valeur à l'Ancien Testament: changeant de front, Augustin se trouve alors amené à affirmer la parfaite concordance des deux testaments" ("Augustin et les juifs," 227ff.). Augustine's apparent tolerance is dictated by the circumstance of simultaneously engaging other contemporaneous heterodox sects; this is an assertion oft repeated in scholarly literature. Only now is the matter of Jewish presence and proselytism being reevaluated, which, in turn, calls into question the theoretical reconstruction formulated by Blumenkranz. See below.

65. For dating, see the benchmark work of Bernhard Blumenkranz, *Die Judenpredigt Augustins: Ein Beitrag zur Geschichte der jüdisch-christlichen Beziehungen in den ersten Jahrhunderten,* Basler Beiträge zur Geschichtswissenschaft 25 (Basel: Helbing & Lichtenhahn, 1946; repr., Paris: Études Augustiniennes, 1973), 207–9, 211.

66. For example, Jeremy Cohen ("Jews as Killers of Christ," *Traditio* 39 [1983]: 1–28, esp. 9–10) credits Augustine with the tradition that "however much the Jews despised Jesus and the truth, their evil derived from their ignorance; from their own perspective, their hostility toward Jesus reflected their love of God....This Augustinian stance remained essentially unchallenged during the late Patristic period." He contends that this Augustinian theme of Jewish ignorance was progressively eclipsed by the accusation of willful deicide made by theologians of the high Middle Ages, Franciscan and Dominican friars chief among them. Cohen does not investigate *CER* or *PER*, and his reading of Augustine's *Tractatus Adversus Iudaeos* is accurately characterized as "selective." See below.

67. See Blumenkranz's *Beschreibung der zeitgenössischen Juden durch Augustin* in his foundational study *Die Judenpredigt Augustins,* 62–68.

68. These works serve to bracket Augustine's career and to provide textual parameters for assessing his attitude toward the Jews. In addition, his *De Diversis Quaestionibus ad Simplicanum* I,2 (hereafter *Ad Simpl.*) will be employed to show the development of his thought by 397, especially concerning election and reprobation. As John Farrelly, OSB, admirably notes, this work "permits us to see exactly how the problem [i.e., of predestination and grace] posed itself to Augustine, the deepest principles of his solution and the secondary matters he looked upon as flowing from these central principles. ...Augustine looks back at the end of his life to this work with predilection and finds in it the principles from which his later teachings on the subject of grace and predestination flow, [therefore] we will with the least chance of error gain an objective understanding of his doctrine by a close study of the pertinent section[s] of this work" (*Predestination, Grace and Free Will* [Westminster, MD: Newman, 1964], 83). An analysis of the Jews, predestination, and election in the entire Augustinian corpus is unnecessary and well beyond the scope and purpose of this present study: a concise comparison and analysis of these topics in Augustine's and Thomas' Romans commentaries. For a thoroughgoing treatment of the Jews and related topics in Augustine's works, see Blumenkranz,

Beschreibung der zeitgenössischen Juden durch Augustin. John Rist ("Augustine on Free Will and Predestination," in *Augustine: A Collection of Critical Essays*, ed. R. A. Markus [Garden City, NY: Doubleday, 1972], 218–52) provides an exceptional, concise analysis of Augustine's positions on predestination, election, and human and divine volition; in fact, he posits that Augustine "did not change his views about the relationship of foreknowledge and predestination after his reply to Simplicanus [and] that means that the doctrine of total dependence [i.e., of all fallen individuals upon divine volition], already explicit in this reply, is maintained consistently until the end of his life" (p. 239). See Margaret H. McCarthy's "Recent Developments in the Theology of Predestination" (S.T.D. diss., Pontificia Universitas Lateranensis, 1995), 5–30, for an analysis of modern interpreters of Augustine on predestination, especially "the problem of reconceiving the universal salvific will [of God, cf. 1 Tim 2.4] with the notion of particular election which Augustine had advanced" (p. 29). She summarizes the contemporary challenges by critics in three categories: "Augustine's theory of particular predestination (i) constrains Augustine to deny the universal salvific will, (ii) is founded on a dualistic conception of the divine design and (iii) is nonpreachable, for it contradicts the *sensus fidelium* and drives the faithful to fatalism and desperation" (p. 9). Thomas refutes i and ii explicitly.

69. See Blumenkranz, *Judenpredigt*, 110ff. and 211, as well as his "Augustin et les Juifs," 233, 235f. Also, Marcel Simon's *Verus Israël: Étude sur les relations entre Chrétiens et Juifs dans l'empire Romain* (Paris: Boccard, 1946), 135–425, 433ff.

With reference to Jewish populations in North Africa, see, e.g., P. Monceaux, "Les colonies juives dans l'Afrique romaine," *Revue des études juives* 44 (1908): 1–28; H. Z. Hirsberg, *A History of the Jews in North Africa* (Leiden: Brill, 1974), 21–40; and Yann LeBohec, "Inscriptions juives et judaïsantes de l'Afrique romain," *Antiquités africaines* 17 (1981): 165–207.

70. Fredriksen, "Excaecati," 322.

71. Ibid., 300–301. See also her doctoral dissertation, "Augustine's Early Interpretation of Paul" (Ph.D. diss., Princeton University, 1979), 1–15.

72. Furthermore, Fredriksen's position underscores the legitimacy of comparing Augustine's *CER* and *PER* with Aquinas' *CRO* for representative positions on the Jews, Judaism, election, and predestination.

73. A *via media* is represented by Marcel Dubois ("Jews, Judaism, and Israel in the Theology of Saint Augustine," *Immanuel* 22/23 [1989]: 178), who writes: "Augustine...was presented with a...troubling problem by the presence of Jews around him, indicative of the presence of an organic Judaism. The New Testament is the fulfillment of the Old, yet the Jews subsist as a people and as a religion. Is this not an indication of a fault in the accomplishment of the divine purpose? Augustine is led to ask the question and enquire what can be the present meaning of the existence of the Jews and Judaism."

74. Fredriksen correctly infers this in *PER* §2 introducing an explanatory

note: "they [Jewish Christians] might not in any way spurn those Gentiles called into the Gospel." Confirmation of her inference is found in *CER*; see below.

75. This thesis is restated in *PER* §64: "[S]ince Paul taught that we do good by the mercy of God,...the Jews should not glory on account of their works, who, when they had received the Gospel, thinking that this should be attributed to their own merit, did not want it to be given to the Gentiles. (2) They ought now cease from their pridefulness and understand that, if we are called to belief not through our own works but through the mercy of God, so that we who believe do good, then they ought not begrudge the Gentiles this mercy as though it had been given to the Jews on account of their previous merit, which is nothing." So too in *Ad Simplicanum* I,2,2: "Et primo intentionem apostoli quae per totam epistulam uiget tenebo quam consulam. Haec est autem, ut de operum meritis nemo glorietur. De quibus audebant Israelitae gloriari, quo datae sibi legi seuissent et ex hoc euangelicam gratiam tamquam debitam meritis suis percepissent, quia legi seruiebant. Vnde nolebant eandem gratiam dari gentibus tamquam indignis...." Clearly, Augustine understood the Apostle's intent in Romans to be a polemic against "meritorious works."

76. *CER* §1,3; see also §11, where Augustine describes the Jews in the Letter to the Hebrews as belligerently railing against Paul.

77. *CER* §1,4, (emphasis mine).

78. As well as deicides; see *CER* §14,6.

79. The further debasement of the Jews is seen in Augustine's philological comparison between the terms *church* and *synagogue*, which he derives from Romans 1.1: "called to be an apostle, set apart for the gospel of God." He writes in §1,2–3: "[T]he Church is so named because it 'calls forth'; the synagogue, because it 'gathers together.' For 'to be called together' is more appropriately said of men, whereas 'to be gathered together' is more appropriately said of animals (which is why the word 'herds'—that is—'gatherings'—is normally used with particular reference to animals). (3) Therefore, although Scripture in many places calls the Church herself God's flock or herd or sheepfold, nevertheless, when men are compared to cattle, it pertains to the old life."

80. *CER* §3: "quoniam credentes in Christum, in quorum numerum vocatus est...."

81. *CER* §4: "They are like the Jews themselves who thought that Christ was the son of David only, ignorant of the preeminence by which he is the Lord of David himself, because he is the Son of God."

82. *CER* §15,5–6: "As for Jewish hostility to the Holy Spirit, Stephen himself is a witness.... (6) And he most clearly told the Jews: 'You have always resisted the Holy Spirit.'"

83. *CER* §20,2–3.

84. *CER* §20,5–6.

85. *CER* §20,4: "And we should attend here to the fact that the Lord himself left open the opportunity for correction and repentance to those same Jews whose blasphemy he condemned."

86. *CER* §23.

87. *PER* §23,12: "illi factis deum negant."

88. See *PER* §30: "By this expression [i.e., 5.20] Paul sufficiently indicated the Jews did not understand why the Law had been given. (2) It was not to bring life, for grace does this through faith. But the Law was given to show what great and tight bonds of sins bound those who presumed to attain righteousness by their own strength."

This assertion of Augustine proceeds from his salvation-historical schema of the Four Stages of Humanity: prior to Law, under the Law, under grace, and in peace. See §§13–18.

89. *PER* §68.

90. *PER* §§7–8.

91. *PER* §66,2.

92. *PER* §60,13: "This argument was used against certain Jews who, once they believed in Christ, both gloried in the works they did before receiving grace and claimed that they had merited this same grace of the Gospel by their own previous good works, though only the person who has already received grace can do good works." Also *PER* §64,2 (see n. 75 above).

93. For there are many men who are not submissive; empty talkers, seducers of the mind, Jews for the most part, who ought to be refuted, who upset entire families teaching things they ought not teach for the sake of filthy lucre.

94. *PER* §84,3–4: "(4) Paul takes up the same point here when he says, 'These men do not serve the Lord Jesus Christ, but their own belly,' and he says of them in another place, 'Their belly is their god.'"

95. Hereafter *AdI*. Citations are from "In Answer to the Jews" in Fathers of the Church 27, trans. Marie Ligouri, IHM (New York: Fathers of the Church, 1955), 387–414. It must be recognized at the outset that Augustine takes up an established genre of Christian literature known as *adversus Judaeos,* evidenced as early as the second century. Clark M. Williamson ("The 'Adversus Judaeos' Tradition in Christian Theology," *Encounter* 39 [1978]: 273–96) concludes that Augustine incorporates the chief characteristics of this literary genre: Jewish blindness, rejection of Christ, reprobation, and the loss of heritage and covenant to Christians. "His original contribution is his development of the idea that the Diaspora of the Jews is willed by God that they may constitute a negative witness to the Church and to Christ among all nations. The wandering Jew, the people who in their desolation and homelessness make a strange witness of unbelief, is his most distinctive contribution to the *Adversus Judaeos* Tradition" (p. 292). Robert S. MacLennan ("Christian Self-definition in the *Adversus Judaeos* Preachers in the Second Century," in *Diaspora Jews and Judaism: Essays in Honor of, and in Dialogue with, A. Thomas Kraabel,* ed. J. Andrew Overman and Robert S. MacLennan, South Florida Studies in the History of Judaism 41 [Atlanta: Scholars Press, 1992], 210) provides four conclusions, although proper to second-century preachers of the *Adversus Judaeos* genre, which may function as criteria to assess Augustine's view of the Jews in *AdI, CER,* and *PER.* MacLennan's conclusions are readily transposed into questions usefully posed

in the process of our inquiry: Is Augustine stating a universally accepted view of Jews and Judaism? Were the Jews of Hippo Regius "at home" and contributing to the general welfare of the city? Is Augustine more concerned with Christian self-definition than with attacking Jews or Judaism? Is Augustine's talk about Jews reflecting immediate experience in his particular time, or are they viewed primarily as "Bible people"?

96. §9. Subsequent generations even did so proleptically "in their parents," §10.

97. §8.

98. §7: "It was not because the unbelievers and the proud had been broken away and the branches were on that account unfruitful and the wild olive of the Gentiles was ingrafted that the root of the Patriarchs and the Prophets died."

99. §9: "The law...which was given them through Moses, on account of which they are quite proudly exalted and by virtue of which they are far better convicted...."

100. §9.

101. As does Paul in Romans 10.21 and 11.10, respectively.

102. §10. Interestingly, Cohen ("Jews as Killers of Christ," 25) cites *AdI* §1,2 and §7,10 to demonstrate that the "*Tractatus* does little more than to enumerate scriptural *testimonia* which demonstrate the truth of Christianity and the blind ignorance of the Jews....Augustine links the blindness of the Jews directly to their crucifixion of Jesus and to their continuing, albeit unwitting, fulfillment and preservation of Old Testament prophecy—precisely the reason for their divinely ordained survival in Christendom." Cohen's benign interpretation of Augustinian texts fails to distinguish between vincible and invincible ignorance. Augustine does not state that the Jews were invincibly ignorant, but because they do not understand their own biblical texts, they scorned the gospel and the apostle Paul. The blindness that came upon Israel was not an inevitable, permanent sort, nor is such the case with the Jews whom Augustine addresses in his own day: "You, in the person of your parents, have killed Christ. For a long time you have not believed in Him and have opposed Him, but you are not yet lost, because you are still alive; you have time now for repentance; only come now. You should have come long ago, of course, but come now; your days are not yet ended; the last day is still to come" (§8,11). What Cohen recognizes in Augustine is the seeming theological incongruity between the blindness of Israel (*sometimes* characterized as ignorance) and the Jews' alleged culpability for the crucifixion of Christ. Cohen recognizes the problem, but incorrectly resolves the difficulty by implicitly defining the Jews' ignorance as invincible. Neither Paul nor Augustine opts for this facile solution. To the contrary, Augustine repeatedly asserts that the Jews' ignorance is a willful misunderstanding of their own scriptural texts *and* a refusal to heed the preaching of Paul and subsequent generations of preachers. Aquinas, by contrast, resolves the seemingly contradictory strands of Augustinian tradition, that is, the Jews' blind ignorance and willful deicide, in *CRO* by means of predestination.

103. *PER* §69,3.

104. I make the distinction between eschatological and metaphorical Israel because the former would theoretically admit of the rehabilitation of historical Israel en masse, as does Paul. Augustine employs the metaphor or symbol of Israel to designate a composite group of the exclusively elect, which does not admit of this possibility. We should not be surprised by Augustine's redefinition—the same phenomenon is seen in his perspective of Law, circumcision, and other Jewish prerogatives. While not strictly an allegorical interpretation, it does exemplify the figure/reality pattern. It is a commonplace exegetical device of the bishop to interpret OT *realia* in this manner.

105. In Ia. 23.6. resp., Thomas cites a similar text from Augustine's commentary on John 6.44 (*Super Joannem* 26 [PL 35:1607]): "Wherefore he draws this one and not that one, seek not to decide if you wish not to err."

106. *Iohannis evangelium CXXIV* (*Corpus Christianorum, Series Latina* [CCSL] 36 [Turnholt: Brepols, 1954], 48.4): "Quia uidebat eos ad sempiternum interitum praedestinatos, non ad uitam aeternam sui sanguinis pretio comparatos." Christ's audience, according to Augustine, is *the Jews* who question him about his origins. See John 10.24. Similarly, Judas ("perditioni praedestinatus" [107.7]) and the world ("quippe ille damnationi praedestinatus merito non cognouit; mundus uero quem per Christum reconciliauit sibi, no merito, sed gratia cognouit" [111.5]) are described as predestined to destruction. He formulates these remarks ca. 413–418 CE. (See p. vii for specific dating of manuscript segments.)

While it is true that Augustine is not slavishly consistent regarding election and reprobation, he is consistent in his evaluation of fallen humanity and the inability of fallen individuals to extricate themselves from the *massa damnata* (see *De Dono Perserverantiae* 35) by the sheer exercise of the will. Augustine maintains that there is no positive impulsion on the part of God in the individual's exercise of the will. In this sense, God does not cause any person to sin. However, because God does not elect a particular person, God *effectively* consigns that person to the permanency of the fallen status, which warrants damnation. Rist ("Augustine on Free Will," 227) states: "As Augustine himself would put it, God does not wish (= cause) the damnation of any man, but in another sense he wishes it, that is, he is willing to let it happen in certain circumstances." Still, the *ratio* of divine election is not illumined, nor is the charge of divine arbitrariness avoided.

5
Election and Predestination in *CRO* 9 and 11

INTRODUCTION

Election is a "certain segregation" enacted by God. The doctrines of election and predestination are closely allied in Aquinas' *ST* Ia. 23. 4., as we have seen. They appear in tandem as Thomas exegetes Romans 9–11.[1] In *CRO* 9, Thomas exegetes Paul's salvific plot line in terms of the election of Jacob and Israel, preparing for the corporate eschatological implications of election and predestination for the Jewish people and the Gentiles in chapter 11. Jacob, the younger, is preferred to Esau not because of any preexisting merit "but according to election, insofar as God with an interior will pre-elect one over the other....However, this is the proposition of predestination...as...above: Ones predestined according to his purpose."[2] The doctrines of predestination and election govern Aquinas' exegesis of Romans 9–11; thereby, he safeguards the integral role of the Jewish people and delineates their relationship to the Peoples newly incorporated into the faith of Israel.

ELECTION IN *CRO* 9

Before Paul analyzes the plight of Israel in Romans 9.6ff., he first delineates the prerogatives of the Jews (v. 4). These claims permit Thomas to maintain the inherent dignity of the Jews and their privilege of divine election,[3] while simultaneously correlating the inclusion of the Peoples under God's predestinating will.

The Prerogatives and Dignity of Israel

While Paul straightforwardly posits the historical prerogatives of Israel (9.4), Aquinas uses these to explicate the dignity of the Jews. He has already stated that the very name of Jew "is honorable."[4] Therefore the once pristine dignity of the Jews, who seemingly are perishing, accounts for the reasonableness and intensity of the apostle's sorrow because "it is a greater evil to have lost a dignity, than not to have had it, as the Gloss says."[5]

Thomas follows the Pauline order of divine prerogatives in 9.4 but classifies them in a threefold schema, in order to explain Israel's *singular* dignity.[6] First Aquinas establishes the Jews' fundamental dignity by their common descent from Jacob; Thomas, citing Deuteronomy 4.7 ("There is no other nation..."), claims that this is an exclusive privilege of this people.[7] Second, he shows the dignity of the Jews from the benefits of God. He lists as the present spiritual benefit the adoption of children as well as a future spiritual benefit, that of glory promised them. (Exodus 4.22 confirms the firstborn status of the Jews and, in Exodus 40.32, God's abiding glory in their midst.) Symbolic benefits are types of present spiritual benefits, namely, covenant, law, and cult.[8] Thomas cites Isaiah 44.1 ("And now listen my servant Jacob, and Israel whom I have chosen...") and thereby illustratively melds divine prerogatives with divine election. The promises pertain to the future spiritual benefit of glory. Indeed, the OT promises fulfilled in Christ were made chiefly to the Jews. Temporal goods promised them signified spiritual goods to be attained (Lev 26.3f.; Deut 28.1–14).[9] Third, the dignity of the Jews derives from their origin, their fathers the patriarchs. Aquinas cites Deuteronomy 4.37 and thereby again asserts their divine election, which he will soon develop: I loved your fathers and I chose their seed. Finally, Paul demonstrates the Jews' dignity by their most significant offspring, the Christ, according to the flesh;[10] here, in §746, Aquinas pointedly reiterates John 4.22: "Salvation is from the Jews."

As important as the Pauline base text is, equally important is the array of other scriptural texts that Aquinas utilizes to explain clearly the dignity of Israel. These biblical texts reassert the Jews' fundamental and singular dignity; their present and future possession of divine benefits, both temporal and spiritual; their firstborn status because of divine election; their progeny (preeminent in Christ); and their essential role in a salvation that comes primarily (if not exclusively) from them. Moreover, these texts demonstrate that Christ and Paul are one with the Jews.[11]

The Election of Israel

According to Thomas, Paul has proven clearly the corporate dignity of the Jews; now the apostle must establish those persons to whom this dignity belongs in particular, which he does in 9.6–13. The Jews' prerogative of ancestry in chapter 9 illustrates a further refinement of principles demonstrated in chapter 4.[12] Paul is unequivocal: "not all who are out of Israel are Israel, nor are the seed of Abraham all children...of Abraham" (v. 6). Repeatedly throughout the commentary, Aquinas warns that carnal descent from Abraham or Jacob does not guarantee salvation.[13] In this regard he aptly represents Paul's understanding of Israel's privilege and its limitations.[14] Despite such caveats, lineal descent from Abraham and Jacob remains (paradoxically) one of the boasts of the Jews. However, dignity belongs to the spiritual seed chosen by God, not merely by virtue of carnal descent from the patriarchs.[15]

Thomas draws out the implications of Paul's allusions in 9.6; he explains how election occurs and whether divine election is unjust.[16] Election occurs in those who are "upright and seeing God through faith";[17] Aquinas sets forth this proposition by means of two comparisons, that is, with Jacob and, subsequently, with Abraham. The fact that election is fulfilled in certain Jews might be seen as demonstrating the steadfastness of the divine purpose. The word of God is proven firm because it has place in *some* who enjoy the prerogatives of Israel.[18] However, the selection of some in the present does not *necessarily* eliminate the comprehensive inclusion of all Israel in the future as a manifestation of God's mercy. Although Abraham's immediate progeny belonged to the people of God, some of the descendants of Isaac did not; specifically, the seed of Esau. Just as not all who are of Abraham's carnal seed are spiritual children (only those who imitate his faith and deeds), so too, neither are all true Israelites in virtue of descent from Jacob (only those who "are upright and see God through faith"). The fidelity of some and the infidelity of others do not nullify the effectiveness of God's word (9.6a); God remains faithful and his gifts to Israel remain intact.

> [I]f because...of the unbelief of some the prerogatives of the Jews were to be taken away, it would follow that the unbelief of man would annul the faithfulness of God, which is unfitting.[19]

The Election of Jacob

Romans 9.10 illustrates the principle of election by means of Jacob. From this example, Thomas makes two brief applications regarding divine election: that the grace of God is not obtained by the merits of the fathers, and that God freely elects one and rejects another. These applications are illustrated by the sons of Abraham and the sons of Isaac alike. Paul, according to Thomas, provides two examples because, regarding the first, the Jews

> were able to impute [election] either to the diversity of mothers, because Ishmael was born from the slave woman and Isaac from the free woman; or to the diversity of the merits of the father, because an uncircumcised one begot Ishmael, but a circumcised man [begot] Isaac. In order that any subterfuge be excluded, [Paul] introduces the examples, where one is chosen and the other of them is rejected, who, not only were begotten from one father but also from one mother and at the same time...from one act of copulation.[20]

Aquinas posits three things that 9.11 teaches: first, Paul designates the time of the promise, specifically, prior to the birth of Jacob and Esau; second, he designates the nature of the promise itself by which God forechose Jacob over Esau; and third, he states that the promise proceeds from the grace of the one calling, not from preexisting merit.[21] The radical freedom of divine election is emphasized, that is, "God himself of his own will pre-elected one over the other...."[22] For Thomas, Paul's inclusion of Genesis 25.23 (v. 12) and Malachi 1.2 (v. 13) reasserts divine election, imports predestination, and designates divine love as the cause of each.

Thomas interprets the text from Genesis 25.23 ("The elder will serve the younger") in 9.12 to function in three ways. First, with regard to their persons (insofar as Esau's malice effects Jacob's good); second, with reference to the progeny of each (insofar as at various times the Idumeans were subject to the Israelites); and third, figuratively, insofar as the Jews ("the elder") serve the Gentiles ("the younger") by "guarding the books from which the testimony of our faith is asserted."[23] The Jews not only are God's firstborn, but they are the preservers of scripture without whom the fullness of faith would be impossible.

Malachi prophesied that God loved Jacob but hated Esau (1.2); according to Thomas, he loved the former because of his good works and hated the latter because of his sins.[24] However, lest God's love for Jacob be construed as the result of preexisting merit in him or in response to Jacob's love for God, Aquinas reasserts that God's initiative in *electio* derives from an eternal *dilectio*.[25]

These arguments are meant to preclude the accusation that God acts capriciously, or worse, unjustly (9.14–18) and imperils the trustworthiness of his word (9.6). Paul himself first recognized the seeming paradox and in *diatribē*-style says: What therefore shall we say, that there is iniquity with God? Far be it! (v.14). One inference could be that God, in electing Jacob (and, by implication, his offspring) and reprobating Esau (and his progeny), acts contrary to distributive justice since the brothers are, in one sense, equals. But for Paul, such an inference is contrary to scripture; for Thomas, it is also contrary to the divine nature. Aquinas resolves the seeming contradiction theologically through Paul's use of Exodus 33.19: I shall have mercy upon whom I have mercy, and I shall offer mercy to whom I shall have mercy. The objection in 9.14 is resolved twofold from this textual authority. God has mercy upon those whom he will because he has judged them worthy of his mercy but not, however, from pre-existent or subsequent merits.[26] The will of God is the *ratio* of election in mercy and therefore the principles of distributive justice do not apply.[27] Since no member of Adam's race *deserves* election no individual right is breached which justice must restore. Mercy granted to some does not abrogate the debt owed by all. In fact, Aquinas returns to Romans 5.12ff. to illustrate this point:

> Therefore since all people because of the sin of the first parents are born liable to damnation, God through his grace liberates them, only by mercy does he free them: and thus to certain ones whom he frees he is merciful, to certain ones whom he does not free he is just; he is wicked to neither however.[28]

For Thomas, according to distributive justice, all persons warrant condemnation. Yet divine volition and mercy save some; others are justly reprobated. Aquinas understands Paul to be using Jacob as the figure for Israel: the primal forebear or eponymous hero for the clan. He moves, as does Paul, from analysis of the particular election of Jacob and the reprobation of Esau to an application pertaining to corporate Israel. Divine mercy therefore may be considered threefold: (1) according to God's will in predestinating, electing to free certain ones; (2) according to the individual's vocation and justification enacted in time; and (3) according to the effect, glory. He succinctly states: Paul "says I shall have mercy, namely by calling and justifying, on whom I have mercy, I shall offer mercy by predestinating [and] finally by glorifying him upon whom I have mercy."[29] Personal striving and pursuit apart from grace do not elicit mercy, nor is one's striving or pursuit solely attributable to divine mercy apart from the integral role of human freedom (v. 16). If the preeminence of grace and divine initiative and mercy are asserted, how do these pertain to the hardening of some and the reprobation of the evil? More specifically, how do these principles apply to the coalescence of a Jewish remnant and to the inclusion of the Gentiles?

The Inclusion of the Gentiles and the Role of Remnant Israel

Aquinas, having asserted the dignity of the Jews and the divine *ratio* for election and reprobation, next analyzes the inclusion of the Gentiles in 9.24ff. He follows Paul's strategy and reflects Paul's arduous struggle to explain the incorporation of the Peoples, the infidelity of Israel, and the role of the remnant. The sometimes conflated *testimonia* from Hosea (vv. 25, 26, 27) and Isaiah (vv. 27, 28, 29, 33) develop the thesis: those chosen and prepared for the riches of his glory come not only from the Jews but also from the Peoples (v. 24). Paul and Thomas treat the election of these respective groups in reverse order.

The Inclusion of the Gentiles

Thomas immediately refers the reader to a similar discussion of Gentile inclusion in Romans 3.29 ("Would God be of the Jews only? And not also of the Peoples? Yes, of the Peoples also"):

> From this it was manifest that God is not only of the Jews, but also of the Peoples, because God is one, who justifies circumcision, that is circumcised Jews from faith and the foreskin, that is the uncircumcised Gentiles, through faith, indeed as it is said Gal 5.6: In Christ Jesus neither circumcision, nor uncircumcision is anything.[30]

Paul's first two citations from Hosea in 9.25–26 prove the proposition stated in v. 24 ("He called them, not only from the Jews but also from the peoples, even us"). Aquinas posits that in the first quotation, Hosea 2.5 ("I shall call the ones not my people, my people, and she who is not my beloved, beloved; and she who obtained not mercy, obtained mercy"), God promises his gifts to the Gentiles; in the second quotation, Hosea 2.1 ("And it shall be in the place where it was said to them: 'You are not my people,' there they will be called sons of the living God"), he promises to them "divine filiation itself."[31]

Significantly, Aquinas isolates three particular "goods" that were "prominent among the Jews" to which "the Gentiles were strangers": divine cult, the privilege of corporate divine election, and freedom from original sin through circumcision.[32]

Because of divine cult, the Jews were called the People of God, "as though his servants and obedient to his precepts."[33] This was in stark contrast to the status of the Gentiles, whom Aquinas characterizes as "strangers" citing Ephesians 2.12 ("Alienated from the society of Israel and strangers to the covenants"). The Gentiles' status is changed through Christ, through whom they were called, so that they might be God's people.

Second, the Gentiles lacked corporate divine election, which excluded them from the spiritual gift of divine love. Thomas cites Hosea 3.1 ("The Lord loves the children of Israel") to confirm Israel's privilege of love, and Ephesians 4.18 ("They were alienated from the life of God on account of the ignorance which was in them") to confirm the Peoples' bereft state. This was changed through the blood of Christ, which brought them near and reconciled them to God.[34]

Third, the Jews enjoyed liberation from original sin conferred in circumcision; the Peoples did not.[35] Thomas first explains the inherent integrity and value of circumcision in the remission of original sin and accompanying punishments in §238. Commenting on 2.25 he writes that Paul

> says, first, Indeed circumcision is of benefit namely for the remission of original sin, whence it is said Gen 17.14: The life of whose flesh the foreskin shall not have been circumcised, etc. However, it is of benefit to you when an adult, if you observe the law....For circumcision was as though a certain profession, obligating a man to the observance of the law.[36]

Already we have seen in the commentary that the covenant marked by circumcision confirms the singular dignity of the Jews as God's people.[37] Circumcision is the exterior sign of that faith; "because faith was the first cause on account of which circumcision and the rest of the legal sacraments proceeded."[38] Circumcision has standing as a true sign when it corresponds to the keeping of the covenant.[39] Yet it did not function *ex opere operato*,[40] nor was it sufficient, in itself, to assure salvation.[41] To the contrary,

> the circumcision of the one transgressing the law may be made uncircumcision...for the true Jew is not he who outwardly is a

Jew, according to carnal generation. [Romans] 9.6: For not all who are from Israel, and afterward he adds, the Israelites are they, who...are children of the promise....Whence if any Jew would be a transgressor of the covenant, his is not a true circumcision, and therefore it is reckoned as uncircumcision.[42]

Aquinas strives to preserve the immanent worth of this Jewish prerogative, while demonstrating the insufficiency of circumcision when perceived merely as a self-assured boast.[43] He maintains that an interior Judaism and an interior circumcision, perceived by God, prevail over exterior signs or judgment of people.[44] In this regard, Paul and Thomas are heirs of a long prophetic tradition decrying Israel's infidelity metaphorically portrayed as uncircumcision of heart (e.g., Jer 4.4; 9.24ff.). This "spiritualization" of carnal circumcision is evident in the commentary.[45] (This sense will eventually predominate in Thomas' later writings.)[46] In *CRO,* however, spiritual circumcision has yet to eclipse this distinctive Jewish prerogative; one in which the Peoples did not share. Circumcision identified adherents to the true cult of God and separated Israel from the Gentiles;[47] it signified the faith of Abraham; it conferred freedom from original sin and accompanying punishment.[48]

However, the discussion of the Gentiles' adoptive status is occasioned by Paul's use of Hosea 2.1 in 9.26.[49] Aquinas uses a prior exposition in Romans 8.14f. to define the children of God, that is, "those who serve God out of love and act by the spirit of God."[50] Not only did the Gentiles not meet such criteria, but they could not be described as even having a servile fear of God that qualified others (albeit in an attenuated sense) as his people. The Jews possessed the dignity of God's children; this was their boast. Now, however, the Peoples (formerly declared "not-my-people" by divine pronouncement and regarded so by the Jews themselves) shall be called children of God "through divine adoption."[51]

The Role of Remnant Israel

Nevertheless, the adoption of the Peoples does not mean the abandonment of Israel. With Isaiah 10.22f. and Isaiah 1.9f., Paul proves the thesis advanced in 9.24 relative to the Jews; here Isaiah cries out on behalf of Israel (v. 27). Paul appropriates the Isaian prophecy of Israel's faithful remnant, a progeny chosen to perdure.[52] Thomas specifies two groups in particular to whom these prophetic texts pertain (believers among the Jews, and the apostles) and the means by which the prophecy is fulfilled, that is, God's word.[53]

According to Thomas, Paul's use of Isaiah 10.22 means that "not all, nor a major part, but [only] a certain few...are left from the fall of others."[54] Here, the dynamic tension and seeming ambiguity become apparent. Although there is a relative paucity of those converted from Israel in comparison with the countless number of her children, nevertheless, a multitude or remnant exists, saved according to the election of grace (11.5).[55]

The word of the Lord, specifically his evangelical word, is the cause of this salvation. Thomas, citing his version of Isaiah 10.22, states that... "a remnant shall be converted from [Israel and that]...the God of armies shall have exercised the consummation and the shortening in the midst of all the earth."[56] Herein he reiterates two points: first, that a remnant shall be saved, and second, that the Lord is the agent who enacts his word.

By using Isaiah 1.9 Paul directly attributes the remnant progeny of Israel to God. Aquinas emphasizes the plight of Israel as a result of her infidelity; something to which Paul only alludes.[57] The gravity of Israel's sin outweighs the sin of Sodom and Gomorrah. Thomas quotes Lamentations 4.6 ("A greater result is the iniquity of my people than the sins of the Sodomites") and Ezekiel 16.48 ("Sodom your sister and her daughter have not done as you and your daughter have done") to prove Paul's assertion from Jewish tradition itself. And yet, just as God in his mercy left...progeny, so too the fact "that the Jews are not wholly exterminated...as the Sodomites, is to be imputed to divine mercy. Lam 3.22: That we are not consumed is of the Lord's mercy."[58]

In 9.30 Paul asks his interlocutor to draw the necessary inferences relative to the Gentiles and to the Jews. The Peoples were alienated from the prerogatives, privileges, and converse of Israel. Their election came not through merits or works, nor that they might observe legal justice, but rather, their adoption came "through the faith of Christ."[59]

Moreover, Israel did not arrive at the status of justice through the law because they did so from works and not from faith (v. 31). Paul melds Isaiah 8.14 and 28.16 in Romans 9.33, and in so doing he posits a twofold causality: divine and human. God has placed a stumbling stone in the midst of Sion, yet "all who believe in him" obtain the reward of justice. In effect, Paul revisits the questions posed in 9.6 ("Has God's word failed?"), 9.14 ("Is there iniquity with God?") and 9.19f. ("Who can resist his will?"). He provides a provisional answer that demands further explanation. Thus, in chapter 10 Paul discusses Israel's choice for or against faith, and in chapter 11 he explains God's role in rejecting and electing Israel.

Throughout chapter 9 Paul has demonstrated the peculiar prerogatives of Israel, of which he himself is a member. The seeming fall of Israel has not nullified the effectiveness of God's word; indeed, the opposite is true: the word of God has been confirmed. God's word is fulfilled in Jacob and the election of some of his descendants. The mercy of God is shown in electing some and hardening others in Israel, and in the adoption of the Peoples. Both groups demonstrate God's wrath, God's power, God's patience, and God's mercy. The preservation of remnant Israel proves that God has not rejected his people. The inclusion of the Gentiles shows forth God's glory in his mercy. God's election and human belief are intertwined for Jew and Gentile alike. Paul the Jew identifies himself with the heritage of his kinsmen, and he agonizes over their plight. Simultaneously, Paul identifies himself with the Peoples, boldly asserting God's merciful call to them and their acquisition of righteousness through faith.

Aquinas both recognizes and exploits Paul's rhetoric. He succinctly summarizes Israel's prerogatives as proof of their singular dignity. Like Paul, he does not discount the function of these benefits nor their inherently positive value in forming Israel as God's people. Faithful to Paul, he ascribes the election of Jew and Gentile to God's mercy—not to preexisting works or merit. In so doing, however, he does not discount the distinctive privileges granted Israel to which the Peoples were foreigners.[60] Earlier Thomas asserted the priority of the Jews *de iure* and *de facto* and spoke of the assumption of the Gentiles into their grace:

> [A]s far as the order of salvation the Jews are first, because promises were made to them, as below 2.3, and into their grace the Peoples are assumed, as though the branch of the wild olive tree were inserted into a good olive tree, as below 11.24. Also, from them our Savior was born. Jn 4.22: Salvation is from the Jews.[61]

Here he reiterates this doctrine and speaks of the Peoples' inclusion into the "converse of Israel." His later commentary on Romans 11.17ff. confirms that the Gentiles are incorporated; they do not supplant remnant Israel, but enter into the promises of Israel.[62] The radical freedom of God exercised in electing Israel and certain Gentiles is the manifestation of his mercy for his glory. Even the repudiation of Christ is apologetically portrayed by Thomas as due to ignorance, because "as it is said 1 Cor 2.8: If they had known, never would they have crucified the Lord of glory."[63]

CORPORATE PREDESTINATION AND ELECTION IN *CRO* 11

Admittedly, Paul equivocates on his use of "Israel." Israel refers explicitly to the whole people, fallen or restored (vv. 1, 7, and 26), or to an implied portion or remnant (vv. 7 and 25). In Romans 11, we see more evidence of the possible corporate implications of predestination and election. Individual election and predestination (characteristic of Romans 9) have receded from consideration; corporate manifestations have moved to the foreground.[64] The shift is evidenced in Romans 11.25b–26a: "a hardening has come upon *part* of Israel, until the *full number* of the Gentiles has come in. And so *all* Israel will be saved."

Thomas similarly equivocates in his terminology in *CRO* 11. Sometimes Aquinas uses *the Jews* as a term for Israel;[65] elsewhere he specifies terms beyond Paul's own usage and contrasts Israel with "the elect of the Jews."[66] The corporate ramifications of election and predestination predominate. Aquinas boldly asserts in §916: "Israel shall be saved, not in a manner individually, but universally."[67] The theme of predestination brackets chapter 11 in §883 and §926.[68] Israel is predestined; Israel is not rejected. How can this be so when Paul has asserted the rejection of Esau (9.13) and pointed toward the distillation of a faithful remnant (11.5)? In other words, how does his seemingly individualistic account of predestination and election fit with corporate election of Israel? More troublesome indeed: how is it possible to claim that the Gentiles have been included in salvation while Israel has seemingly fallen away, and then conclude that God did not reject his people (11.1)? In response to these and other theological conundrums, here Thomas avoids supersessionism concerning Israel and the Jews, and offers a solution by means of predestination and election in *CRO* 11.

In §871 Thomas reminds the reader of certain principles articulated earlier in the commentary: that the remnant are elect; they are so by the grace of God and not by works; God acts freely in choosing. These, of course, proceed from divine *predilectio*; "that is, as far as the ones elected out of that people...[for] if they are most beloved by God it is reasonable that they be saved by God."[69] Thomas builds upon the example provided by Paul in Romans 11.2–4 of Elijah and the prophets of Baal. The existence of a remnant does not nullify God's election of Israel as his people, or compel a limited salvation of *only* a remnant; rather, the distillation of a remnant is God's doing in the present day as it was in the past. God's remnant in Paul's day, still chosen by grace, reinstantiates God's prior choices in Israel's history. In other words, God has acted thusly before in Israel and does so in the present.[70] In the latter case, as in the former, the fall of the Jews is not universal;[71] it is not irreparable;[72] it does not revoke Israel's prerogatives or singular dignity, but rather God has hardened some (11.7) for the benefit of others. Thomas summarizes the matter succinctly by citing John 15.16: You did not choose me, I chose you. Such hardening of a portion of Israel is attributed to God for two other purposes: to effect the salvation of the Peoples, and to incite the rest of Israel to jealousy.[73] This individual hardening *ex Deo* is nothing other than a covert theology of corporate predestination.

The Fall of the Jews

In §879 Thomas makes these implicit principles of predestination explicit insofar as the fall of the Jews is not an end in itself (that would contravene the divine goodness), occasions the salvation of others (as contingent effects), and will not remain forever (because while useful, it is reparable).[74] Indeed, following Paul, Aquinas unabashedly asserts that their fall is advantageous for the whole world, "and thus, if God, on account of the benefit (*utilitatem*) for the whole world permitted the Jews to be wanting and to diminish, much more will he fulfill their downfalls on account of the benefit for the whole world."[75] The providence of God is operative in the fall of the Jews, the inclusion of the Gentiles, and the ultimate restoration of Israel—all essential components of τὸ μυστήριον τοῦτο (Romans 11.25). Indeed, Paul's ministry is perceived as a sign of the reparable character of the fall of Israel.[76] Moreover, the converted Jews will be the cause of the repristinated fervor of the Gentiles at the end of time because the Peoples are "believers who decrease in ardor."[77] Lest Gentile inclusivity be seen as supplanting the singular dignity of Israel, three *exempla* set forth by Paul are analyzed by Thomas.

Lump, Root, and Olive Tree Imagery

In 11.13 Paul directly addresses the Gentiles, and from vv. 16ff. he uses images to remind them of the contours of their inclusion and the preeminence of the Jews. Thomas specifies aspects of the metaphors beyond that which Paul himself supplies.

For example, regarding 11.16 Aquinas specifies the portion of the lump as referring to the apostles who "are taken by God from the people of the Jews....And...if the Apostles are holy, it follows that the people of the Jews is holy."[78] Moreover, Thomas interprets the holy root as being the patriarchs, so "also the Jews are holy who proceeded from them as branches."[79] Yet Paul refers neither to the apostles nor to the patriarchs in v. 16f. How do these claims function in the logic of Thomas' argument? Aquinas suggests that the sanctity of believing Jews perdures or, at the very least, exists *in potentia*.

In §893 Thomas qualifies the argument:

> But it must be said that the Apostle does not speak here of actual holiness; for he does not intend to show the unbelieving Jews to be holy, but [he speaks] concerning potential sanctity. For nothing prohibits them to be repaired in holiness, the fathers of whom and the sons of whom are holy. Or it is able to be said that they who imitate them are especially branches of the patriarchs, accordingly Jn 8.39: "If you are the sons of Abraham, do the works of Abraham."[80]

No medieval Christian would deny the holiness of the apostles; no medieval Jew or Christian would deny the holiness of the patriarchs. In the former example, by means of inductive logic, and in the latter, by means of deductive logic, Jewish sanctity is defended.

Thomas' treatment of the third example (Rom 11.17–24) is more extensive than the previous two. In many ways, Aquinas is more severe in his criticism of and warnings to the Gentiles; one suspects that there is a contemporary, implied audience that is non-Jewish in character. For example, in §§895–97 he forbids the Gentiles to boast against the *remaining* or excised Jews. In fact, the Gentiles are in greater peril than the Jews insofar as they have received a dignity far above their former abject status; what they construe as preferment is illusory and vainglorious.[81] The Peoples have been grafted into a cultivated olive tree "and promoted to the society of that people and the patriarchs and the apostles and the prophets."[82] Gentileness (*gentilitas*) is not more precious than Jewishness. And the unbelief that caused the breaking-off of certain branches is not peculiar to Jews alone. Unbelief also threatens Gentiles.

Furthermore, the Gentiles (unfruitful, wild, unnatural branches) have been grafted "into the faith of the Jews, against nature, that is against the general course of nature."[83] This olive tree is the Jews and it bears "abundant spiritual fruits....Jer 11.6: The Lord called your name, an abundant olive tree, beautiful, fruitful [and] splendid."[84] The Gentiles enjoy no preferment. Once again the actual status of Jews and Gentiles—branches alike—is relativized except insofar as "the root" (v. 18) preexists and perdures. The very possibility of the Gentiles' salvation comes into being only because of the Jews. The now familiar refrain of John 4.22 recurs here: salvation is from the Jews. Thomas grounds his argument historically, but also looks toward the future restoration of the Jews to their proper dignity:

> If...this was done against nature, how much more these who are according to nature, that is who belong to the people of the Jews by natural origin, shall be inserted into its own olive tree, that is, led back to the dignity of their own people, Mal the last [4.6]: He will turn the hearts of fathers toward their sons, and the hearts of sons toward their fathers.[85]

What accounts for Aquinas' insistence on the Jews' sanctity, their priority *de iure* and *de facto* vis-à-vis the Gentiles, as well as his concern for their restoration? Is this simply a close textual reading of Paul? In other words, what undergirds these metaphors and unites *CRO* 11 theologically for Thomas? The mystery of predestination and election as illustrated by the hardening of a part of Israel and by Paul's eschatological schema accounts for the theological unity.

The Blindness and the Restoration of the Jews

Paul states that a πώρωσις[86] has come upon a part of Israel (11.25). Thomas equates the fall of particular Jews with blindness (§915) and makes oblique reference to 11.8 and to 11.11. His understanding of Paul's eschatology is straightforward: the fall of a portion of Israel permits some Gentiles to enter into salvation; the status quo will continue until the full number of the Peoples have entered in, and then all Israel, collectively, shall be saved.[87] (Perhaps this will occur as a *sanatio in radice*?) Throughout the eschatological scenario God is an active agent, selecting, blinding (or hardening), whose motive is the manifestation of his mercy.

Several themes from Romans 9 are reprised by Paul and Thomas. As God hardened Pharaoh's heart (9.17–18), so also he effects a hardness or blindness in Israel. As God manifested his mercy then (9.15; 9.18), so does he show mercy now and in the future (9.30f.). The offer of salvation to the Jews through Christ signifies election and liberation from fault or punishment. Some "are converted as though with a certain violence.... However he says he will banish impiety from Jacob for the purpose of showing the ease of the conversion of the Jews at the end of the world."[88] The disbelief of some Jews occasioned God's mercy toward the Gentiles, so that, at some future time, the Jews might obtain mercy as well.[89] The Jews remain elect because God chose the fathers and the sons freely

(11.28); the call of God and his gifts are without repentance (11.29). Thomas specifies that "the call here is taken for election"[90] and it perdures,

> for someone would be able to say by opposing this that the Jews, if formerly they were most beloved...on account of the fathers, nevertheless, the hostility which they employed against the Gospel prohibits [it] lest in the future they be saved. But this the Apostle asserts to be false, saying for the gifts and the call of God are without repentance since concerning this God does not repent....Ps 110.4: The Lord swore, and he will not repent.[91]

For Thomas, as we have seen, the action of God in predestination and election is the manifestation of his goodness and mercy; now, however, those on whom he has mercy are Jews and Gentiles alike. To accomplish this end

> God consigned, that is, he permitted to enclose all, that is every type of person, Jews as much as Gentiles, in disbelief, just as in a certain chain of error...so that in every race of humankind his mercy may have a place....*For this distribution is done for the individual races and not for the individual of the races.* However, for this reason God wishes all to be saved through his mercy, so that from this they may be brought low and his salvation may not be ascribed to themselves but to God. Hos 13.9: Your perdition is from you, O Israel, only from me is your help. Above 3.19: So that every mouth may be stopped up, and the whole world may be subject to God.[92]

We now must ask: Does Aquinas' understanding of election and his reading of Romans 9 and 11 derive from the Augustinian tradition, or, more pointedly, does it not preclude a supersessionist resolution to the Jew–Gentile debate?

ELECTION IN AUGUSTINE'S *PER* AND *CER*

Augustine did not equate those who are called with the elect—as a superficial reading of Romans 8.29 might suggest. The elect, rather, are those individuals who are called according to the purpose of God (which signifies, for him, the foreknowledge and predestination of God). The elect are identical with the justified because God's foreknowledge and predestination cannot be frustrated. "Nor did God predestine anyone except him whom *he knew would believe* and would follow the call. Paul designates such persons 'the elect.' For many did not come, though they have been called."[93] At this stage in Augustine's career the specific difference between the elect and the called is foreseen faith which, for him, is illustrated in Romans 9.11–13 and the election of Jacob. These verses provide a salient contrast to Aquinas' interpretation because Augustine locates the specific difference between the brothers, Jacob and Esau, in Jacob's future act of belief.

Jacob and Esau: Romans 9.11–13

Augustine, particularly in *PER*, is concerned to safeguard the sovereignty of God's election and the integrity of human free will against the Manichaeans while providing a *ratio* for the salvific predestination of some. The election of Jacob over Esau provides him with a case study. Because Romans 9.11 ("they were not yet born and had done nothing either good or bad") clearly excludes the merit of preceding works as eliciting God's election of Jacob, Augustine locates the defining difference between the brothers in the future act of believing foreseen by God.[94] Augustine faces a self-imposed dilemma. God cannot elect anyone's works, since these are the consequence of the gift of the Holy Spirit given to *de facto* believers. Moreover, since "all are equal prior to merit, and no choice can be made between absolutely equal things" the distinguishing element must be found in God's foreknowledge by which "he chose faith, so that he chooses precisely him whom he foreknew would believe in him."[95] In his attempt to safeguard the integrity of the human response to the *vocatio Dei*, Augustine asserts that "belief is our work" in contradistinction to subsequent, meritorious good deeds flowing from the bestowal of the Spirit.[96] Later, in *PER* §62 Augustine refines his position and

> speaks of the *prima merita fidei* or the *prima merita impietatis* according to the character of [one's] free response to the divine *vocatio*. The scheme of divine call and human response permits him to retain just enough merit on man's part to vindicate the choice of some and the rejection of others on God's part.[97]

By the mid-390s, Augustine substitutes (in effect) a merit of faith for the merit of works in order to account for divine election.[98] In *PER*

§60 we saw this principle applied to particular "Jews who, once they believed in Christ, both gloried in the works they did before receiving grace and claimed that they merited this same grace of the gospel by their own previous good works." Their former life merited them nothing (like their Gentile counterparts) except damnation as sinners because of humankind's solidarity with Adam and his sin.[99]

The election of particular individuals instantiates a twofold manifestation of divine mercy. Citing Romans 9.15,[100] Augustine delineates two stages of God's manifestation of mercy that correlate with the divine call and the giving of the Holy Spirit.[101] Later he will reinterpret the example of Jacob and Esau as applicable to corporate Israel; here, however, Augustine's focus is decidedly individualistic.[102] God's foreknowledge results in the election of faith, and the subsequent bestowal of the Holy Spirit enables the believer to be compassionate "so that [one] can do good works through love."[103] Like Paul (Rom 9.14) Augustine precludes any hint of divine injustice in God's selecting worthy objects of his mercy; but he does so by considering the obverse proposition of election: divine reprobation.[104] Some contemporary commentators on Augustine contend that

> God's predestination of the saved as well as of the damned—and contrary to the view sometimes expressed, Augustine does speak of the predestination of the damned [*Iohannis evangelium tractatus* CXXIV 48.4, 6; 107.7; 111.5]—is eternal and timeless....Predestination to damnation is simply the withholding by God of grace from those he does not will to save.... [T]hey are predestined because God foreknows that he will not give them the grace to be saved.[105]

We must examine the accuracy of this statement and other related assertions that God's positive will effects reprobation.

Reprobation: The Negative Thesis

As Jacob exemplified belief and divine election, correlatively, Pharaoh exemplifies hardness of heart and reprobation. To be consistent, Augustine must characterize Pharaoh's hardness of heart (9.17–18) as punishment for prior infidelity. "For as with the chosen (not works but faith initiating merit so that through the gift of God they do good), so with the condemned: infidelity and impiety initiate their meriting their penalty."[106] The theological dilemma for the bishop of Hippo is to preserve God's initiative in election from taint of injustice and from direct entanglement in human disobedience, which, seemingly, is semi-autonomous. (The resolution of the problem, of course, will have implications for conceptualizing the disobedience of the Jews and their corporate, ongoing role in salvation history.[107]) Augustine's solution, as we shall see, is both provisional and unsatisfactory.[108]

The execution of evil deeds, whether by Pharaoh or others, derives from the punishment in which God abandons the individual to the consequences of unbelief, so that they "work evil through his chastisement. Nevertheless, [one's] free will remains, whether for belief in God so that mercy follows, or for impiety followed by punishment."[109] In *PER* the desertion of such persons to their own pursuits hardens impiety and simultaneously accounts for the divine decision to withhold mercy from them. Interestingly, Augustine cites Romans 1.28 ("And since they did not see fit to acknowledge God, God handed them over to a base mind so that they did unseemly things") to illustrate the abandonment of Pharaoh based on the universal experience of humanity apart from God and mired in sin. Augustine knew that should he eliminate foreseen faith and foreseen unbelief as the motive of election and reprobation respectively, the alternative of divine causality and responsibility looms threateningly on the theological horizon.[110]

Vessels of Shame and Wrath

Augustine cautions that inquiry into the election of some and the hardening of others, the "merits of faith and impiety," is reserved for the "spiritual."[111] He reiterates, negatively, that since "God has made some vessels for honorable use and some for dishonorable, it is not for [anyone] to discuss, whoever...still lives according to this lump, that is, who is wise by earthly senses and fleshly wisdom."[112] In Pharaoh, Augustine's themes converge: hardness of heart and the hidden merits of impiety render him a vessel of wrath made for destruction. What is significant, however, is that Pharaoh's destruction is ordered toward the remedy of others, specifically, those "whom [God] had decided to free from error,"[113] not only Jews but Gentiles as well. Augustine implicitly alludes to divine providence insofar as he invests Pharaoh's obduracy with a purpose beyond itself. A similar argument is advanced in *PER* §70 regarding the Jews who "did not sin so as to fall, that is, only to fall as a punishment, but so that this fall itself would be profitable to the Gentiles for salvation." Indeed, in tender terms, Augustine describes the Jews' fall as precious indeed.

CONCLUSION

Augustine and Aquinas are both close readers of Paul, and some of the agreement between their respective commentaries derives simply from a straightforward recapitulation of him. For example, each commentator underscores the need for the Gentiles to avoid self-congratulatory smugness at their newfound status.[114] Both agree that an interior, "spiritual" Judaism takes precedence over exterior, "legal" observances (e.g., circumcision): "qui in abscondito Iudaeus est, et circumcisio cordis in spiritu non littera, cuius laus non ex hominibus sed ex Deo est (Romans 2.29)."

There is, as well, substantial doctrinal agreement exhibited between Augustine and Aquinas that is not attributable simply to a close adherence to the Pauline text. While Aquinas is far more concerned than Augustine to ground Israel's prerogatives in historical *realia*, both Christian theologians see the fullness of these privileges realized in Christianity. Law, circumcision, cult, and other divine gifts were entitlements possessed by the Jews *in figura*. Thomas sublates[115] the prerogatives of Israel, while Augustine views them as superseded once Christ comes. Both commentators maintain the testamentary witness of the Jews. Augustine and Thomas agree that the choice of some persons is attributable, ultimately, to God's mercy;[116] the reprobation of others, to God's justice.[117]

Thomas shapes the doctrinal legacy of Augustine on predestination, election, and the role of the Jews in the *ST* and *CRO*. In fact, of all cited authorities in Ia. 23. 1–8, the Doctor of Grace is quoted most frequently, indeed, almost exclusively. (In *CRO* Thomas cites Augustine as an authority no fewer than fifty-three times.)

"Augustine," Thomas writes in *ST* Ia. 23. 1, "describes predestination as the purpose of taking pity."[118] Aquinas engages him on specific principles as he advances the discussion, for example, "predestination [is] the destination of one who exists."[119] For Thomas, it need not be taken as a real sending and can apply to what "does not yet exist, because of the precedence predestination implies."[120] Predestination "is a preparation for God's benefits"[121] and "a prevision of God's benefits,"[122] but, for Aquinas, in a qualified sense—that is, on the part of God, who "conceived the plan ordaining persons to salvation."[123] The predestined are elect, even "those who do not yet exist are chosen by God and he makes no mistake."[124] Thomas recognizes the limits of human intelligibility of the divine *ratio* of election, using Augustine's caution: "wherefore he draws this one and not that one, seek not to decide if you wish not to err"[125] and that "another will not get [the crown] unless the man has lost it."[126] He agrees with Augustine that "the number of those predestined is fixed, and can be neither increased nor diminished,"[127] but specifies that "we have to hold that the number is fixed, not only at a figure, but also to whom it includes."[128]

We have seen these texts and other doctrinal principles of Augustine functioning in Thomas' *CRO*, and by our ongoing comparisons with *PER*, *CER*, *AdI*, and *Ad Simpl.* we witnessed Thomas' correction and development of them. Nonetheless, Thomas substantially excludes several of the chief premises of Augustine asserted in *PER* and *CER*, namely: that the primary purpose of the letter is a theological articulation of the relationship between works and grace (Thomas understands it to be the instruction and coalescence of Jews and Gentiles in Rome, not a dispute about grace and free will); second, that election is subsequent to the *vocatio Dei* and justification (rather, for Aquinas, the interior call and temporal election to grace are simultaneous[129]); third, that election proceeds from foreseen faith; fourth, that Jewish prerogatives are allegorical foreshadowings of Christian realities (Thomas strives mightily to ground them in literal, historical *realia*); fifth, that reprobation is generated by prior, even secret, infidelity resulting in manifest obduracy that cannot be remedied;[130] and finally, that Israel has been replaced by Christians of Jewish or Gentile provenance. Even Paul, according to Augustine, has been taken from his kinsmen and called into the number of Gentiles "whom he had *placed before the Jews* from whom he had been set apart...."[131] This statement accords neither with Paul's self-description in Romans nor with Aquinas' understanding of Paul, whose ancestry and status as elect *and* Jewish are a recurring theme.

It is equally important to acknowledge what Augustine does not say, in contradistinction to Thomas. Although the two commentators agree that the fall of the Jews collectively considered occasions the salvation of the Gentiles, nowhere does Augustine state that the Jews' fall is temporary or reparable (as does Aquinas in *CRO* §879). Since Israel has been redefined by Augustine, historical Israel need not be restored—indeed, cannot be restored because foreseen obduracy demands reprobation.[132] Moreover, Augustine does not cite John 4.22 (or any substantially equivalent text) with reference to the fall of the Jews or the inclusion of the Gentiles. Rather, he is concerned to explain the essence of Matthew 22.14: How is it that many are called but few are chosen?

Augustine, unlike Aquinas, cannot explain adequately the temporal "tension" that Paul himself articulates in Romans regarding the fall and restoration of Israel. The prerogatives and *singular* dignity of Israel are subverted and are replaced, or at the very least redefined, by him. Except for Christ's lineal descent from the patriarchs, what once were marks of the Jews' excellence (e.g., covenant, cult, and circumcision) are relegated to the status of prefigurements or routinely allegorized.[133] For Thomas, the fall of the Jews is not universal; it is not irreparable, and it does not revoke Israel's prerogatives or dignity. God hardens a portion of Israel to effect the salvation of the Peoples and to incite the rest of Israel to jealousy. It is not impossible that God, having accomplished his ends, would freely restore all Israel in his mercy; in fact, that is precisely what Paul asserts and what Augustine avoids. Even Augustine's distinction between the *vocatio Dei* and *electio* cannot account for the irrevocable quality of God's call and gifts to Israel, nor their "purposive disobedience," nor their being an object of mercy once again: "For God has consigned all to disobedience, that he may have mercy upon all" (Rom 11.32).

The continuity and differences between Augustine and Aquinas are apparent regarding predestination and election, as are their application of these doctrines to the Jews and Israel. Indeed, one witnesses in Augustine's commentaries a continual exegetical erosion of the Jews' status and role in salvation history. And yet Paul does not claim that "all Gentiles shall be saved"—this privilege is ascribed solely to the Jews. Aquinas grapples with the apostle's unequivocal assertion. In so doing he proves himself no mere tradent of Augustine on these matters; there is profound disagreement between Thomas' *CRO* and Augustine's Romans commentaries.

In this chapter, by comparison and contrast, we have seen that Thomas is no mere transmitter of Augustine's policy of testamentary tolerance toward the Jews, nor is he a continuator of Augustinian supersessionism. Earlier we investigated the ecclesial and social context in which Thomas wrote his *CRO*, as well as his position on select issues pertaining to the Jews in *ST*. Most importantly, however, we confirmed that predestination and election serve as the hermeneutical keys to understanding Aquinas' *CRO*. Failure to recognize the centrality of these concepts necessarily skews any assessment of Aquinas and the Jews. In the following chapter, I will compare Thomas' view of Romans 9–11 with the interpretation of contemporary exegetes, not only to feature his contribution to the commentary tradition but also to rediscover Aquinas as an apt dialogue partner in the current discussion concerning Paul's letter and Jewish–Christian relations. The pre-Reformation theological tradition that Aquinas' *CRO* represents preserves the corporate eschatological role of the Jewish people and the Gentiles, as well as the individual's appropriation of salvation through justification by faith. Thomas asserts that

"Gentileness" is not more precious than "Jewishness." The individual's justification by faith does not preempt corporate aspects of salvation or soteriology. Thomas' *CRO* is uniquely poised to make a contribution in the contemporary debate to the traditionalist and revisionist readers of Romans 9–11; this is the subject to which we now turn our attention.

NOTES

1. Especially in §§759–65 in chapter 9 and in §§862–63, 923–26 in chapter 11.

2. ...sed secundum electionem, id est inquantum ipse Deus spontanea voluntate unum alteri praelegit....Hoc autem est propostitum praedestinationis, de quo ibidem....Predestinati secundum propositus ecus.

3. §748f.

4. "Quantum autem ad gentem dicit Si autem tu cognominaris Iudaeus, quod est honorabile..." (§225). Notable is Thomas' etymology of the name as well as his use of John 4.22 ("Salvation is from the Jews") as a scriptural warrant for the honorific title.

5. Deinde cum dicit Qui sunt Israëlitae ostendit Iudaeorum dignitatem, ut eius tristitia videretur esse rationabilis propter pristinam dignitatem populi pereuntis—*propensius enim malum est dignitatem perdidisse, quam non habuisse,* ut dicit Glossa—et non solum ex affectu carnali procedens (§742).

6. In response to the rhetorical question posed by Paul in 3.1 ("What advantage is there for the Jew?"), Thomas lists the prerogatives of the Jew differently. He writes: "[I]t is more for him both as regards quantity...and as far as concerns number. For they have something more both in contemplation of divine things...and according to the disposition of temporal things....For [the Jew] has more as far as concerns the Fathers, as far as concerns the promises and as regards progeny. Below 9.4: Of whom is the adoption of the children of God and the glory and the covenant. And in any of these, there is not a small excellence, but a great one....For the greatest good for a person is...that one may adhere to God and be instructed by God" (§249). The Jews were instructed by God and his oracles were given over to them "as if to friends" (§250).

7. §743.

8. For example, the covenant may signify the pact of circumcision given to Abraham (Gen 17.2) or the New Testament preached first to Israel (Matt 15.24). The law clearly means the Mosaic legislation (Sir 24.33). Cult signifies the exclusive worship of God in contrast to pagan idolatry.

9. §744.

10. Although Aquinas posits a threefold proof, the Christ and his inherent dignity are a further development of the Jews' prerogative of progeny.

11. Aquinas completes this section (*CRO* §§735–47) with a brief refuta-

tion of four heresies that contradict Christ's lineage: Manicheanism, Valentianism, Nestorianism, and Arianism. Each of his arguments depends on the assertion of Christ's descent from the Jews, "according to the flesh."

12. See, for example, §243, wherein Aquinas draws the analogy between lineal descent and external circumcision in order to thwart false assurance that each prerogative might engender: "Non enim est verus Iudaeus ille qui in manifesto Iudaeus, id est secundum generationem carnalem. Infra IX.6: Non omnes qui ex Israel sunt hi sunt Israëlitae et postea subdit sed qui filii sunt promissionis. Et similiter etia neque est vera circumcisio illa quae est manifesta in carne."

13. See, e.g., §169.

14. Conversely in chapter 11 (e.g., §900f.) Aquinas amplifies Paul's admonition to Gentile Christians against smug complacency because of their own election, as we shall see. These reprimands reprise themes introduced in Romans 2.1f. and assert that divine selection occurs within the fold of the Gentiles as well as the Jews.

15. [I]sta dignitas non pertineat ad eos qui processerunt ex antiquis patribus carnaliter sed ad spirituale semen quod est a Deo electum (§748). Moreover, the election that bestows such dignity pertains to Jews and Gentiles alike. Aquinas delays discussion of this assertion until §796.

16. He reiterates that election, by which God prefers one person to another, issues not from works but from the grace of the one calling ("non ex operibus, sed ex gratia vocantis") and then procedes to inquire into the justice of such preferential treatment ("inquirit de iustitia huius electionis") (§765).

17. [P]rimo per comparationem ad Iacob, dicens Non enim omnes qui sunt ex Israël, id est ex Iacob secundum carnem progeniti, hi sunt veri Israëlitae ad quos pertinent Dei promissa, sed illi qui sunt recti et videntes eum per fidem.

...Secundo ostendit idem per comparationem ad Abraham, dicens Neque omnes qui sunt carnale semen Abrahae, sunt spirituales Abrahae filii, quibus Deus benedictionem repromisit, sed solum illi qui eius fidem et opera imitantur (§750).

18. Aquinas will discuss the "remnant of Israel." See §871f.

19. [Q]uia si per incredulitatem quorundum praerogativa Iudaeorum tolleretur, sequeretur quod incredulitas hominis fidem Dei evacuaret, quod est inconveniens (§253).

20. Possent autem hoc adscribere vel diversitati matrum, quia Ismaël natus est de ancilla et Ysaac de libera; vel diversitati meritorum patris, quia Ismaëlem genuit incircumcisus Ysaac autem circumcisus. Ut igitur omne subterfugium excludatur, inducit exempla, ubi unus eligitur et alius reprobatur eorum, qui non solum ab uno patre sed etiam ab una matre sunt geniti et eodem tempore, imo ex uno concubitu (§756).

21. §§758–60. Thomas also uses this text to refute the teachings of the Manichees, Pelagians, and Origen.

22. ...ipse Deus spontanea voluntate unum alteri praelegit... (§759).

23. ...custodientes libros ex quibus nostrae fidei testimonium perhibetur. Io V.39: Scrutamini scripturas et ipse sunt que testimonium perhibent de me (§761).

24. Thomas makes a distinction between the eternal predestination of Jacob and the reprobation of Esau: predestination prepares for glory, reprobation is the preparation of punishment. However, God punishes the evil that people have from themselves and rewards the just because of the merits that come from him. He cites Hosea 13.9: "Your destruction is from you, O Israel, only in me is your help" (§764).

25. §762. As we have seen above, Aquinas defines *electio, predestinatio*, and *dilectio* in §763.

26. Aquinas refutes the resolutions proffered by Origen and Pelagius insofar as merits are an effect of predestination. The infusion of grace by God accounts for the justification of the individual as well as the use of the grace given. See §§771–73. This does not nullify human freedom, "since God moves all things, but by diverse modes, insofar as namely whatever thing is moved by God is according to the mode of its nature ('unumquodque movetur a Deo secundum modum suae naturae'). And thus a person is moved by God for willing and pursuing through the mode of free will" (§778).

27. "The will of God is the cause of every good which is in the creature and in this manner the good by reason of which one creature is preferred to another through the mode of election, follows upon the will of God" (§763).

28. Cum igitur omnes homines propter peccatum primi parentis nascantur damnationi obnoxii, quos Deus per gratiam suam liberat, sola misericordia liberat. Et sic quibusdam est misericors, quos liberat, quibusdam autem iustus, quos non liberat, neutris autem iniquus (§773).

It should be noted that this division occurs posterior in the order of explanation to "the Fall."

29. ...dicit miserebor, scilicet vocando et iustificando, cui misereor, praedestinando et misericordiam prestabo, finaliter glorificando eum cui misereor vocando et iustificando (§774).

30. [E]x hoc manifestum est quod Deus est non solum Iudaeorum, sed et Gentilium, quoniam quidem unus est Deus qui iustificat circumcisionem, id est Iudaeos circumcisos ex fide et praeputium, id est Gentiles incircumcisos, per fidem ut enim dicitur Gal V.6: In Christo Iesu neques circumcisio aliquid est neque praeputium (§319).

31. "...ipsam divinam filiationem" (§798). Also see §800: "Deinde cum dicit Et erit in loco, etc., inducit aliam auctoritatem quae habetur Osea I.10: in qua eis repromittitur dignitas filiorum Dei...."

32. Est autem considerandum quod a tribus bonis quae in Iudaeis eminebant, gentiles erant alieni, quorum primum erat divinus cultus, ratione cuius Iudei dicebantur populus Dei....

Secundum est privilegium divine electionis....

Tertium est liberatio a peccatis originali quae Iudaeis in circumcisione conferebatur... (§799).

33. "...quasi ei servientes et eius praeceptis obedientes" (§799). Further, "it must be said that he was the God of the Jews only through a special cult exhibited by them to God, whence in Ps 76.2: God is known in Judea" (§319).

34. Aquinas cites Eph 2.13 and Rom 5.10, respectively. See below regarding this prerogative.

35. Sed huius liberationis [i.e., from original sin by circumcision] gentiles non erant participes (§799). Cf. §335: ...peccatum originale pluraliter significatur. Vel propter plures homines, in quibus multiplicatur originale peccatum, vel potius quia virtute continet in se quodammodo omnia peccata.

36. Dicit ergo primo Circumcisio quidem prodest scilicet ad remissionem peccati originalis. Unde dicitur Gen XVII.14: Anima cuius praeputii caro circumcisa non fuerit, etc. Sed tibi adulto tunc finaliter prodest, si legem observes sicut religiosis prodest professio, si regulam observent. Circumcisio enim erat quasi quaedam professio, obligans homines ad observantiam legis.

37. Also in *ST* Ia IIae. 102.5 Thomas writes: "For this profession and imitation of Abraham's faith to be fixed in the hearts of the Jews, they received in their bodies a sign that could not be forgotten. Hence it is written, My covenant shall be in your flesh for a perpetual covenant."

38. ...quia fides fuit prima causa ex qua processit circumcisio et caetera sacramenta legalia (§320).

39. Non est autem signum verum, nisi ei respondeat signatum (§243).

40. Et ideo melius dicendum est quod circumcisio ex ipso opere operato non habebat virtutem effectivam, neque quantum ad remotionem culpae, neque quantum ad operationem iustitiae: sed erat solum iustitiae signum,...sed per fidem Christi, cuius circumcisio signum erat, auferebatur peccatum originale et conferebatur auxilium gratiae ad recte agendum (§349).

41. See, e.g., §§109, 210, and 237.

42. [C]ircumcisio praevaricantis legem fit praeputium....Non enim est verus Iudaeus ille qui in manifesto Iudaeus, id est, secundum generationem carnalem. Infra IX.6: Non omnes qui ex Israel sunt hi sunt Israëlitae et postea subdit sed qui filii sunt promissionis....Unde si quis Iudaeus esset transgressor foederis, non esset vera circumcisio, et ideo reputatur in praeputium (§243).

43. §322. Ironically, it also provides an advantage to the Jew, illustrated in the person of Abraham, who "discovered in accordance with carnal circumcision and the rest of the works of the law" that he was not justified by means of the works of the law (understood as exterior deeds) (§324).

44. Unde relinquitur quod interior Judaismus et circumcisio praevalet exteriori. Et hoc est quod dicit cuius, scilicet interioris circumcisionis, laus non est ex hominibus, sed ex Deo (§245).

45. Et similiter circumcisio vera est, quae est cordis in spiritu, id est, per Spiritum Sanctum facta, per quod superfluae cogitationes et affectiones a corde praecinduntur....Phil III.3: Nos sumus circumcisio, qui spiritu Deo servimus (§244).

46. Richard Schenk, OP, in "Thomas Aquinas and Robert Kilwardby on the Sacrament of Circumcision" in *Ordo sapientiae et amoris: Image et mes-*

sage de saint Thomas d'Aquin à travers les récentes études historiques, herméneutiques et doctrinales; Hommage au Professeur Jean-Pierre Torrell, OP, à l'occasion de son 65e anniversaire, ed. Carlos-Josaphat Pinto de Oliveira, Studia Friburgensia n.s. 78 (Fribourg: Editions Universitaires, 1993), 555–93, overstates the case: "When Thomas returned to Naples in 1272, he continued to work privately on the *tertia pars*, using the fruit of his second lecture on the Letter to the Romans and the first ten chapters of First Corinthians. The tendency which had begun already with his first lecture series on Paul continued: without denying the literal sense to the cult of the older covenant, its meaning was ever more exclusively defined by the younger one. The *verus Judaeus*, the *vera circumcisio*, *interior Judaismus et circumcisio* means a life in Christ" (pp.13–14). He cites as evidence, for example, Romans 2, lect. 4; Romans 3, lect. 1; and Romans 4, lect. 2. Nowhere in the first two subsections does Thomas' argument favor Schenk's thesis. To the contrary, in the first, Aquinas explicitly qualifies the time frame of the subject matter under discussion: "Indeed what the Apostle said [Gal 5.2]: If you be circumcised, Christ will benefit you nothing, he speaks as far as the time after the grace of the Gospel was divulged; indeed, here he speaks as far as concerns the time before the passion of Christ, during which circumcision had standing" (§238). Throughout the *lectio* Thomas correlates *vera circumcisio* with observance of the law, both exteriorly and interiorly. He then compares the nonobservant Jew to the Gentile who observes the law by nature. In Romans 3, lect. 1 Thomas asserts that interior circumcision does not annul the advantages of the Jews nor render unfitting exterior circumcision, "since it was given over by God, who says in Isa 48.17: I the Lord am teaching you useful things" (§247). Only in Romans 4, lect. 2 (§349) does Thomas state that circumcision is the "sole sign of justice...but through the faith of Christ, of whom circumcision was the sign; original sin was being taken away and the help of grace was being conferred to act rightly." In this description circumcision functions proleptically. However, in the same article Thomas quotes the authority of Bede: "[I]t should be known that...circumcision in the law was providing the same salutary help of a cure against the wound of original sin that baptism was accustomed to work in the time of revealed grace." Clearly, §349 demonstrates that the cult of the older covenant was increasingly defined by the cult of the younger one—but not exclusively so. The Romans commentary marks the beginning of this tendency in Aquinas. However, evidence of the inherent value of circumcision and other Jewish prerogatives exists alongside Christian prerogatives. What is remarkable, in my estimation, is Aquinas' efforts as a medieval Christian theologian to preserve the inherent value of the privileges of Israel at all. The ambivalence and dynamic tension exhibited in Thomas' commentary between the two dispensations mimic Paul's own struggle in chapters 9–11 of the original letter.

47. §341 and especially §347: "[P]er hoc signum populus ille Deum colens, ab omnibus aliis populis distingueretur. Et inde est quod mandavit Dominus circumcidi filios Israël, qui inter alias nationes erant habitaturi, qui prius in deserto solitarii manentes circumcisi non erant."

48. Thomas clearly struggles to preserve the Jewish prerogative of circumcision *in illo tempore*, by recognizing its literal and spiritual character, incumbent obligations, and consequent effects. Aquinas does not discount circumcision as a distinctive privilege of the Jews, but in *CRO* he begins to sublate bodily circumcision by means of a spiritual circumcision to be done through Christ. This is not surprising. See, e.g., §348. He, like Paul, teaches that the Peoples were not beneficiaries of this manifestation of God's mercy until Christ.

49. For Aquinas, Hosea 1.10.

50. Gentiles autem non solum non dicebantur filii, quod pertinet ad eos qui ex amore Deo serviunt et "spiritu Dei aguntur," ut supra cap. VIII.14 dictum est, sed etiam nec digni erant ut populi Dei dicerentur, quod pertinere poterat etiam ad eos qui acceperant spiritum servitutis in timore (§800).

51. §800. In §364 Thomas earlier explained: "ea quae non sunt, id est, Gentiles vocat, scilicet ad gratiam, tamquam ea quae sunt, id est, tamquam Iudaeos. Infra IX.24: Vocabo non plebem meam, etc. Significat autem Gentiles per ea quae non sunt, quia erant omnino alienati a Deo."

52. A more detailed exposition by Paul of the remnant's composition and role awaits 11.5, which Aquinas himself notes in §803.

53. §801.

54. Reliquiae salvae fient, id est non omnes, nec maior pars, sed aliqui pauci qui relinquentur ex excidio aliorum (§802).

55. The multitude and the remnant alike prove God's fidelity in fulfilling his promises. In §800f. Thomas develops the argument advanced in §253: "Alio modo potest intelligi de fide qua Deus in se fidelis est implens promissa....Haec autem fidelitas evacuaretur si per quorumdam incredulitatem accideret quod nihil amplius esset Iudaeo. Promiserat enim Deus populum illum multiplicare et magnificare, ut patet Gen XXII.16: Multiplicabo semen tuum."

56. Habetur autem haec auctoritas Is. X.22, ubi secundum litteram nostram sic dicitur:...reliquiae convertentur ex eo....Consummationem enim et abbreviationem Dominus Deus exercituum faciet in medio omnis terrae (§805).

57. Commenting on 4.17, Thomas stated that when Paul "says Who gives life to the dead, etc., he shows by whom the promise of this sort may be fulfilled, saying, Who, namely God, gives life to the dead, that is to the Jews, who were dead in [their] sins, acting against the law, he gives life through faith and grace so that they might attain the promise to Abraham. Jn 5.21: Just as the Father raises the dead and gives life, etc." (§364).

58. Et ideo quo Iudaei non sunt totaliter exterminati sicut Sodomitae, est divinae misericordiae imputandum. Thr. III.22: Misericordiae Domini quis non sumus consumpti (§806).

59. Iustitiam autem quae ex fide est, non eam quae in operibus consistit. Non enim ad hoc Gentes conversae sunt, ut legalem iustitiam observent, sed ut iustificentur per Christi fidem. Supra III.22: Iustitia Dei per fidem Iesu Christi (§808). "The faith of Christ" does not mean the faithfulness of Jesus (i.e., fiduciary faith) as some contemporary exegetes interpret Romans 3.20. For Thomas, the phrase signifies faith *in* Jesus.

60. Later in chapter 15 (see §1157) Thomas will qualify this assertion when, speaking of the conversion of Jews and Gentiles, he attributes the former to divine truth and the latter to divine mercy: "[B]ecause of the fact that [Paul] ascribes the call of the Jews to divine truth does not exclude mercy, because the Apostle, born from the Jews, says in 1 Tim 1.13: I obtained mercy. And the very fact that God made promises to the fathers concerning the salvation of descendants was of mercy. Also similarly through the fact that he ascribes the vocation of the Peoples to mercy, he does not exclude entirely divine truth, because this indeed pertained to divine truth, that he fulfilled his proposition concerning the salvation of the Peoples....Yet a certain mode of truth, namely for the fulfillment of promises, is considered in the call of the Jews which is not considered in the call of the Peoples, to whom promises were not made."

61. Sed quantum ad ordinem salutis Iudaei sunt primi, quia eis promissiones sunt factae, ut infra III.2 dicitur, et in eorum gratia sunt Gentiles assumpti, ac si ramus oleastri insereretur in bonam olivam, ut dicitur infra XI.24. Ex his etiam Salvator natus est. Io. IV.22: Salus ex Iudaeis est (§101).

62. See, e.g., §204: [M]anifestat in bonis, et ponit primo duo, eadem supra dixerat scilicet, gloriam et honorem. Tertium vero, scilicet pacem, ponit loco incorruptionis, quam includit pacem, et multa alia comprehendit.

...Is. XXXII.18: Sedebit populus meus in pulchritudine pacis in tabernaculis fiducie in requie opulenta. Et in his etiam primatum Iudaeis attribuit, quia eis sunt primo promissa, et in eorum promissiones Gentes introierunt. Io. IV.38: Alii laboraverunt et vos, etc.

63. After exegeting Isa 28.16 as the "principal authority" signifying Christ as the foundation stone of church, Thomas examines Isa 8.14. He comments: "hinc sumitur medium auctoritatis quo dicit lapidem offensionis et petram scandali, ut offensio referatur ad ignoranciam, quia, ut dicitur I Cor II.8: Si cognovissent, numquam Dominum gloriae crucifixissent" (§812). See chapter 3 and the discussion of Jewish culpability in the crucifixion of Christ found in *ST* IIIa. 47.5.

64. Earlier in §813, commenting on Romans 10.1, Thomas refers to the election of the Gentiles as well as some Jews and provides an analysis of the Jewish people's fall. It is preparatory for the sustained discussion in chapter 11.

65. §882.

66. §872. I do not think that Thomas is influenced here by the Johannine meaning of the term "the Jews," especially since John 4.22 figures prominently in his rhetoric. The identification of "the Jews" with Judaism's religious officialdom was seen in chapter 3.

67. Et huic concordat quod infra subdit de futuro remedio Iudaeorum, cum dicit Et tunc, scilicet cum plenitudo Gentium intraverit, Israël salvus fiet, non particulariter sicut modo, sed universaliter, Os I.7: Salvo eos in Domino Deo eorum.

68. "[I]t must be said that the gift here is taken for a promise, which is

made in accordance with the foreknowledge and predestination of God. However the call...is taken for election, because on account of the certitude of both, what God promises, now in a certain way he gives: the ones whom he chose, now by a certain mode he calls."

69. Vel intelligendum est secundum electionem, id est quantum ad electos ex illo populo, sicut supra eodem dictum est, Electio consecuta est. Si autem sunt Deo charissimi, rationabile est quod a Deo salventur, secundum illud Is. LXIV.4: Oculus non vidit, Deus, absque te quae praeparasti (§923).

70. At this juncture, it is particularly important to remind the reader that God's choice is between Jew and Jew, not between Christian and Jew. Rather, God chooses within Israel, as 11.1–10 makes clear. What is radically new is that he also chooses from among the Gentiles (11.11). While the intramural choice within Israel establishes a distinctive faithful remnant from among God's chosen people, the choice of some from among the Gentiles relativizes the status between Jew and Gentile. The choice of the former does not cancel their corporate dignity or status; the choice of the latter bestows a derivative dignity. It is my contention that Aquinas extends these theological principles to his contemporaries as well.

71. Postquam Apostolus ostendit Iudaeorum casum esse miserandum, non tamen totaliter excusabilem..., hic ostendit casum Iudaeorum non esse universalem. See §§861–62, wherein Aquinas cites Paul, proselytes, the sons of Jacob (particularly the tribe of Benjamin), and the many other elect (*multis alios electos*) as proof.

72. Deinde cum dicit Absit solvit quaestionem [i.e., Numquid sic offenderunt ut caderent?] et primo secundum primum intellectum ostendens casum Iudaeorum fuisse utilem; secundo solvit quaestionem quantum ad secundum intellectum, ostendens casum Iudaeorum esse reparabilem, ibi Quod si delictum illorum, etc. (§880). See also §§883, 888, 893, and elsewhere.

73. In §882 Thomas offers four interpretations of the Jewish–Gentile rivalry. It is significant that in 11.11 Thomas alludes to 11.25 in order to remind the reader that despite the rivalry and fall of the Jews, in fact, all Israel shall be saved.

74. In §881 Thomas, commenting on 11.11, teaches that the Jews' fall effects the salvation of the Gentiles by means of the death of Christ, the rejection of the apostles, and the subsequent Jewish Diaspora. The shedding of Christ's blood, the apostles' preaching mission to the Gentiles after a largely unsuccessful Jewish mission, and the spread of the books and prophecies concerning the Christ derive from the seeming fall of the Jews.

75. Et sic, si Deus propter ultilitatem [*sic*] totius mundi permisit Iudaeos delinquere et diminui, multo magis implebit ruinas eorum propter totius mundi utilitatem (§884).

76. Et ideo dicendum est quod sic erat sibi commissa praedicatio Gentilium, ut ad eam ex necessitate teneretur, sicut ipse dicit I Cor IX.16....Nec tamen

erat ei prohibitum Iudaeis praedicare, quamvis ad hoc non teneretur. Et secundum hoc eorum saluti insistendo, ministerium suum honorificabat; quod quidem non faceret, si casum eorum irreparabilem reputaret (§889).

77. Gentiles enim fideles qui tepescent. Matt XXIV.12...vel etiam qui totaliter cadent decepti ab Antichristo, Iudaeis conversis in pristinum fervorem restituentur. Et etiam sicut Iudaeis cadentibus, Gentiles post inimicitias sunt reconciliati, ita post conversionem Iudaeorum, imminente iam fine mundi, erit resurrectio generalis, per quam homines ex mortuis ad vitam immortalem redibunt (§890).

78. Dicitur autem delibatio id quod ex massa pastae sumitur, quasi ad probandum. Sunt autem Apostoli ex gente Iudaeorum assumpti a Deo, sicut delibatio ex massa. Et ideo si Apostoli sunt sancti, consequens est quod gens Iudaeorum sit sancta. I Petr. II.9: Gens sancta, populus acquisitionis (§891).

79. §892.

80. "Sed dicendum quod Apostolus hic non loquitur de actuali sanctitate. Non enim intendit ostendere Iudaeos incredulos esse sanctos sed de sanctitate potentiali. Nihil enim prohibuit eos reparari in sanctitate, quorum patres et quorum filii sunt sancti. Vel potest dici quod illi sunt sancti specialiter rami Patriarcharum, qui eos imitantur, secundum illud Io. VIII.39: Si filii estis Abrahae, opera Abrahae facite." Unbelief is not specified as unbelief *in Christ*, although this may be implied when one looks ahead to 11.20. But the subsequent argument with its exhortation to imitate the patriarchs seems sufficient to prove his point at this juncture. In either case, however, Thomas points ahead to the restoration of the Jews for "nothing prohibits them to be repaired in holiness."

81. Promotio autem alicuius tanto magis consuevit eum magis extollere in vanam gloriam, quanto ex viliori statu elevatur....Et ideo praemittit abiectum statum, de quo assumpit erant, dicens Tu autem Gentilis... (§895).

82. Sic ergo promoti sunt Gentiles ad societatem illius populi, et Patriarcharum et Aposotolorum et Prophetarum (§896).

83. Et insertus in bonam olivam id est, in fide Iudaeorum, contra naturam, id est contra communem cursum naturae. Non enim consuevit ramus arboris malae inseri in bonam arborem, sed potius e converso (§910).

84. Oliva quidem dicitur ipsa gens Iudaeorum propter uberes fructus spirituales, quos attulit. Ier. XI.6: Olivam uberem, pulchram, fructiferam, speciosam vocavit Dominus nomen tuum (§896).

85. Si...hoc factum est contra naturam, quanto magis hi qui sunt secundum naturam, id est qui naturali origine pertinent ad gentem Iudaeorum, inseretur suae olivae, id est reducentur ad dignitatem gentis suae, Mal. ult. [IV.6]: Convertet corda patrum ad filios, et corda filiorum ad patres eorum (§911).

86. This term means a hardening or, metaphorically, an obtuseness or blindness.

87. See Francis Martin, "Et sic omnis Israel salvus fieret, Rom 11,26," *Estudios Bíblicos* 21 (1962): 127–50, which traces the interpretation of this phrase in patristic literature. For an alternate view, see F. Refoulé, "...*Et ainsi tout*

Israël sera sauvé": Romains 11,25–32 (Paris: Éditions du Cerf, 1984), who provides an exegetical and rhetorical study of 11.25–32. He concludes (p. 273): "Selon notre interprétation, Paul n'announce donc pas en Rm 11.25–26 le salut d'Israël comme peuple, mais seulement celui de ces Juifs pieux, de ces hassidim qui, avant l'annonce de l'Évangile, pouvaient être considérés comme consitutant le Reste, l'Israël de l'élection. Autrement dit, le 'mystère' exprimait l'espoir de Paul de voir ces derniers se convertir avant la Parousie du Christ."

88. Unde utrumque refertur ad liberationem a culpa sed dicit Qui eripiat, propter paucos, qui nunc difficulter quasi cum quadam violentia convertuntur. Amos III.12: Quomodo si eruat pastor de ore leonis duo crura, aut extremum auriculae, sic eruentur filii Israël. Dicit autem avertet impietatem a Iacob, ad ostendendum facilitatem conversionis Iudaeorum in finem mundi (§919).

89. §931.

90. §923.

91. Deinde cum dicit Sine poenitentia enim etc., excludit obviationem.

Posset enim aliquis obviando dicere quod Iudaei, et si olim fuerint charissimi propter patres, tamen inimicitia, quam contra Evangelium exercent, prohibet ne in futurum salventur. Sed hoc Apostolus falsum esse asserit, dicens sine poenitentia enim sunt dona et vocatio Dei,...quia de hoc Deus non poenitet.... Ps CIX.5: Iuravi Dominus, et non poenitebit eum (§924).

92. Conclusit enim Deus, id est concludi permisit, omnia, id est omne hominum genus, tam Iudaeos quam Gentiles in credulitate, sicut in quadam catena erroris....ut omnium misereatur, id est ut in omni genere hominum sua misericordia locum habeat....Fit enim hac distributio pro generibus singulorum et non pro singulis generum. Ideo autem Deus vult omnes per suam misericordiam salvari, ut ex hoc humilientur et suam salutem non sibi, sed Deo adscribant. Os XIII.9: Perditio tua, Israël, tantummodo ex me auxilium tuum, supra III.19: *Ut omne os obstruatur, et subditus fiat omnis mundus Deo* (emphasis mine) (§932).

93. *PER* §55 (emphasis mine).

94. In *Ad Simpl.* I,2,3 he gives great emphasis to the simultaneous conception of the twins in order to establish irrefutably their equality in nature ("Simul enim ambo uno tempore ille seuit, eodem tempore ila concepit") while expressly denying meritorious works or foreseen faith as the motive of divine election.

95. *PER* §60. This dilemma recurs in *Ad Simpl.* I,2,4 ("Si enim nullo merito electus est Iacob nondum natus et nihil operatus, nec omnino eligi potuit nulla existente differentia qua eligeretur") but has a different resolution from the Romans commentaries.

96. In *PER* §61 he rephrases and clarifies this assertion: "God did not elect those doing good works, but those who believed, with the result that he enabled them to do good works. *It is we who believe and will*, but he who gives to those believing and willing the ability to do good works through the Holy Spirit..." (emphasis mine). Although he repeats a similar formula in *Ad Simpl.*

I,2,5 ("nec credit aliquis nisi libera uoluntate") he employs it to probe more deeply into the question of the function of human free will and belief in God's election of Jacob. As Gerard O'Daly concisely states: "even the elect cannot be rewarded for something for which they are not responsible" ("Predestination and Freedom in Augustine's Ethics," in *The Philosophy in Christianity,* ed. Godfrey Vesey [Cambridge: Cambridge University Press, 1989], 91). Augustine couples Romans 9.15 ("So it depends not upon [one's] will or exertion, but upon God's mercy") with Phil 2.12–13 ("work out your own salvation with fear and trembling; for God is at work in you, both to will and to work for his good pleasure") to demonstrate that "ipsam bonam voluntatem in nobis operante deo fieri." The human ability to will rightly accompanies God's gift of mercy but follows God's call. See *Ad Simpl.* I,2,12.

97. William Babcock, "Augustine's Interpretation of Romans (A.D. 394–396)," *Augustinian Studies* 10 (1979): 64 n. 68. This divine scheme is modified in *Ad Simpl.* I,2,13, wherein the distinction is made between those called *congruenter*, who are the elect, and those not called in the same manner: "Ad alios autem uovatio quidem peruenit, sed quia talis fuit, qua moueri non possent nec eam capere apti essent, uocati quidem dici potuerunt sed non electi...." The human response, though free, is in keeping with the manner of the divine calling. Matthew 22.14 ("For many are called but few are chosen") serves to ground the distinction as in *PER* §55.

James Wetzel ("Pelagius Anticipated: Grace and Election in Augustine's *Ad Simplicianum*," in *Augustine: From Rhetor to Theologian*, ed. J. McWilliam [Waterloo, ON: Wilfrid Laurier University Press, 1992], 121–32) characterizes the human will in Augustine's thought as conflicted, perverse, or obdurate to account for a *congrua vocatio*. Persons with a conflicted will are those who cannot act on their recognition or desire for a life of blessedness; those whose will is perverse do not have any inner turmoil and their choices lead them away from a life of beatitude. Nonetheless, in each instance God can "effect a conversion from these pathological conditions." However, the individual "afflicted with obduracy rejects God's influence and becomes one of the many who are called but not chosen" (pp. 124–25). As we shall see, these theological differentiations, whether Augustine's *congruenter/non-congruenter* or Wetzel's threefold classification of human volition, ultimately do not avoid the specter of divine injustice or arbitrariness.

98. Babcock, "Augustine's Interpretation," 64. In *Ad Simpl.* I,2 Augustine sees that this position is subject to the same critique that he has directed against works: "Si igitur electio per praescientiam, praescuit autem deus fidem Iacob, unde probas quia non etiam ex operibus elegit eum? si propterea qua nondum nati erant et nondum aliquid egerant bonum seu malum, ita etiam nondum crediderat aliquis eorum."

Both Babcock ("Augustine's Interpretation," 66) and Paula Fredriksen ("Excaecati Occulta Justitia Dei," *Journal of Early Christian Studies* 3 [1995]: 308) note that in *Ad Simpl.* I,2 Augustine relocates the specific difference between Jacob and Esau in the manner in which *God calls* not in their respective responses of faith and unbelief, nor within *occultissimis meritis* of individuals. Instead, the *ratio* of election resides within God "aequitate occultissima et ab humanis sensibus remotissima iudicat..." (*Ad Simpl*. I,2,16), therefore "illi enim electi qui congruenter vocati, illi autem qui non congruebant neque contemperabuntur vocationi non electi, quia non secuti quamvis vocati" (*Ad Simpl*. I,2,13). See discussion below, especially as this pertains to the obverse of the proposition of election: reprobation.

99. This is especially clear in *Ad Simpl*. I,2,16, wherein he writes: "Sunt igitur omnes homines—quando quidem, ut apostolos ait, *in Adam omnes moriuntur*, a quo in uniuersum genus humanum origo ducitur offensionis dei—una quaedam massa peccati supplicium debens diuinae summaeque iustitiae...."

100. That is, in his own version, which reads: "I will have mercy on whom I will have had mercy, and I will show him compassion on whom I will have had compassion." Fredriksen cautions that "Augustine's exegesis demands strict attention to Latin sequence of tenses" (*Augustine on Romans: Propositions from the Epistle to the Romans, Unfinished Commentary on the Epistle to the Romans*, Society of Biblical Literature Texts and Translations 23, Early Christian Literature 6 [Atlanta: Society of Biblical Literature, 1982], 33).

101. "'I will have mercy...on whom I will have had mercy.' God was merciful to us the first time when he called us while we were still sinners. 'On whom I will have had mercy...so that I called him,' and *still* 'I will have mercy on him' yet again once the man has believed. Yet how does God have mercy this second time? He gives to the believing seeker the Holy Spirit" (*PER* §61).

102. In *Ad Simpl*. the contrary is true; the bishop of Hippo, following Paul's strategy in Romans 9, applies these principles of election to corporate humanity (I,2,16), Jews and Gentiles (I,2,19), and to those to be justified (I,2,22).

103. *PER* §61. Not surprisingly, in *Ad Simpl*. the process of election differs because the inception of divine activity does not occur with the foreknown faith (or works) of an individual. The purpose of God is to justify those who believe; election, in this scheme, does not precede justification (see I,2,6). "Augustine, probably because of the distinction between the called and the chosen in the parable of the guests invited to the feast [Matt 22.1–14]..., says that this temporal choice (by which he means a choice for heaven) presupposes justification" (John Farrelly, OSB, *Predestination, Grace and Free Will* [Westminster, MD: Newman, 1964], 85). Augustine writes: "...quia cui misertus erit deus ut eum vocet, miserebitur eius ut credat, et cui misericors fuerit ut credat, misericordiam praestabit, hoc est faciet eum misericordem, ut etiam bene operetur." God, through a "certain hidden equity" bestows mercy upon some and not upon others. Those upon whom God bestows mercy are those called and given faith for belief unto justification which, in turn, results in election because of the actualizing of good works by the believer. These persons are those called *congruenter*, whose wills are freely conformed to the call and gift of faith. He explains this further: "Ut uelimus enim et suum esse uoluit et nostrum, suum uocando

nostrum sequendo. Quod autem uoluerimus solus praestat, id est posse bene agere et semper beate uiuere" (I,2,10). *PER* §62, although less precise, provides a rationale for reprobation: "Therefore clearly, we do good deeds not by our own willing or running but by the mercy of God, although our will (which alone can do nothing) is also present." Those who do not receive mercy are called nonetheless, but in such wise as to be obstinate or hardened to believing; these are the reprobate.

104. In *Ad Simpl.* I,2,15 there is a provisional development of the topic dictated by Paul's rhetorical strategy so that "non ab illo inrogetur aliquid quo sit homo deterior, sed tantum quo sit melior non erogetur."

105. O'Daly, "Predestination and Freedom," 90.

106. *PER* §62.

107. The initial hardening of Israel is purposive, namely, the inclusion of the Gentiles. Unlike the hardening of Pharoah whose obduracy remains intact, however, divine providence must also account for the subsequent restoration of the Jews as integral to the eschatological trajectory sketched by Paul.

108. He recognizes the inadequacy of the formulation, not only as it pertains to Esau but especially relative to Pharaoh. In *Ad Simpl.* I,2,14 he exposes substantially the weakness of the argument advanced in *PER*: "Quod si tanta quoque potest esse obstinatio uoluntatis, ut contra omnes modos uocationis obdurescat mentis euersio, quaeritur, utrum de diuina poena sit ipsa duritia, cum eum deus deserit non sic uocando, quomodo ad fidem moueri potest. Quis enim dicat modum quo ei persuaderetur ut crederet etiam omnipotenti defuisse?"

Augustine confronts a similar problem regarding the semiautonomy of human volition in *Encheiridion* 26,100 and, in particular, 27,103 ("quia necesse est fieri si voluerit"). John Rist summarizes Augustine's resolution in this way: "Augustine argues [that] salvation is independent of man's fallen will; it is a matter of God's omnipotence. God has mercy on those whom he will. When God wills that [an individual] be saved, the matter is settled. [That one] is saved; [one's] evil will is turned to good. The text 'God wishes all...to be saved' must be interpreted to mean that all those who are saved are saved by God's will. If God wishes [one's] salvation, salvation follows of *necessity*....Augustine's perverse reading of the text...is not limited to the *Encheiridion* and thus cannot be explained away as a slip" ("Augustine on Free Will and Predestination," in *Augustine: A Collection of Critical Essays*, ed. R. A. Markus [Garden City, NY: Doubleday, 1972], 238). I believe that the fundamental argument preexists in his Romans commentaries.

109. *PER* §62.

110. This difficulty is particularly clear in *Ad Simpl.* I,2,14–16. While reasserting that hardening of certain individuals derives from some divine penalty (I,2,14) Augustine also teaches that God does not act unjustly, whether the debt due God is exacted (rendering some reprobate) or remitted (as in the case of the elect). Since all are "una quaedam massa peccati supplicium debens diuinae summaeque iustitiae, quod siue exigatur siue donaretur, nulla est iniq-

uitas" (I,2,16). Nevertheless, this reformulation of *PER* §62 does not delineate the criteria "employed" by God in the election of some, nor the hardening of others (properly understood). Why Esau or Pharaoh or some Jews fall into the latter category "quibus misericordiam non esse praebendam...occultissima et ab humanis sensibus remotissima..."; nevertheless, "aequitate...judicat" (ibid.). Eventually Augustine interprets the hardening of Pharaoh (or any other individual) "as God's refusal of mercy and not an impulsion to sin" (Farrelly, *Predestination,* 87), but this does not illumine the *ratio* of God's selectivity. Does Augustine cry, "Mystery!" too soon?

111. *PER* §62,15–17.

112. *PER* §62.23. One senses that Augustine spiritualizes the theological task because no satisfactory resolution of the problem is at hand. Rist writes: "Augustine takes refuge behind the Pauline *O altitudo* and the other scriptural texts which indicate that God's ways are past finding out. But his attempt to escape the difficulties in which he is involved is unsatisfactory....But...Augustine has got himself into...difficulties about justice through an *unwillingness to take scriptural texts about the desire for universal salvation seriously. Because he has been unable to relate these texts to a theory about the divine 'will', he is prepared to abandon the texts*" ("Augustine on Free Will," 240–41; emphasis mine). Rist and I came to similar conclusions quite independently. Although *PER* and *CER* form the background to *Ad Simpl.* and other texts that he explicitly addresses, Rist fails to assess these commentaries in his survey.

113. *PER* §63,2.

114. Augustine writes in *PER* §66 regarding Romans 10.1 ("Brethren, my heart's desire and my prayer to God for them is that they might be saved"): "Here Paul begins to speak of his hope for the Jews, lest the Gentiles in their turn dare to grow haughty toward them. (2) For just as he had to refute the pride of the Jews because they gloried in their works, so also with the Gentiles, lest they wax proud as if they had been preferred over the Jews." As we have seen, this is a familiar, oft-repeated caveat of Thomas as well.

115. "[W]hat sublates goes beyond what is sublated, introduces something new and distinct, puts everything on a new basis, yet so far from interfering with the sublated or destroying it, on the contrary needs it, includes it, preserves all its proper features and properties, and carries them forward to a fuller realization within a richer context" (Bernard Lonergan, SJ, *Method in Theology* [New York: Herder & Herder, 1972], 241).

116. Cf. *ST* Ia. 23.5. resp. and *PER* §61.

117. Cf. *ST* Ia. 23.5. resp. and *PER* §60,14 as well as §62,15–17.

118. This definition is seen not only in Ia. 23.1. obj. 3. and 5. ad 2., but also in *CRO* §700. Cf. *De diversis quaest.* I, 2 (PL 40:115).

119. Ia. 23. 2. obj. 2. Cf. *De diversis quaest.* I, 2 (PL 40:114).

120. Ia. 23. 2. ad. 2.

121. Ia. 23. 2. obj. 3. Cf. *De dono perserverantiae* 14 (PL 45:1014).

122. Ia. 23. 2. *sed contra.* Cf. *De dono perserverantiae* 14 (PL 45:1014).

123. Ia. 23. 2. ad 4.
124. Ia. 23. 4. ad 2. Cf. *Sermones ad populum* XXVI, 4 (PL 38:173).
125. Ia. 23. 4. ad 5. Cf. *Super Joannem* 26 (PL 35:1607); John 6.44.
126. Ia. 23. 6. obj. 1. Cf. *De correptione et gratia* 13 (PL 44:940).
127. Ia. 23. 7. *sed contra*. Cf. *De correptione et gratia* 13 (PL 44:940).
128. Ia. 23. 7. resp. Aquinas does not invoke the authority of Augustine only in articles 3 ("utrum Deus aliquem hominem reprobet") and 8 ("utrum praedestinatio possit juvari precibus sanctorum"). As we have seen already, Thomas does not conceive of reprobation as a positive act of the divine will. Since the role of divine volition in reprobating individuals is not as clear in Augustine, this may account for the absence of authoritative texts from his *corpus* in these articles.
129. See chapter 4 for the order of divine love, election, and predestination.
130. Thomas, unlike Augustine, consistently denies that God's positive will is the cause of reprobation.
131. *CER* §3 (emphasis mine).
132. In fact, Augustine and Aquinas diverge on the very image that Paul advances in 11.16 to demonstrate Jewish prerogatives: the image of the lump. As we have seen above, Augustine exploits the image in *Ad Simpl.* to depict the corruption of original sin, in which all humanity partakes. Aquinas, by contrast, specifies the portion as the apostles and the lump as the people of the Jews. "And...if the Apostles are holy, it follows that the people of the Jews is holy" (*CRO* §891).
133. Marcel Dubois conceives of this differently, namely, not as development but rather as opposition "between flesh and spirit or letter and spirit. Within this perspective one witnesses a strange reversal of the literal sense and historical reality." And yet he recognizes an oscillation between two approaches to the OT and Judaism; the first is positive insofar as it prefigures the New, the second is negative insofar as it a mere shadow "portrayed as an imperfection, deprivation, or absence of reality" ("Jews, Judaism, and Israel in the Theology of Saint Augustine," *Immanuel* 22/23 [1989]: 178, 204).

6
The Contribution of Aquinas' *Commentary on Romans* to the Contemporary Debate on Romans 9–11

INTRODUCTION: TRADITIONALIST VS. REVISIONIST INTERPRETATIONS OF ROMANS 9–11

The theological doctrine of forensic justification has functioned since the Reformation as the dominant hermeneutical prism through which Paul's Letter to the Romans has been exegeted. Critics of this standard interpretation of Romans contend that such selective theological refraction occluded Paul's primary thesis of the letter, namely, the inclusion of the Gentiles into God's plan of salvation. This inclusion put all people on par with the Jews. Nevertheless, for such interpreters of Romans 9–11, justification of the individual (whether Jew or Gentile) remains an important subsidiary theme, insofar as it accounts for the particular instantiation of the corporate status of Jews and Gentiles, respectively.

Since Krister Stendahl's programmatic address to the American Psychological Association thirty-seven years ago, entitled "Paul and the Introspective Conscience of the West,"[1] there has been an ongoing reassessment and, as many scholars would contend, a gradual recovery of the letter's original purpose (although not always freed from the strictures of Reform and Counter-Reform theological polemic[2]). In that address, Stendahl warned all scholars against "modernizing" scriptural texts in the process of exegesis, by which he meant that "sayings which meant originally one thing later on were interpreted to mean something else, something which was felt to be more relevant to human conditions of later times."[3] Stendahl sketched a history of paradigm shifts of interpretation pertaining to Romans, from Augustine to the present day, focusing especially on the developing hermeneutic of the "introspective conscience." According to Stendahl, the paradigmatic shift in interpretation away from viewing Jewish–Gentile relations (generally) and Romans 9–11 (in particular) as the climax of the letter toward the introspective conscience extrapolated from Romans 7.19 radically skewed the letter's original frame of reference. Stendahl writes: "When Paul was concerned about the possibility for Gentiles to be included in the messianic community, his statements are now read as answers to the quest for assurance about [one's] salvation out of a common human predicament."[4] Additionally, he states: "So drastic is the reinterpretation once the framework of 'Jews and Gentiles' is lost, and the Western problems of conscience become its unchallenged and self-evident substitutes."[5]

Exegetical interpretations arise in response to questions posed by the prevailing *Zeitgeist*; Rudolf Bultmann's existentialist Paul is a notable modern example to illustrate this point. In the current debate over the letter two dominant types persistently characterize exegesis of Romans:[6] a *traditionalist* approach, which posits "justification by faith alone" in Christ as the fundamental thesis statement (articulated in Rom 1.16–17), emphasizing individual assent and salvation;[7] and a *revisionist* approach, which locates Romans 9–11 as the material focus of the letter and maintains the corporate privileges of Israel while declaring the distinct but equal status of the Gentiles in God's universal plan of salvation.[8] Hybrid approaches occur as well, some of which merge individual decision for faith and forensic justification within one salvific framework,[9] thereby allowing for two equivalent ways of personal salvation within the distinct corporate entities of Israel and the Gentiles.[10]

Practical theological corollaries derive from these speculative, exegetical determinations. Theologians who assert justification *sola fide* as the thrust of Romans generally emphasize God's impartiality and relativize the distinctive status of Jews and Gentiles because only one way exists in the personal economy of salvation: faith in Christ. If faith in Christ alone warrants salvation, no ongoing rationale exists for the Jews' historical prerogatives nor for the maintenance of Jewish rites of worship. In other words, the historical priority of the Jews as the covenant people no longer assures priority in the present offer of salvation: usually it is expressed that the favored status of Jews has been superseded altogether by the "new Israel," the Christian church. The post-Reformation traditionalist view

> is that...Torah and Christ are mutually exclusive categories....
> The traditional view is that the exclusiveness is chronological
> or sequential: once Christianity appears on the scene the Torah
> is either abrogated or appropriated by Christianity at its true
> spiritual level. In either case, whether rejected or replaced,
> Judaism forfeits its privilege as the chosen people of God. The
> Torah is no longer, *if indeed it ever was,* the basis of salvation
> or redemption, whether for the Jew or Gentile.[11]

However, Jews are tolerated as a pool of potential converts. In extreme form, such theological deconstruction of Israel's dignity fomented the most virulent anti-Judaism historically, and abets contemporary anti-Semitism.

> It was the doctrine of the divine rejection of Israel which, of
> all anti-Jewish teachings, was the most pernicious in terms of
> its practical applications. Cast off by God, they were to be
> despised by [humanity]. Jews were to dwell apart, have their
> opportunities for earning a livelihood restricted, wear special
> clothing, have no Christian servants, limit their social contacts with Christians....With the passage of time, the condemnations grew more severe.[12]

Theologians who locate the material center of Romans in chapters 9–11 posit God's faithfulness to the covenant people while simultaneously legitimizing a way of salvation for the Gentiles, distinct yet equal to that of the Jews. For some exegetes, Romans concerns "*missiology, not soteriology.* [It]...is a tractate on mission, not just in terms of outreach, but in terms of how Paul's bringing the message to the Gentiles fits into God's total plan."[13] While faith in Christ remained the essential point of access for the Peoples, Paul neither nullified nor abrogated the covenantal rights and obligations of the Jews.[14] Indeed, in the extreme form of this position, the Mosaic covenant perdures as a *sufficient* vehicle for faith and salvation for the Jews. The Gentiles enter into salvation by a parallel track, that is, without the yoke of the Mosaic Law. Gager, for example, succinctly states this position:

> Paul never explicitly equates Israel's salvation with conversion to Christianity, but even more...he uses faith (*pistis*) not
> just of Christians but of Jews as well. Rom 3.30 asserts that

God "will justify the circumcised on the ground of their faith and the uncircumcised because of their faith."...Paul uses faith here not as the equivalent of faith in Christ but as a designation of the proper response to God's righteousness, whether for Israel in the Torah or for Gentiles in Christ.[15]

The theological corollary is, of course, universalism.[16]

Stendahl theorizes that "Rom 9–11 is not an appendix to [chapters] 1–8, but the climax of the letter."[17] He holds that emphasis on the "introspective conscience" and forensic justification as the solution to humanity's common plight is rooted profoundly in an Augustinian anthropology. As we have seen, Jeremy Cohen and John Y. B. Hood posit, analogously, that forms of anti-Judaism have their precursors in the same Augustinian school of interpretation. For example, Cohen explicitly claims that "the Roman Church's attitude toward the Jews emanated from what may be termed Augustinian theology of Judaism."[18] Indeed,

> the dispersion and degradation of the Jews, if insured by the regnant Church, would both alleviate the problems of Jewish encroachments upon Christianity and enhance the value of their survival—by emphasizing the deplorable wretchedness of their error. The elements of this Augustinian approach toward the Jews and Judaism determined the basic stance of virtually all early medieval Christian polemics against the Jews.[19]

Hood states: "Just as Augustine's views on free will, predestination, and Trinitarian dogma remained paradigmatic for a thousand years, so too his ideas on Judaism and the Jews dominated the medieval debate."[20] However, we have seen that Aquinas corrects and develops the received theological tradition of Augustine regarding predestination, election, and the role of the Jewish people. It is precisely as a pre-Reformation resource that Thomas' *CRO* warrants consideration in the contemporary debate on Romans 9–11.

AQUINAS' *COMMENTARY ON ROMANS* 9–11: SUMMARY CONCLUSIONS

In the history of confessional doctrines, the concern for individual justification gradually eclipsed the corporate implications of the Christ-event (for Jews and Gentiles alike) articulated in Romans. I contend that the post-Reformation emphasis on the individual's justification by faith (subjectively experienced) coalesced with the earlier phenomenon of anti-Judaism to denigrate definitively the corporate role of the Jews and to reinforce theological supersessionism: namely, that Christian believers supersede Jews as the *verus Israel*.[21] As we have seen, Hood, Cohen, and others claim that Thomas Aquinas was a faithful transmitter and, indeed, proponent of this Augustinian tradition relative to the Jews. We have also seen that this is an inaccurate assessment of Aquinas, especially in terms of his Romans commentary. Thomas' anthropology is not Augustinian.[22] Neither does Aquinas view Romans through the hermeneutical prism of forensic justification. Instead, he utilized the controlling concept of divine providence and, particularly, the theological categories of predestination and election to delineate the relationship between Jew and Gentile, as well as the ongoing role of the Jews in salvation history.[23]

The student of Thomas must resist modernizing him in order to respond to the challenge of contemporary Jewish–Christian dialogue or our own prevailing *Zeitgeist* in academe. This is particularly true in analyses of Thomas' biblical commentaries in general and especially his *Commentary on Romans*. To modernize Aquinas would mean that we are twice removed from Paul's resolution of the Jew–Gentile and Jewish–Christian/Gentile–Christian problem.

We have seen that Aquinas defends the corporate soteriological status of the Jews throughout his commentary. In addition, we have seen that in *CRO* (as well as in other Thomistic texts) predestination and the ancillary doctrine of election account for the ongoing role and status of the Jews as a privileged, temporal manifestation of God's eternal will. God's election of the Jews and the call of the Gentiles retain a temporal tension or ambiguity that Paul recognized and struggled to articulate in corporate and individual aspects. Thomas preserved the inherent ambiguity of the apostle and sought to provide an explicit theological rationale for the soteriological interdependence of Jews and Gentiles and, by implication, of his Jewish and Christian contemporaries.

An analysis of Thomas' exegesis of Romans 9–11 was the focus of this study: I contend that Aquinas faithfully preserves Paul's perspective and resolution of the role of the Jews in salvation history and, by so doing, implicitly opposes the incipient anti-Judaism arising in the medieval Christian society. Thomas repeatedly asserts in his commentary that "salvation is from the Jews (Jn 4.22)."[24] While not equivocating on the decisive revelation of God in Christ Jesus, Thomas exploits the equality of preceding guilt and the necessity of subsequent faith for Gentile and Jew alike—so essential to Paul's resolution of the Jew–Gentile conflict. Throughout his work Aquinas maintains the inherent dignity of the Jews as God's chosen people and their vital role in salvation history;[25] he cautions non-Jews against smug self-confidence and promises the future remedy of the Jews when "all Israel shall be saved, not in a manner partly, but universally."[26]

This study investigated how Aquinas' commentary on Paul's letter is to be read in the theological context of medieval, anti-Jewish polemic and repressive trends directed against the Jews by civil and ecclesial entities. Thomas Aquinas may well have been aware of the rise of anti-Judaism manifested in the attack on Talmud and the writings of Moses Maimonides, as well as the strictures imposed upon the Jewish community by secular and ecclesial authorities. It is difficult to imagine that Thomas could be completely ignorant of the Jewish counterpolemical literature engendered by the formal public disputations between Jews and Christians sanctioned by church or state. These events, appraised in tandem with the Jews' ongoing concern for group identity and cohesion (often characterized by their detractors as intolerance of Christians and Jewish exclusivity), make Thomas' *CRO* and *ST* all the more remarkable. In both works, his theological positions concerning the Jews are frequently in opposition to prevailing social trends; his affinity for the writing of Rabbi Moses, whom he cites among the list of venerable authorities in the *ST*,[27] is but one case in point. Although Aquinas is constrained in *CRO* by a *lectio continua,* he consistently acknowledges the debt of Gentiles to the Jews and, by extension, a reciprocal debt of Christians to Jews. In sum, both corporate entities are essential to the culmination of salvation history. Paul is a Jew; Aquinas is a faithful commentator on the apostle.

Although chapters 9–11 of *CRO* were the chief concern of the study, references to the role of the Jews elsewhere in the commentary supplemented the primary texts under consideration. Furthermore, auxiliary texts from the Thomistic corpus nuanced the doctrines of predestination, election, and the role of the Jewish people in Romans 9–11. The task, methodologically considered, has been primarily one of internal description, that is, discerning the controlling concepts that Thomas employed in order to define the passage under consideration in Romans 9–11 and assessing his use of authoritative references that serve to explicate its meaning.[28] However, we also have investigated the commentary's theological importance relative to the medieval Jewish–Christian polemic in light of the contemporary debate on the purpose of Romans.

I have argued that *CRO* represents a significant resource for the development of a reading of Romans that sustains a positive theological appraisal of the Jewish people. In chapter 2 we saw that the contemporary scene in which Thomas found himself writing was shaped by an ecclesial policy toward the Jews that was becoming increasingly hostile. In chapter 3, I advanced the argument that, while Aquinas addresses many of the same sociotheological issues that are found in the *Sicut* tradition and elsewhere, he goes beyond the *status quo* (an ever-eroding tolerance). We learned that Aquinas did not merely tolerate Jewish presence in society, but that he upheld the Jews' legitimate, divinely appointed role in an overwhelmingly Christian milieu. In successive chapters (4 and 5), I argued that predestination and election remain the key concepts for understanding Thomas' exegesis of Romans 9–11 and the relationship between Jews and Gentiles. In addition, close analysis of Augustine's *Unfinished Commentary on the Epistle to the Romans* and his *Propositions from the Epistle to the Romans* (as well as other works) provided the means to ascertain his putative theological influence on Aquinas and how (*pace* Cohen, Hood, and others) Thomas significantly differs from Augustine's construal of predestination and election, and the ongoing role of the Jewish people in salvation history. Contemporary reappraisals of medieval anti-Judaism frequently reproach Thomas for an allegedly negative, supersessionistic view of the Jews; these critics selectively interpret Aquinas' writings, largely ignoring his most sustained treatment of Jew–Gentile relations found in *CRO* 9–11. Analysis of these chapters, in particular, has demonstrated that Thomas is not anti-Jewish: he remains faithful to the plot line established by Paul.

Aquinas' commentary on Romans 9–11 should be read in a nontraditionalist manner and in a social context of medieval, anti-Jewish polemic and repressive trends against the Jews. By doing so, we avoid modernizing Aquinas and heed Stendahl's warning. We also discover (or rediscover) a significant voice that should be heard in the contemporary exegetical debate. Thomas' hermeneutical keys to understanding Romans 9–11 are readily applicable to the contemporary Jewish–Christian dialogue: it is God who predestines and elects; it is God who grants Jew and Gentile their privileged status; it is God who saves "all Israel" once the "fullness of the Gentiles" has entered into salvation, and it is God to whom the synagogue and the church are accountable. "If God is faithful, then this faithfulness has to extend to Israel's past, present and future."[29] The recent Vatican document "We Remember: A Reflection on the 'Shoah'"[30] provides a fitting conclusion to this study of *CRO* 9–11:

> Looking to the future of relations between Jews and Christians, in the first place we appeal to our Catholic brothers and

sisters to renew the awareness of the Hebrew roots of their faith. We ask them to keep in mind that Jesus was a descendant of David; that the Virgin Mary and the Apostles belonged to the Jewish people; that the Church draws sustenance from the root of that good olive tree on to which have been grafted the wild olive branches of the Gentiles (cf. Rom 11.17–24); that the Jews are our dearly beloved brothers, indeed in a certain sense they are "our elder brothers."

...We wish to turn awareness of past sins into a firm resolve to build a new future in which there will be no more anti-Judaism among Christians or anti-Christian sentiment among Jews, but rather a shared mutual respect, as befits those who adore the one Creator and Lord and have a common father in faith, Abraham....[T]he spoiled seeds of anti-Judaism and anti-Semitism must never again be allowed to take root in any human heart.

NOTES

1. Stendahl's essay was published in *Harvard Theological Review* 56 (1963): 199–215 as the English translation of a 1960 presentation in Swedish. The article and the rejoinder to Ernst Käsemann's criticism of Stendahl's thesis (see *Perspectives on Paul*, trans. by Margaret Kohl [Philadelphia: Fortress, 1971], 60–78) also appear in Krister Stendahl, *Paul among Jews and Gentiles and Other Essays* (Philadelphia: Fortress, 1976).

2. See, for example, Scott Hafemann, "The Salvation of Israel in Romans 11.25–32: A Response to Krister Stendahl," *Ex Auditu* 4 (1988): 38–58, esp. 55, where he writes: "However we may understand the contrasts between 'faith' and the 'law' and 'grace' and 'works' in these texts, it cannot be denied that the parallel between 9.30–33 and 11.5–7 indicates that Paul's doctrine of *justification by faith alone* is to be applied equally to both Gentiles and Jews....Hence arguments may differ concerning how close to the center of Paul's theology his doctrine of justification by faith actually is, but Stendahl has moved it too far away."

3. Stendahl, "Introspective Conscience," 214.

4. Ibid., 206.

5. Ibid., 207.

6. Exegetical methods applied to Romans have yielded a vast body of literature and will, undoubtedly, generate far more. I refer the reader to two representative commentaries of the Reform and Roman Catholic traditions, namely, Ernst Käsemann, *Commentary on Romans*, trans. Geoffrey W. Bromiley (Grand Rapids: Eerdmans, 1980); and Joseph A. Fitzmyer, *Romans: A New Translation*

with Introduction and Commentary (Anchor Bible 33; Garden City, NY: Doubleday, 1993). I have chosen to limit my review of the contemporary literature to those approaches that explicitly analyze the role of the Jews in Romans 9–11. See John G. Gager, *Origins of Anti-Semitism: Toward Judaism in Pagan and Christian Antiquity* (New York: Oxford University Press, 1983) for a trenchant analysis of the modern debate (pp. 13–34), as well as his *Reinventing Paul* (Oxford: Oxford University Press, 2000). See also the work of Stendahl, E. P. Sanders (e.g., *Paul and Palestinian Judaism: A Comparison of Patterns of Religion* [Philadelphia: Fortress, 1977]), Rosemary Radford Ruether (e.g., *Faith and Fratricide: The Theological Roots of Anti-Semitism* [New York: Seabury, 1974], and Lloyd Gaston (e.g., "Paul" in *Anti-Semitism and the Foundations of Christianity,* ed. A. Davies [New York: Paulist Press, 1979], 48–71). Despite the array of methods represented in exegeting these three chapters of Romans, most scholars are proponents of either the "traditionalist" or the "revisionist" position. These two polarities admit of some variation, and, where relevant, the distinctive contributions to the argument are noted.

7. Perhaps the foremost contemporary proponent of the existentialist decision for faith is Ernst Käsemann, who, commenting on 1.16-17 states that this "verse speaks of faith only as a decision,...but the very dubious speculation about a 'supra-individual phenomenon' must be strenuously resisted....Rather faith is an appropriation of the eschatological public proclamation made to the whole world and to each individual. Each person is placed in a situation of personal responsibility" (*Romans*, 23). See also C. K. Barrett (*The Epistle to the Romans*, Harper's New Testament Commentaries [New York: Harper & Row, 1957], 175), who subordinates Romans 9–11 to the interpretive lens of *sola fides*: "In the second as in the first half of the epistle Paul writes about God and his strange mercy in offering...justification on the basis of faith alone, but his portrayal of divine freedom and grace is determined by somewhat different sets of circumstances." See John Murray, *The Epistle to the Romans*, 2 vols., New International Commentary on the New Testament (Grand Rapids: Eerdmans, 1959), 2:xii–xvi for similar subordination of these chapters to Rom 1.16–17.

8. The preeminent contemporary proponent of this view is Krister Stendahl. He provides a concise articulation of the revisionist thesis and its implications for Jewish–Christian relations in *Final Account: Paul's Letter to the Romans* (Minneapolis: Fortress, 1995).

9. See, e.g., Walter B. Russell, "An Alternative Suggestion for the Purpose of Romans," *Bibliotheca Sacra* 145 (1988): 174–84, esp. 180, which posits a "cross-cultural" starting point for exegeting Romans rather than a "theological, conscience-oriented perspective," one that is "more outward-looking and more activistic than introspective in basic orientation." Russell's proposed purpose statement for the letter exemplifies one such hybrid approach: "In an exhortative letter confronting their Jewish/Gentile relationships, Paul challenged the Roman churches to participate fully in God's present harvest of all peoples by showing that their ethnocentrism opposed God's eternal plan of justifying people by faith,

of giving them new life in the Spirit, and of mercifully placing them in His redemptive plan."

10. John G. Lodge utilizes reader-response criticism of Romans 9–11 to delineate soteriological principles that are either "anti-Israel" or "pro-Israel." The dynamic between the implied author and the audience in the former category reinforces the incompatibility of Christ and the Mosaic Law, as well as the supersession of Israel by the church. The pro-Israel dynamic accepts the compatibility of Christ and the Mosaic Law and recognizes two legitimate ways of salvation for Jew and Gentile. The reader-response method permits Lodge to posit the coexistence of *both* groups in Rome and, by implication, in the present. Fundamentally, "[t]he point for pro-Israel implied readers is that they must accept that the hardening of Israel is part of God's plan for both Gentiles and Jews. The point for anti-Israel implied readers is that *both* the λεῖμμα [i.e., Jews, like Paul, who believe in Jesus Messiah] and the λοίποι [i.e., Jews who do not believe in Jesus Messiah] remain 'Israel.' The question then becomes: What ongoing relationship do the implied readers have to this Israel?" (*Romans 9–11: A Reader-Response Analysis*, University of South Florida International Studies in Formative Christianity and Judaism 6 [Atlanta: Scholars Press, 1996], 215). Elizabeth Johnson ("Jews and Christians in the New Testament: John, Matthew, and Paul," *Reformed Review* 42 (1988/1989): 113–28) recognizes Paul's irresolution of the Jew–Gentile relationship as intentional because he ultimately sees the dilemma as God's problem (p. 120). She theorizes that Paul keeps two principles in tension throughout Romans 9–11, specifically, that God is impartial to Jews and Gentiles, and that he is faithful to Israel. Johnson posits a three-stage response to the theological dilemma. In 9.6 Paul repeats the standard Jewish election theology, but includes the election of Gentiles as well in 9.24; second, this impartial righteousness (9.30) offered the Gentiles is a *skandalon* for Israel, although theirs was meant to be an inclusive covenant; and, third, although the offer of impartial mercy is accepted by some Jews (11.1ff.), the Jews who do not believe (who constitute the majority) are part of God's plan to effect the Gentile mission (pp. 119–20). Johnson, while seeing the corporate and individual dimensions of Romans 9–11, sometimes wrongly recasts the Jew–Gentile relationship as a Jewish–*Christian* problem. For example, she writes (p. 120): "Ultimately, the problem of Jews and Christians is *God's* problem, and Paul is willing to let God solve it." This characterization seems anachronistic, at best. Nevertheless, she succinctly interweaves the interdependent roles of Jews and Gentiles according to Paul and in contradistinction to positions taken in the Gospels according to Matthew and John.

11. Gager, *Origins of Anti-Semitism,* 213 (emphasis mine).

12. Frank Talmage, *Disputation and Dialogue: Readings in the Jewish-Christian Encounter* (New York: KTAV, 1975), 7. Talmage characterizes medieval Christian polemical literature as transferring covenantal promises from the old Israel to the new: "It was the Gentile Church who were the children of Abraham, the first Christian, who was himself saved by faith and not by the

Mosaic law. Jacob was the church; Esau the rejected Synagogue....[A]ll prophecies of redemption and consolation were applied to Christians; all prophecies of chastisement to the Jews. The Jews were entitled only to divine wrath but not to divine love" (pp. 6–7).

13. Stendahl, *Final Account*, 41. See also Paul S. Minear's analysis of Rom 1.1–17 and 15.14–33 (*The Obedience of Faith: The Purposes of Paul in the Epistle to the Romans*, Studies in Biblical Theology, Second Series 18 [Naperville, IL: Allenson, 1971], 37) as proof of Paul's overall missiological purpose.

14. Lloyd Gaston, for example, holds this view. Jesus was primarily the fulfillment of God's promises to Israel in order that the Jews would be a light to the nations. He maintains that Paul did not advocate the abandonment of Torah but struggled to legitimize a separate way of salvation for the Gentiles apart from Torah observance. See Lloyd Gaston, "Israel's Enemies in Pauline Theology," *New Testament Studies* 28 (1982): 400–423, and "Abraham and the Righteousness of God," *Horizons in Biblical Theology* 2 (1980): 39–68. More recently, Mary Ann Getty ("Paul and the Salvation of Israel: A Perspective on Rom 9–11," *Catholic Biblical Quarterly* 50 [1988]: 456–69), upon a careful analysis of Paul's summary statements in 11.25–32, argued convincingly that the Apostle to the Gentiles does not spiritualize nor replace "historical, real, physical Israel, [his] own kinspeople" through the inclusion of the Gentiles (p. 465). She rejects allegations of "Pauline anti-Judaism" based on substitutionary theories and because the "term...risks attributing to Paul a modern anti-Semitic bias" (p. 456 n. 4). For Getty, the misconstrual of Romans is attributable to severing the letter from its first-century missiological moorings and transforming it into a timeless treatise on justification by faith. Rather, "Paul does not speak of Israel being rejected by God. He never speaks of the Torah as having been abrogated, nor of the Gentiles or Christians assuming Israel's place" (p. 468 n. 31). See also her earlier article "Paul on the Covenants and the Future of Israel," *Biblical Theology Bulletin* 17 (1987): 92–99. Cf. J. Louis Martyn, "Paul and His Jewish-Christian Interpreters," *Union Seminary Quarterly Review* 42 (1988): 9, who prescinds from the question of any explicit missiology in Romans 9–11, but sees Paul primarily asserting two corporate realities: "(a) God's election of Israel is fundamentally the paradigm for God's election of all humanity; (b) the power that God's gospel is now exerting on all of humanity is fundamentally the paradigm for the power that God's mercy will ultimately exert on all Israel." Martyn contends that substitutionary theories or supersessionism are, therefore, alien to Paul.

15. Gager, *Origins of Anti-Semitism*, 261–62.

16. Barnabas Lindars succinctly delineates the difficulty faced by Paul: the inclusion of the Peoples into God's plan of salvation through faith in Jesus threatened an *exclusion of unbelieving Jews*. Romans 9–11 responds to the challenge of Jewish unbelief by showing "that the unbelief of the Jews has actually worked positively toward the fulfillment of God's universal salvation by forc-

ing the church to evangelize the Gentiles. By the same token...the unbelief of the Jews is only temporary, and...God's promises to them will not fail (511)." Lindars provides an assessment of Jewish warrants for Pauline universalism ("The Old Testament and Universalism in Paul," *Bulletin of the John Rylands University Library of Manchester* 69 [1986]: 511–27). Paul resolves the tension between Jewish/Gentile believers in Jesus as Messiah and nonbelieving Jews by extending the range of application of familiar texts (some of which he conflates, e.g., Hos 2.23 and 1.9–10), exploiting verbal ambiguities (e.g., the use of τέλος in Rom 10.4), and appropriating scriptural warrants utilized in the early kerygma or apologetic preaching (e.g., Ps 69.22f.). He writes: "Paul's concept of universal salvation had precedents in prophetic passages of the Old Testament, in some strands of contemporary Jewish thought, and some of the remembered sayings of Jesus. But these were often ambiguous, and there is no evidence for a considered theological treatment of the problem" (p. 526). By these and other means, Paul fashions a rationale to account for his universalist perspective. However, as a theological corollary, universalism per se neither implies nor prohibits religious conversion, since, for example, Jewish unbelief is not specified as *unbelief in Christ*. Possession of the Law does not preclude the exercise of divine mercy. Cf. Lester J. Kuyper, "The Hardness of Heart According to a Biblical Perspective," *Scottish Journal of Theology* 27 (1974): 459–74, for universalism argued from Paul's negative thesis expressed in Rom 9.17f., 11.7f., 11.25f., and 11.32: "For God has consigned all [people] to disobedience that he may have mercy upon all (11.32). This all includes Israel in her hardened heart, as well as Gentiles in their former disobedience" (p. 465). For a contrasting view, see J. Munck, "Israel and the Gentiles in the New Testament," *Journal of Theological Studies* n.s. 2/1 (1951): 3–16, where he sketches the emergence of a "reverse particularism" that supplants the original universalism, "the representative universalism preached by Jesus, the earliest disciples, and Paul [so] that Israel, that is, the Jewish people is no longer granted a decisive place in the history of salvation" (p. 16).

17. Stendahl, "Introspective Conscience," 205.

18. Jeremy Cohen, *The Friars and the Jews: The Evolution of Medieval Anti-Judaism* (Ithaca: Cornell University Press, 1982), 19.

19. Ibid., 20.

20. John Y. B. Hood, *Aquinas and the Jews*, Middle Ages Series (Philadelphia: University of Pennsylvania Press, 1995), 10.

21. The use or claim of prefigurement in exegeting the New Testament does not, of itself, necessitate substitutionary theories or supersessionism. The work of J. W. Aageson ("Typology, Correspondence, and the Application of Scripture in Romans 9–11," *Journal for the Study of the New Testament* 31 [1987]: 51–72) is useful to illustrate the point. Aageson claims that, excluding "Rom 5.12–21 and perhaps I Cor 10.1–13 the language of 'type', 'antitype', and historical linkage is neither adequate nor helpful in describing the basic framework with which Paul came to use scripture" (p. 53). He prefers the term *cor-*

respondence, which correlates the truth of a scriptural assertion (whether concerning persons or events) to contemporary persons or events. In this way, historical linkage is neither necessitated nor precluded, nor is the integrity of the scriptural assertion about persons or events compromised. For example, "Israel according to the flesh and Israel according to the promise are intended to correspond...to Israel according to physical descent and Israel according to 'faith.' There is no suggestion in 9.6–13 that Paul understood the Christian community as having superseded Israel; on the contrary, he argues that the Christian community is the embodiment of Israel, that is, Israel understood as the 'people of promise'" (p. 55). Although the claim of prefigurement implicitly demands historical linkage, it does not necessarily impugn nor replace scriptural truth claims about persons or events. In fact, prefigurement in theology or exegesis depends radically upon these *realia* for correspondence. Although Aquinas employs prefigurement as one category of exegetical method in his commentary that does not make him, *de facto*, a proponent of supersessionism nor permit him to impugn or ignore the role of the Jews. To the contrary, his concern for the literal meaning of the scriptural text required an irrevocable bond between the two testaments.

22. A profitable future study would consider Thomas' predominant application of Aristotelian philosophy as opposed to Augustine's use of Platonic philosophy to inform each commentators' exegesis regarding Jews and Judaism, in tandem with (Christian) anthropology. Jeremy Cohen already hints at the importance of these philosophical substrates in shaping his analysis of Augustine and Thomas, respectively (*Living Letters of the Law: Ideas of the Jew in Medieval Christianity* [Berkeley and Los Angeles: University of California Press, 1999]).

23. For contemporary commentators utilizing a similar hermeneutical key, see G. B. Caird, "Predestination—Romans IX–XI," *Expository Times* 68 (1957): 324–27; R. Bring, "Paul and the Old Testament: A Study of the Ideas of Election, Faith and Law in Paul, with Special Reference to Romans 9.30–10.13," *Studia Theologica* 25 (1971): 25–28); and C. K. Barrett, "Romans 9.30–10.21: Fall and Responsibility of Israel," in *Essays on Paul* (London: SPCK, 1982), who writes: "Perhaps the most common view [of Romans 9–11] is that after a predestinarian account of the fall of Israel in 9.1–29, 9.30–10.21 provides a complementary account of the same lapse in which the fault is laid squarely at Israel's door, and in turn leads to a synthesis in chapter 11 in which Paul states his hope for Israel's future" (p. 132). Unlike contemporary commentators, however, Aquinas provides a comprehensive systematic, theological account of predestination and election in his *ST*, which illumines his application of these concepts in his *CRO*.

24. See, e.g., §§101, 225, 746, 881, 897, 918.

25. E.g., §§859ff., 879ff.

26. §916.

27. To quote Warren Zev Harvey, "Maimonides and Aquinas on Interpreting the Bible," in *Proceedings of the American Academy for Jewish Research*

55 (1988): 76: "In co-opting the radical, potentially subversive [Arabic Aristotelian] philosophy into his theology, Aquinas made felicitous use of Rabbi Moses. He portrayed him as a harmonious blend of Jew and Aristotelian. Aquinas wrote about Maimonides words similar to those he wrote about Augustine. Augustine, he wrote, accepted from Plato everything that did not contradict *fides* [*ST* Ia. 84.5]. Maimonides, he wrote, sought to make concord between Aristotle and *sacra scriptura* [*ST* Ia. 50.3]." This is true, despite the fact that "Dominicans examined Maimonides' writings and publicly burned some of them in 1232" (Hood, *Aquinas and the Jews,* 340).

Our knowledge of the history of the Maimonidean controversy ca. 1233 is woefully inadequate. However, it is also highly likely that Rabbi Moses' *Guide of the Perplexed* was also consigned to destruction along with Talmudic literature in 1244, replicating the earlier condemnation originally generated by anti-Maimunist propagandists. Despite the condemnation of the *Guide* in the first half of the thirteenth century by Jewish and Christian authorities alike, it is remarkable that Aquinas cites Rabbi Moses in the *ST* so frequently. See, e.g., Ia *pars*, qq. 50. 3. resp., 66. 1. ad 3, 68. 1. ad 1, 69. 1. ad 5., 74. 3. ad 3 and ad 4, as well as several citations in the discussions pertaining to ceremonial precepts (Ia IIae. 101–2).

28. Primarily with reference to the commentary itself, e.g., John 4.22.

29. See Joseph Sievers, "'God's Gifts and Call Are Irrevocable': The Interpretation of Rom 11:29 and Its Uses" in *Society of Biblical Literature: 1997 Seminar Papers* (Atlanta: Society of Biblical Literature, 1997), 337–57; also his longer treatment in *Annali di storia dell'esegesi* 14, no. 1 (1997): 342–81; citation from 337. Sievers provides a concise review of the text's use by modern and contemporary commentators, as well as "church documents." He aptly notes that "important impulses for further exegetical and theological reflection have come through the teachings of Vatican II [e.g., *Nostra Aetate* 4] and of Pope John Paul II," who taught in an address to the Jewish leaders of Mainz (November 17, 1980) that the Old Covenant has never been revoked (350). The direction given by the council and by the late pope must guide every effort in interreligious dialogue to explore the relationship of the covenants, one to another, and to understand the irrevocable character of the "gifts and calling of God" (Rom 11:29). Thus, the question must be posed: Is the argument that the Jews *post Christum natum* will be saved solely by their role and conversion in the eschaton now subordinate to the irrevocable character of the covenant and election by God?

30. Vatican Commission for Religious Relations with the Jews, "We Remember: A Reflection on the 'Shoah,'" *L'Osservatore Romano* [Vatican City], March 18, 1998, p. 7.

Selected Bibliography

REFERENCE WORKS

Bauer, W. *A Greek-English Lexicon of the New Testament and Other Early Christian Literature.* Translated and revised by W. F. Arndt, F. W. Gingrich, and F. W. Danker. 2nd edition. Chicago: University of Chicago Press, 1979.

Blass, F., and A. Debrunner. *A Greek Grammar of the New Testament and Other Early Christian Literature.* Translated and revised by R. W. Funk. Chicago: University of Chicago Press, 1961.

Deferrari, R. J. *A Latin-English Dictionary of St. Thomas Aquinas.* Boston: Daughters of Saint Paul, 1960.

Hammond, N. G. L., and H. H. Scullard. *The Oxford Classical Dictionary.* Oxford: Clarendon, 1970.

Harvey, Warren Zev. "Maimonides and Aquinas on Interpreting the Bible." *Proceedings of the American Academy for Jewish Research* 55 (1988): 59–77.

Index Thomisticus [CD-ROM]: *Sancti Thomae Aquinatis operum omnium indices et concordantiae in quibus verborum omnium et singulorum formae et lemmata cum suis frequentiis et contextibus variis modis referuntur.* Stuttgart-Bad Cannstatt: Frommann-Holzboog, 1974–80.

Kittle, G., ed. *Theological Dictionary of the New Testament.* 10 volumes. Translated by G. W. Bromiley. Grand Rapids: Eerdmans, 1964–76.

Metzger, Bruce. *A Textual Commentary on the Greek New Testament.* London: United Bible Societies, 1971.

Novum Testamentum: Graece et Latine. Edited by K. Aland et al. Stuttgart: Deutsche Bibelgesellschaft, 1994.

PRIMARY LITERATURE CITED

Aquinas, Thomas, Saint. *Opera Omnia: cum hypertextibus in CD-ROM.* Roberto Busa. Milan: Editoria Elettronica Editel, 1992.

———. *Scriptum Super Libros Sententiarum.* 4 volumes. Edited by R. P. Mandonnet, OP (vols. 1 and 2), and M. F. Moos, OP (vols. 3 and 4). Paris: Lethielleux, 1929–47.

———. *Summa Theologiae.* 61 volumes. General Editor, Thomas Gilby, OP. London: Eyre & Spottiswoode; New York: McGraw-Hill, 1964–76.

———. *Super Epistolas S. Pauli Lectura.* 8th rev. ed. Edited by P. Raphaelis Cai, OP. Rome: Marietti, 1953.

———. *Super Evangelium S. Ioannis.* 5th rev. ed. Edited by P. Raphaelis Cai, OP. Rome: Marietti, 1952.

Augustine, Aurelius, Saint. *De Civitate Dei.* 7 volumes. Edited by G. E. McCracken et al. Loeb Classical Library. Cambridge, MA: Harvard University Press, 1957–60.

———. *De Diversis Quaestionibus ad Simplicanum.* Edited by A. Mutzenbecher. Corpus Christianorum Series Latina 44. Turnholt: Brepols, 1970.

———. *Epistolae Ad Romanos Inchoata Expositio* and *Expositio Quarundum Propositionum ex Epistolae ad Romanos.* In *Augustine on Romans: Propositions from the Epistle to the Romans, Unfinished Commentary on the Epistle to the Romans.* Translated by Paula Fredriksen Landes. Society of Biblical Literature Texts and Translations 23, Early Christian Literature 6. Atlanta: Society of Biblical Literature, 1982.

———. *In Answer to the Jews.* Translated by Marie Liguori, IHM. Fathers of the Church 27, 387-414. New York: Fathers of the Church, 1955.

———. *Iohannis Evangelium.* Edited by D. R. Willems, OSB. Corpus Christianorum Series Latina 36. Turnholt: Brepols, 1954.

———. *Retractiones.* Translated by M. I. Bogan. Fathers of the Church 60. Washington, DC: Catholic University of America Press, 1968.

SECONDARY LITERATURE CITED

Aageson, J. W. "Typology, Correspondence, and the Application of Scripture in Romans 9–11." *Journal for the Study of the New Testament* 31 (1987): 51–72.

Babcock, William. "Augustine's Interpretation of Romans (A.D. 394–396)." *Augustinian Studies* 10 (1979): 55–74.

Barrett, C. K. *The Epistle to the Romans.* Harper's New Testament Commentaries. New York: Harper & Row, 1957.

———. "Romans 9.30–10.21: Fall and Responsibility of Israel." In *Essays on Paul.* London: SPCK, 1982.

Blumenkranz, Bernhard. "Augustins et les juifs: Augustine et le judaïsme." *Recherches Augustiniennes* 1 (1958): 225–41.

———. "Le *De Regimine Judaeorum:* ses modèles, son exemple." In *Aquinas and Problems of His Time,* edited by G. Verbeke and D. Verhelst, 101–17. Leuven: Leuven University Press, 1976.

———. *Die Judenpredigt Augustins: Ein Beitrag zur Geschichte der jüdisch-christlichen Beziehungen in den ersten Jahrhunderten.* Basler Beiträge zur Geschichtswissenschaft 25. Basel: Helbing & Lichtenhahn, 1946.

Boguslawski, Steven. Review of *Aquinas and the Jews,* by John Y. B. Hood. *Journal of Ecclesiastical History* 48 (October 1997): 346–47.

Boyle, Leonard. "De regimine Judaeorum ad Ducissam Brabantiae." *Proceedings of the Patristic, Mediaeval, and Renaissance Conference* 8 (1983): 25–35.

Broadie, Alexander. "Medieval Jewry through the Eyes of Aquinas." In *Aquinas and Problems of His Time,* edited by G. Verbeke and D. Verhelst, 57–68. Leuven: Leuven University Press, 1976.

Chazan, Robert, ed. *Church, State, and Jew in the Middle Ages.* Library of Jewish Studies. New York: Behrman House, 1980.

Cohen, Jeremy. *The Friars and the Jews: The Evolution of Medieval Anti-Judaism.* Ithaca: Cornell University Press, 1982.

———. "Jews as Killers of Christ." *Traditio* 39 (1983): 1–28.

———. *Living Letters of the Law: Ideas of the Jew in Medieval Christianity.* Berkeley and Los Angeles: University of California Press, 1999.

———. "Towards a Functional Classification of Jewish Anti-Christian Polemic in the High Middle Ages." In *Religionsgespräche im Mittelalter,* edited by Bernard Lewis and Friedrich Niewöhner, 93–114. Wiesbaden: Harrassowitz, 1992.

Cranfield, C. E. B. *A Critical and Exegetical Commentary on the Epistle to the Romans.* 2 volumes. International Critical Commentary. Edinburgh: T. & T. Clark, 1979.

Davies, W. D. "Paul and the People of Israel." *New Testament Studies* 24 (1977–78): 4–39.

Dinkler, Erich. "The Historical and the Eschatological Israel in Romans Chapters 9–11: A Contribution to the Problem of Predestination and Individual Responsibility." *Journal of Religion* 33 (1956): 109–27.

DiNoia, J. Augustine, OP. "Providence." *Our Sunday Visitor's Encyclopedia of Catholic Doctrine,* edited by Russell Shaw, 546–50. Huntington, IN: Our Sunday Visitor, 1997.

Domanyi, Thomas. *Der Römerbriefkommentar des Thomas von Aquin: Ein Beitrag zur Untersuchung seiner Auslegungsmethoden.* Bern: Lang, 1979.

Dubois, Marcel. "Jews, Judaism, and Israel in the Theology of Saint Augustine." *Immanuel* 22/23 (1989): 162–214.

———. "Thomas Aquinas on the Place of the Jews in the Divine Plan." *Immanuel* 24 (1990): 241–66.

Farrelly, John. *Predestination, Grace and Free Will.* Westminster, MD: Newman, 1964.

Fitzmyer, Joseph A. *Romans: A New Translation with Introduction and Commentary.* Anchor Bible 33. Garden City, NY: Doubleday, 1993.

Fredriksen (Landes), Paula. "Augustine's Early Interpretation of Paul." Ph.D. diss., Princeton University, 1979.

———. "Excaecati Occulta Justitia Dei." *Journal of Early Christian Studies* 3 (1995): 299–324.

———. "Paul and Augustine: Conversion Narratives, Orthodox Traditions, and the Retrospective Self." *Journal of Theological Studies* n.s. 37 (1986): 3–34.

Gager, John G. *Origins of Anti-Semitism: Attitudes Toward Judaism in Pagan and Christian Antiquity.* New York: Oxford University Press, 1983.

Garrigou-Lagrange, R. *Predestination.* Translated by Dom Bede Rose, OSB. St. Louis: Herder, 1946.

Gaston, Lloyd. "Abraham and the Righteousness of God." *Horizons in Biblical Theology* 2 (1980): 39–68.

———. "Israel's Enemies in Pauline Theology." *New Testament Studies* 28 (1982): 400–423.

———. "Paul." In *Anti-Semitism and the Foundations of Christianity,* edited by Alan Davies, 48–71. New York: Paulist Press, 1979.

Getty, Mary Ann. "Paul and the Salvation of Israel: A Perspective on Romans 9–11." *Catholic Biblical Quarterly* 50 (1988): 456–69.

———. "Paul on the Covenants and the Future of Israel." *Biblical Theology Bulletin* 17 (1987): 92–99.

Grayzel, Solomon. "Changes in Papal Policy Toward the Jews in the Middle Ages." In *Proceedings of the Fifth World Congress of Jewish Studies,* volume 2, edited by Pinchas Peli, 43–54. Jerusalem: Hacohen, 1972.

———. *The Church and the Jews in the XIIIth Century.* 2 volumes. New York: Hermon, 1966 (vol. 1); Detroit: Wayne State University Press, 1989 (vol. 2).

———. "The Papal Bull *Sicut Judeis.*" In *Studies and Essays in Honor of Abraham A. Neuman,* edited by Meir Ben-Horin, B. D. Weinryb, and S. Zeitlin, 243–80. Leiden: Brill, 1962.

———. "Popes, Jews, and Inquisition: From 'Sicut' to 'Turbato.'" In *Essays on the Occasion of the Seventieth Anniversary of Dropsie University,* edited by A. I. Katsh and L. Nemoy, 151–88. Philadelphia: Dropsie University, 1979.

Hafemann, Scott. "The Salvation of Israel in Romans 11,25–32: A Response to Krister Stendahl." *Ex Auditu* 4 (1988): 38–58.

Hailperin, Herman. *Rashi and the Christian Scholars.* Pittsburgh: University of Pittsburgh Press, 1963.

Hood, John Y. B. *Aquinas and the Jews.* Middle Ages Series. Philadelphia: University of Pennsylvania Press, 1995.

Käsemann, Ernst. *Commentary on Romans.* Translated by G. W. Bromiley. Grand Rapids: Eerdmans, 1980.

———. *Perspectives on Paul.* Translated by Margaret Kohl. Philadelphia: Fortress, 1971.

Katz, Jacob. *Exclusiveness and Tolerance.* London: Oxford University Press, 1961.

Kuyper, Lester J. "The Hardness of Heart According to Biblical Perspective." *Scottish Journal of Theology* 27 (1974): 459–74.

Lasker, D. J. *Jewish Philosophical Polemics against Christianity in the Middle Ages.* New York: KTAV, 1977.

Lindars, Barnabas. "The Old Testament and Universalism in Paul." *Bulletin of the John Rylands University Library of Manchester* 69 (1986): 511–27.

Lodge, John G. *Romans 9–11: A Reader-Response Analysis.* University of South Florida International Studies in Formative Christianity and Judaism 6. Atlanta: Scholars Press, 1996.

Lukens, Michael. "Saint Thomas' Letter on the Jews." In *Conflict and Community: New Studies in Thomistic Thought,* edited by Michael Lukens, 165–201. New York: Lang, 1992.

Maccoby, Hyam. *Judaism on Trial: Jewish-Christian Disputation in the Middle Ages.* London and Toronto: Associated University Presses, 1982.

MacLennan, Robert S. "Christian Self-definition in the *Adversus Judaeos* Preachers in the Second Century." In *Diaspora Jews and Judaism: Essays in Honor of, and in Dialogue with A. Thomas Kraabel,* edited by J. Andrew Overman and Robert S. MacLennan, 209–24. South Florida Studies in the History of Judaism 41. Atlanta: Scholars Press, 1992.

Martin, Francis (Francisco Javier Caubet Iturbe). "Et sic omnis Israel salvus fieret, Rom 11,26." *Estudios Bíblicos* 21 (1962): 127–50.

Martyn, J. Louis. "Paul and His Jewish-Christian Interpreters." *Union Seminary Quarterly Review* 42 (1988): 1–15.

McCarthy, Margaret H. "Recent Developments in the Theology of Predestination." S.T.D. diss., Pontificia Universitas Lateranensis, 1995.

Minear, Paul S. *The Obedience of Faith: The Purposes of Paul in the Epistle to the Romans.* Studies in Biblical Theology. Second Series 18. Naperville, IL: Allenson, 1971.

Munck, J. "Israel and the Gentiles in the New Testament." *Journal of Theological Studies* n.s. 2/1 (1951): 3–16.

Murray, John. *The Epistle to the Romans.* 2 volumes. New International Commentary on the New Testament. Grand Rapids: Eerdmans, 1965.

O'Daly, G. "Predestination and Freedom in Augustine's Ethics." In *The Philosophy in Christianity,* edited by Godfrey Vesey, 85–93. Cambridge: Cambridge University Press, 1989.

Refoulé, F. *"...Et ainsi tout Israël sera sauvé": Romains 11,25–32.* Paris: Éditions du Cerf, 1984.

Rist, John M. "Augustine on Free Will and Predestination." In *Augustine: A Collection of Critical Essays,* edited by R. A. Markus, 218–52. Garden City, NY: Doubleday, 1972.

Rogers, Eugene F. "A Theological Procedure in the *Summa Theologiae.*" Ph.D. diss., Yale University, 1992.

Ruether, Rosemary Radford. *Faith and Fratricide: The Theological Roots of Anti-Semitism.* New York: Seabury, 1974.

Russell, Walter B., III. "An Alternative Suggestion for the Purpose of Romans." *Bibliotheca Sacra* 45 (1988): 174–84.

Schenk, Richard. "Thomas Aquinas and Robert Kilwardby on the Sacrament of Circumcision." In *Ordo sapientiae et amoris: Image et message de saint Thomas d'Aquin à travers les récentes études historiques, herméneutiques et doctrinales; Hommage au Professeur Jean-Pierre Torrell, OP, à l'occasion de son 65e anniversaire,* edited by Carlos-Josaphat Pinto de Oliveira, 555–93. Studia Firburgensia n.s. 78. Fribourg: Editions Universitaires, 1993.

Schmidt, K. L. "προορίζω." *Theological Dictionary of the New Testament,* edited by Gerhard Kittel and Gerhard Friedrich, translated by Geoffrey W. Bromiley, 5:452–56. Grand Rapids: Eerdmans, 1964–76.

Sievers, Joseph. "'God's Gifts and Call Are Irrevocable: The Interpretation of Rom 11:29 and Its Uses." In *Society of Biblical Literature: 1997 Seminar Papers,* 337–57. Atlanta: Society of Biblical Literature, 1997.

Simon, Marcel. *Verus Israël: Étude sur les relations entre Chrétiens et Juifs dans l'empire Romain.* Paris: Boccard, 1946.

Smalley, Beryl. *The Study of the Bible in the Middle Ages.* Oxford: Clarendon, 1941.

———. "Use of the Spiritual Sense of Scripture in Persuasion and Arguments by Scholars in the Middle Ages." *Recherche de théologie ancienne et médiévale* 52 (1985): 44–63.

Stendahl, Krister. *Final Account: Paul's Letter to the Romans.* Minneapolis: Fortress, 1995.

———. *Paul among Jews and Gentiles and Other Essays.* Philadelphia: Fortress, 1976.

———. "Paul and the Introspective Conscience of the West." *Harvard Theological Review* 56 (1963): 199–215.

Stroumsa, Gedaliahu G. "Religious Contacts in Byzantine Palestine." *Numen* 36 (1989): 16–42.

Talmadge, Frank. *Disputation and Dialogue: Readings in the Jewish-Christian Encounter.* New York: KTAV, 1975.

Tomasic, Thomas M. "Natural Moral Law and Predestination in St. Thomas Aquinas: An Incurable Contradiction?" In *The Medieval Tradition of Natural Law,* edited by Harold J. Johnson, 179–89. Kalamazoo, MI: Medieval Institute, 1987.

Torrell, Jean-Pierre. *Saint Thomas Aquinas.* Volume 1, *The Person and His Work.* Translated by Robert Royal. Washington, DC: Catholic University of America Press, 1996.

Vatican Commission for Religious Relations with the Jews. "We Remember: A Reflection on the 'Shoah.'" *L'Osservatore Romano* [Vatican City], March 18, 1998, 6–8.

Walter, Nicholaus. "Zur Interpretation von Römer 9–11." *Zeitschrift für Theologie und Kirche* 81 (1984): 172–95.

Weisheipl, James A. *Friar Thomas D'Aquino: His Life, Thought, and Work.* Garden City, NY: Doubleday, 1974.

Wetzel, James. "Pelagius Anticipated: Grace and Election in Augustine's *ad Simplicianum.*" In *Augustine: From Rhetor to Theologian,* edited by J. McWilliam, 121–32. Waterloo, ON: Wilfrid Laurier University Press, 1992.

Williamson, Clark M. "The '*Adversus Judaeos*' Tradition in Christian Theology." *Encounter* 39 (1978): 273–296.

Wyschogrod, Michael. *The Body of Faith: Judaism as Corporeal Election.* Minneapolis: Seabury, 1983.

Yearley, Lee H. "St. Thomas Aquinas on Providence and Predestination." *Anglican Theological Review* 49 (1967): 409–23.